GO MATH!

HOUGHTON MIFFLIN HARCOURT

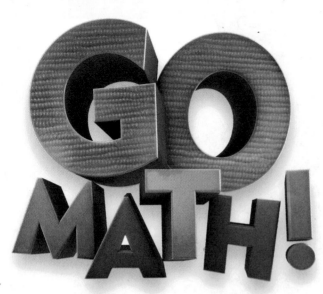

HOUGHTON MIFFLIN HARCOURT

ISBN 978-0-547-35201-5

10 11 12 13 14 15 16   0877   21 20 19 18 17 16 15 14

4500472136   ^ B C D E

Dear Students and Families,

Welcome to **Go Math!**, Grade 2! In this exciting mathematics program, there are hands-on activities to do and real-world problems to solve. Best of all, you will write your ideas and answers right in your book. In **Go Math!**, writing and drawing on the pages helps you think deeply about what you are learning, and you will really understand math!

By the way, all of the pages in your **Go Math!** book are made using recycled paper. We wanted you to know that you can Go Green with **Go Math!**

Sincerely,

The Authors

Made in the United States
Text printed on 100% recycled paper
By using this paper in a typical print run,
we achieved the following environmental benefits:
• Trees Saved: 797
• Air Emissions Eliminated: 89,748 pounds
• Water Saved: 439,641 gallons
• Solid Waste Eliminated: 66,317 pounds

*Environmental impact estimates calculated using
the Environmental Defense Fund Paper Calculator.
For more information, visit www.papercalculator.org*

GO MATH!

Authors

Juli K. Dixon
Professor of Mathematics Education
University of Central Florida
Orlando, Florida

Matt Larson
Curriculum Specialist for Mathematics
Lincoln Public Schools
Lincoln, Nebraska

Miriam A. Leiva
Founding President, TODOS:
    Mathematics for All
Distinguished Professor
    of Mathematics Emerita
University of North Carolina Charlotte
Charlotte, North Carolina

Thomasenia Lott Adams
Professor of Mathematics Education
University of Florida
Gainesville, Florida

Contributing Author

Anne M. Goodrow
Associate Professor, Elementary Mathematics
Rhode Island College
Providence, Rhode Island

Number and Place Value

 DIGITAL PATH Go online! Your math lessons are interactive. Use *i*Tools, Animated Math Models, the Multimedia *e*Glossary, and more.

© Houghton Mifflin Harcourt Publishing Company

Focal POINT

Developing an understanding of the base-ten numeration system and place-value concepts

Math Story

Whales

Social Studies

Look for these:

REAL WORLD

H.O.T.
Higher Order Thinking

Use every day for Standards Practice.

v

Big Idea 2

© Houghton Mifflin Harcourt Publishing Company

Focal POINT

Developing quick recall of addition facts and related subtraction facts and fluency with multidigit addition and subtraction

Math Story

All About Animals

Look for these:

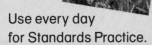

Higher Order Thinking

Use every day for Standards Practice.

vi

Addition, Subtraction, Multiplication, and Data

DIGITAL PATH Go online! Your math lessons are interactive. Use *i*Tools, Animated Math Models, the Multimedia *e*Glossary, and more.

4 2-Digit Addition 153

Big Idea 3

DIGITAL PATH Go online! Your math lessons are interactive. Use *i*Tools, Animated Math Models, the Multimedia *e*Glossary, and more.

9 Length 373

Math Story

Look for these:

Higher Order Thinking

Use every day for Standards Practice.

12 Geometry and Patterns 517

Whales

by John Hudson

Focal POINT Developing an understanding of the base-ten numeration system and place-value concepts

Some scientists study whales. Different kinds of whales swim along the west coast of the United States of America.

A scientist sees 8 blue whales.

Blue whales are the largest animals on Earth.

Social Studies

Where is the United States of America on the map?

North America

Alaska

Pacific
Ocean

Canada

Atlantic
Ocean

United States
of America

N

W E

S

0 500 1,000 Miles
0 500 1,000 Kilometers

Mexico

Map Legend
— Border

The scientist also sees 13 humpback whales.

Humpback whales sing underwater.

Did the scientist see more humpback whales or
more blue whales? more _____ whales

Social Studies

Where is the Pacific Ocean on the map?

3

Whales also swim along the east coast of Canada and the United States of America. Pilot whales swim behind a leader, or a *pilot*. A scientist sees a group of 29 pilot whales.

Social Studies

Where is Canada on the map?

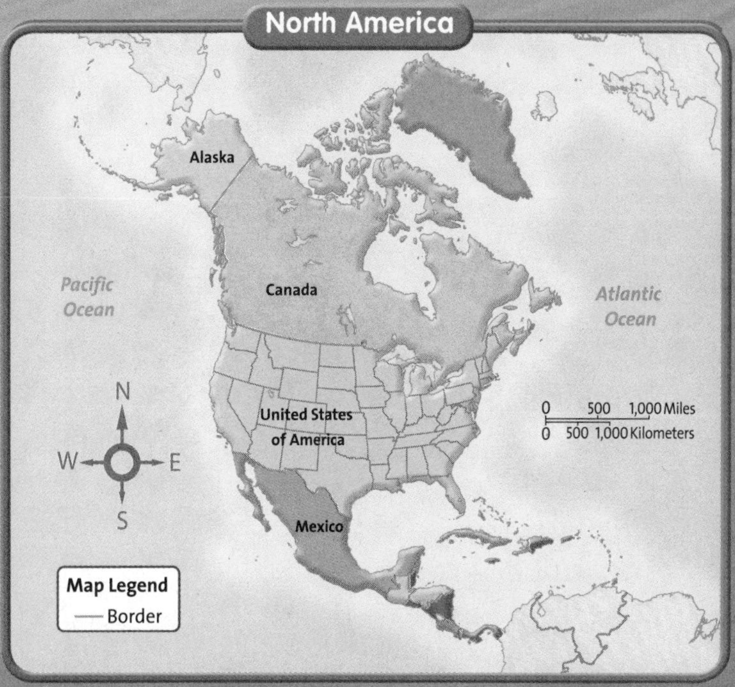

Alaska

Pacific
Ocean

Canada

Atlantic
Ocean

United States
of America

0   500   1,000 Miles
0   500 1,000 Kilometers

N
W   E
S

Mexico

Map Legend
— Border

Fin whales are fast swimmers. They are the second-largest whales in the world.

A scientist sees a group of 27 fin whales.

How many tens are in the number 27?

_____ tens

Social Studies

Where is the Atlantic Ocean on the map?

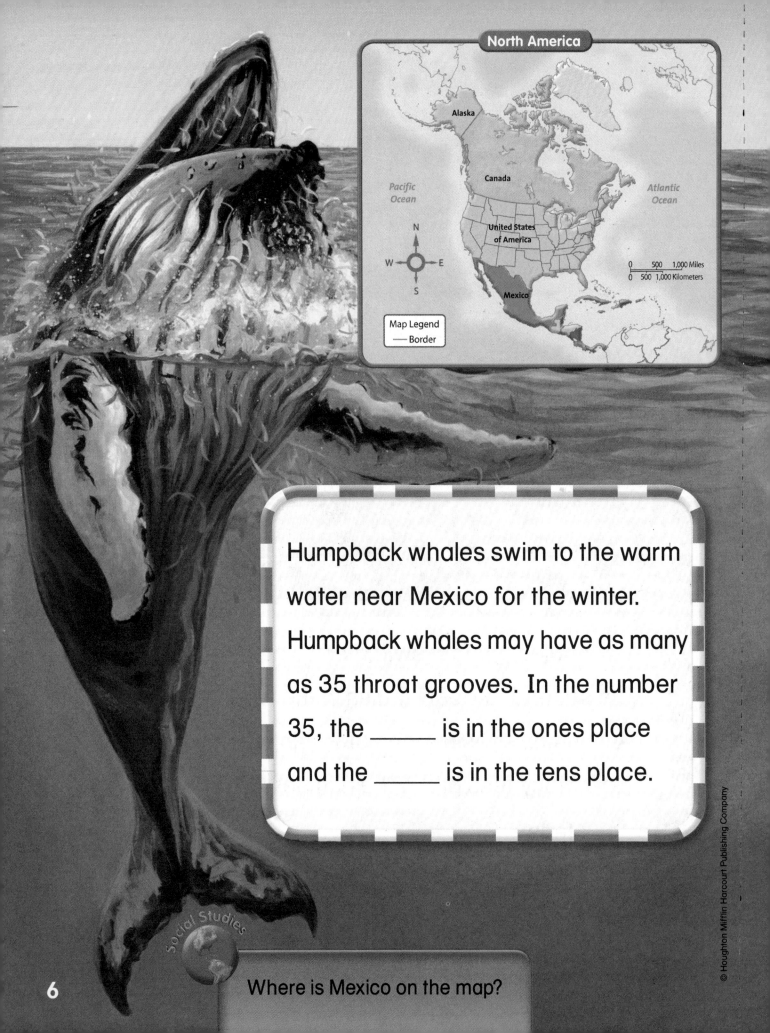

Alaska

Canada

Pacific
Ocean

Atlantic
Ocean

United States
of America

N
W — E
S

0   500   1,000 Miles
0   500 1,000 Kilometers

Mexico

Map Legend
— Border

Humpback whales swim to the warm water near Mexico for the winter. Humpback whales may have as many as 35 throat grooves. In the number 35, the _____ is in the ones place and the _____ is in the tens place.

Social Studies

Where is Mexico on the map?

6

Write About the Story

Look at the pictures. Draw and write your own story. Compare two numbers in your story.

Vocabulary Review

more	greater than
fewer	tens
less than	ones

_____

_____

_____

_____

_____

The Size of Numbers

The table shows how many young whales were seen by scientists.

Young Whales Seen	
Whale	**Number of Whales**
Humpback	34
Blue	13
Fin	27
Pilot	43

1. Which number of whales has a 4 in the tens place?

   _____

2. How many tens and ones describe the number of young blue whales seen?

   _____ ten _____ ones

3. Compare the number of young humpback whales and the number of young pilot whales seen.

   Write > or <.

   34 ◯ 43

4. Compare the number of young fin whales and the number of young blue whales seen.

   Write > or <.

   27 ◯ 13

 Write a story about a scientist watching sea animals. Use some 2-digit numbers in your story.

Curious About Math with Curious George

At a farmers' market, many different fruits and vegetables are sold.

If there are 3 groups of 10 watermelons on a table, how many watermelons are there?

Show What You Know

Model Numbers to 20

Write the number that tells how many.

1.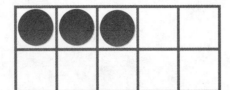

_____

2.

_____

Tens

Write how many tens. Write the number.

3.   _____ tens

_____

4. 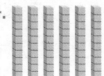 _____ tens

_____

Compare 2-Digit Numbers

Write **is greater than**, **is less than**, or **is equal to**.

5.

26 _____ 62.

6.

50 _____ 35.

Family note: This page checks your child's understanding of important skills needed for success in Chapter 1.

GO Online Assessment Options
Soar to Success Math

Name _____

Vocabulary Builder

Visualize It

Fill in the boxes of the graphic organizer.
Write sentences about **ones** and **tens**.

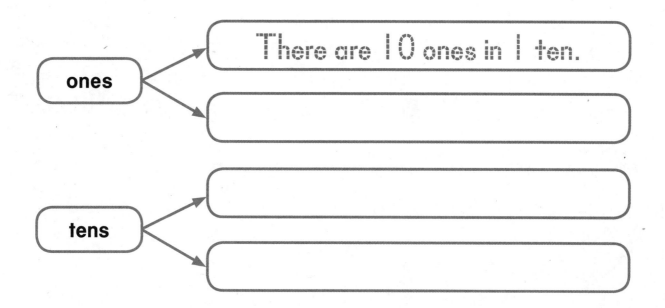

ones → There are 10 ones in 1 ten.

tens →

Understand Vocabulary

Look at the hundred chart.

1. Start on 10. Use yellow to shade the numbers as you count on by **tens** to 80.

2. Start on 1. Use blue to shade the numbers as you count on by **ones** to 8.

1	2	3	4	5	6	7	8	9	10
11	12	13	14	15	16	17	18	19	20
21	22	23	24	25	26	27	28	29	30
31	32	33	34	35	36	37	38	39	40
41	42	43	44	45	46	47	48	49	50
51	52	53	54	55	56	57	58	59	60
61	62	63	64	65	66	67	68	69	70
71	72	73	74	75	76	77	78	79	80
81	82	83	84	85	86	87	88	89	90
91	92	93	94	95	96	97	98	99	100

GO Online • eStudent Edition
• Multimedia eGlossary

 **Game**

Three in a Row

Materials • 15 • 15 ⚪ •

Play with a partner.

1. Choose a leaf. Read the number on the leaf. Use ▥▥▥▥▥ ▤ to model the number.

2. Your partner checks your model. If your model is correct, put your ⚫ on the leaf.

3. Take turns. Try to get 3 ⚫ in a row.

4. The first player with 3 ⚫ in a row wins.

5	28	13	19	20
25	15	29	8	12
11	9	30	16	24
22	23	17	27	10

Name _____

Understand Place Value

Essential Question How do you know the value of a digit?

Listen and Draw  REAL WORLD

Write the numbers.
Then choose a way to show the numbers.

Tens	Ones

Tens	Ones

Math Talk
Explain why the value of 5 is different in the two numbers.

 FOR THE TEACHER • Read the following problem. Have children write the numbers and show how they chose to represent them. Tyler collects baseball cards. The number of cards that he has is written with a 2 and a 5. How many cards might he have?

Chapter 1

Model and Draw

0, 1, 2, 3, 4, 5, 6, 7, 8, and 9 are **digits**.
In a 2-digit number, you know the value of
a digit by its place.

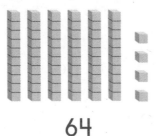

64

Tens	Ones
6	4

6 tens   4 ones

The digit **6** is in
the tens place. It
tells you there are
6 tens, or 60.

The digit **4** is in
the ones place. It
tells you there are
4 ones, or 4.

Share and Show

Circle the value of the red digit.

1.   26

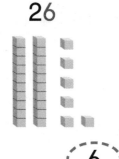

60   (6)

2.   58

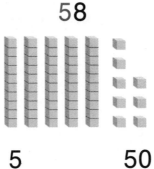

5   50

3.   40

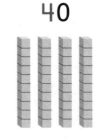

40   4

4.   73

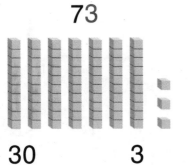

30   3

⊘5.   24

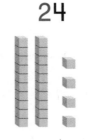

2   20

⊘6.   61

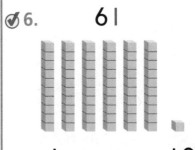

1   10

On Your Own

Circle the value of the red digit.

7. 51

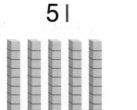

1   10

8. 49

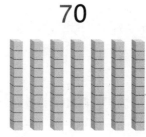

90   9

9. 70

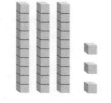

7   70

10. 18

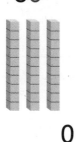

1   10

11. 65

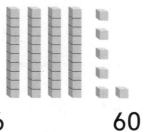

50   5

12. 33

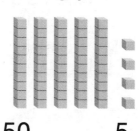

30   3

13. 30

10   0

14. 46

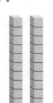

6   60

15. 54

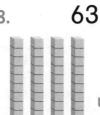

50   5

H.O.T. Look at the digits of the number.
Draw quick pictures for the missing blocks.

16. 47

17. 52

18. 63

PROBLEM SOLVING

Write the 2-digit number that matches the clues.

19. My number has 7 ones and 3 tens.

My number is _____.

20. My number has no ones and 4 tens.

My number is _____.

21. My number has 3 tens.

It has more than 7 ones.

It does not have 9 ones.

My number is _____.

22. My number has 8 tens.

It has more than 7 ones.

It has more ones than tens.

My number is _____.

23. My number has more ones than tens.

One of the digits is 2.

One of the digits is 6.

My number is _____.

24. **H.O.T.** My number has double the number of ones as tens.

The sum of the digits is 3.

My number is _____.

25. ⭐ **Test Prep** Henry has 45 crayons.
What is the value of the digit 5 in this number?

- ○ 4
- ○ 5
- ○ 9
- ○ 50

 TAKE HOME ACTIVITY • Write the number 56. Have your child tell you which digit is in the tens place, which digit is in the ones place, and the value of each digit.

16 sixteen

Expanded Form

Essential Question How do you describe a
2-digit number as tens and ones?

 **Listen** REAL WORLD

Use ▭▭▭▭▭ ▭ to model each number.

Tens	Ones

Math Talk

Explain how you know how many tens and ones are in the number 29.

FOR THE TEACHER • After you read the following
problem, write 38 on the board. Have children
model the number. Mac used 38 stickers to
decorate a book of photos. How can you model 38
with blocks? Continue the activity for 83 and 77.

What does 23 mean?

Tens	Ones
‖	°°°

The 2 in 23 has a value of 2 tens, or 20.
The 3 in 23 has a value of 3 ones, or 3.

23 = ____ tens ____ ones

23 = ____ + ____

Share and Show

Draw quick pictures to show the number.
Describe the number in two ways.

1. 37

37 = ____ tens ____ ones

37 = ____ + ____

2. 54

54 = ____ tens ____ ones

54 = ____ + ____

✓ 3. 16

16 = ____ ten ____ ones

16 = ____ + ____

✓ 4. 60

60 = ____ tens ____ ones

60 = ____ + ____

On Your Own

Draw quick pictures to show the number.
Describe the number in two ways.

5. 48

48 = ____ tens ____ ones

48 = ____ + ____

6. 31

31 = ____ tens ____ one

31 = ____ + ____

7. 59

59 = ____ tens ____ ones

59 = ____ + ____

8. 75

75 = ____ tens ____ ones

75 = ____ + ____

 H.O.T. Write the missing number.

9. ____ = 40 + 3

10. 82 = ____ + 2

11. 56 = ____ tens 6 ones

12. ____ = 6 tens 8 ones

13. 97 = 90 + ____

14. ____ = 70 + 9

PROBLEM SOLVING

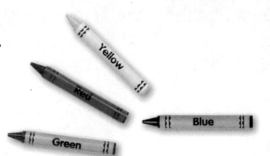

H.O.T. Use crayons. Follow the steps.

15. Start at 51 and draw a green line to 43.

16. Draw a blue line from 43 to 34.

17. Draw a red line from 34 to 29.

18. Then draw a yellow line from 29 to 72.

1 ten 5 ones	30 + 2
4 tens 3 ones	20 + 9
10 + 2	3 tens 4 ones
70 + 2	5 tens 1 one
	7 + 2

19. ⭐ **Test Prep** Which of these is another way to describe 85?

- ○ 80 + 5
- ○ 50 + 8
- ○ 8 + 5
- ○ 50 + 80

TAKE HOME ACTIVITY · Ask your child to write 89 as tens plus ones. Then have him or her write 25 as tens plus ones.

20 twenty

FOR MORE PRACTICE:
Standards Practice Book, pp. P5–P6

Name _____

Different Ways to Write Numbers

Essential Question What are different ways to write a 2-digit number?

Listen and Draw REAL WORLD

Write the number. Then write it as tens and ones.

_____ tens _____ ones

_____ + _____

_____ + _____

_____ tens _____ ones

FOR THE TEACHER • Read the following problem. Taryn counted 53 books on the shelves. How many tens and ones are in 53? Continue the activity with the numbers 73, 35, and 40.

Math Talk
In 44, do both digits have the same value? **Explain.**

Model and Draw

A number can be written in different ways.

seventeen

1 ten 7 ones

10 + 7

17

ones	teen words	tens
0 zero	11 eleven	10 ten
1 one	12 twelve	20 twenty
2 two	13 thirteen	30 thirty
3 three	14 fourteen	40 forty
4 four	15 fifteen	50 fifty
5 five	16 sixteen	60 sixty
6 six	17 seventeen	70 seventy
7 seven	18 eighteen	80 eighty
8 eight	19 nineteen	90 ninety
9 nine		

Share and Show

Look at the examples above.
Then write the number another way.

1. thirty-two

   _____

2. 20 + 7

   _____

3. 63

   _____ tens _____ ones

4. ninety-five

   _____ + _____

5. 5 tens 1 one

   _____

6. seventy-six

   _____ + _____

7. 20 + 8

   _____

8. 8 tens 0 ones

   _____

Name _____

On Your Own

Write the number another way.

9. 2 tens 4 ones

_____

10. thirty

_____ tens _____ ones

11. 80 + 5

_____

12. 54

_____ + _____

13. twelve

_____ + _____

14. 90 + 9

_____ tens _____ ones

15. 7 tens 8 ones

_____

16. 40 + 1

_____

H.O.T. What numbers are missing on the number line? Show the missing numbers as tens and ones.

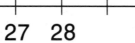

25   27 28   31 32   34

17. _____ tens _____ ones

18. _____ tens _____ ones

19. _____ tens _____ ones

20. _____ tens _____ ones

TAKE HOME ACTIVITY • Write 20 + 6 on a sheet of paper. Have your child write the 2-digit number. Repeat for 4 tens 9 ones.

Name _____

 # Mid-Chapter Checkpoint

Concepts and Skills

Circle the value of the red digit. (pp.13–16)

1. 62	2. 78	3. 37
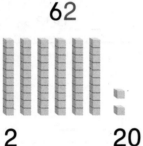	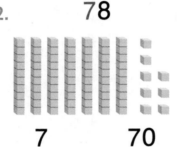	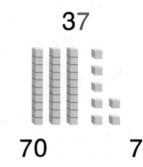
2 20	7 70	70 7

Draw quick pictures to show the number.
Describe the number in two ways. (pp. 17–20)

4. 35

35 = _____ tens _____ ones

35 = _____ + _____

5. 53

53 = _____ tens _____ ones

53 = _____ + _____

Write the number another way. (pp. 21–23)

6. 8 tens 6 ones

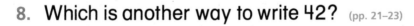

7. sixty-one

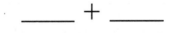

⭐ Test Prep

8. Which is another way to write 42? (pp. 21–23)

○ 2 tens 4 ones

○ 40 + 2

○ forty

○ 4 + 2

Name _____

Different Names for Numbers

Essential Question How can you show the value of a number in different ways?

Listen and Draw

Use ▭▭▭▭▭ ▪ to show the number.
Make trades to show the number a different way.
Record the tens and ones.

_____ tens _____ ones

_____ tens _____ ones

_____ tens _____ ones

FOR THE TEACHER • Read the following problem. Drew has 21 pennies. What are some different ways he can show 21 with blocks? Have children start with 21 ones blocks. Then have them make trades and record the number of tens and ones in each of their models.

Math Talk
Describe the trades you made for different models.

Chapter 1

Model and Draw

These are some different ways to show 32.

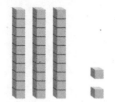

__3__ tens __2__ ones

__30__ + __2__

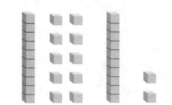

__2__ tens __12__ ones

__20__ + __12__

__1__ ten __22__ ones

__10__ + __22__

Share and Show

Math Board

Write how many tens and ones.
Then write the number as tens plus ones.

✓ 1. **28**

_____ tens _____ ones

_____ + _____

_____ ten _____ ones

_____ + _____

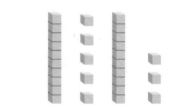

_____ tens _____ ones

_____ + _____

✓ 2. **35**

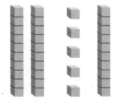

_____ tens _____ ones

_____ + _____

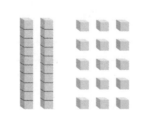

_____ tens _____ ones

_____ + _____

_____ tens _____ ones

_____ + _____

On Your Own

Write how many tens and ones.
Then write the number as tens plus ones.

3. 43

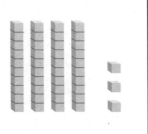

____ tens ____ ones

____ + ____

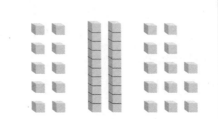

____ tens ____ ones

____ + ____

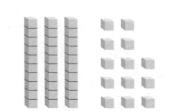

____ tens ____ ones

____ + ____

4. 30

____ tens ____ ones

____ + ____

____ tens ____ ones

____ + ____

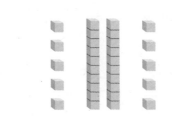

____ tens ____ ones

____ + ____

5. 41

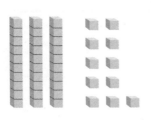

____ tens ____ ones

____ + ____

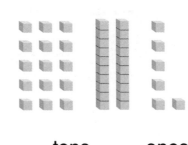

____ tens ____ ones

____ + ____

____ tens ____ one

____ + ____

6. **H.O.T.** Anna used these blocks
to show 57. What is wrong with the
model? Cross out extra blocks or
draw quick pictures for missing blocks.

PROBLEM SOLVING

Circle the answer for each riddle.

7. A number has the digit 4 in the ones place and the digit 7 in the tens place. Which of these is another way to write this number?

$40 + 7$ $70 + 4$

$4 + 7$

8. **H.O.T.** A number is shown with 3 tens and 27 ones. Which of these could be the number?

thirty

thirty-seven

fifty-seven

Fill in the blanks to make each sentence true.

9. _____ tens _____ ones is the same as $90 + 3$.

10. 2 tens 18 ones is the same as _____ + _____ .

11. 5 tens _____ ones is the same as _____ + 17.

12. ⭐ **Test Prep** Which of these is another way to write 48?

○ eighty-four

○ $40 + 80$

○ $4 + 8$

○ $40 + 8$

TAKE HOME ACTIVITY · Write the number 45. Have your child write or draw two ways to show this number.

FOR MORE PRACTICE:
Standards Practice Book, pp. P9–P10

Name _____

Make a List • Tens and Ones

Essential Question How does making a list help you solve a problem?

Gail needs to buy 32 pencils. She can buy single pencils or boxes of 10 pencils. What are the different ways Gail can buy 32 pencils?

Unlock the Problem REAL WORLD

What do I need to find?

ways she can

buy 32 pencils

What information do I need to use?

She can buy _____single_____ pencils

or ___boxes of 10___ pencils.

Show how to solve the problem.

Draw quick pictures to show 32 in different ways.
Complete the chart to list the ways.

Boxes of 10 pencils	Single pencils
3	2
2	12
1	
0	

HOME CONNECTION • Your child made a list to organize information. The list shows the different solutions to the problem.

© Houghton Mifflin Harcourt Publishing Company

Try Another Problem

Make a list to solve.

- What do I need to find?
- What information do I need to use?

1. Sara is putting away a pile of 36 crayons. She can pack them in boxes of 10 crayons or as single crayons. What are the different ways Sara can pack the crayons?

Boxes of 10 crayons	Single crayons

2. Mr. Winter is putting 28 chairs away. He can put them away in stacks of 10 chairs or as single chairs. What are the different ways Mr. Winter can put away the chairs?

Stacks of 10 chairs	Single chairs

Math Talk

Explain how making a list helped you solve the first problem.

Share and Show

Make a list to solve.

✓ 3. Lucy is packing 25 carrot sticks for a picnic. She can pack them in bundles of 10 sticks or as single sticks. What are the different ways Lucy can pack the carrot sticks?

Bundles of 10 sticks	Single sticks

✓ 4. Stickers are sold in packs of 10 stickers or as single stickers. Mr. Keys wants to buy 43 stickers. What are the different ways Mr. Keys can buy the stickers?

Packs of 10 stickers	Single stickers

5. Devin is sorting his 29 baseball cards. He can pack them in boxes of 10 cards or as single cards. What are the different ways Devin can sort the cards?

Boxes of 10 cards	Single cards

On Your Own

Solve. Write or draw to explain.

6. Mr. Link needs 30 cups. He can buy them in packs of 10 cups or as single cups. What are the different ways Mr. Link can buy the cups?

Packs of 10 cups	Single cups

7. **H.O.T.** Zack has 6 marbles. Olivia gives him some more. Now he has 13 marbles. How many marbles did Olivia give him?

_____ marbles

8. ⭐ **Test Prep** Lee can pack her toy cars in boxes of 10 cars or as single cars. Which of these is a way that she can pack her 24 toy cars?

○ 4 boxes of 10 cars and 2 single cars

○ 1 box of 10 cars and 24 single cars

○ 3 boxes of 10 cars and 14 single cars

○ 2 boxes of 10 cars and 4 single cars

TAKE HOME ACTIVITY · Have your child explain how he or she solved one problem on this page.

FOR MORE PRACTICE:
Standards Practice Book, pp. P11–P12

Name _____

Even and Odd Numbers

Essential Question How are even numbers and odd numbers different?

Use 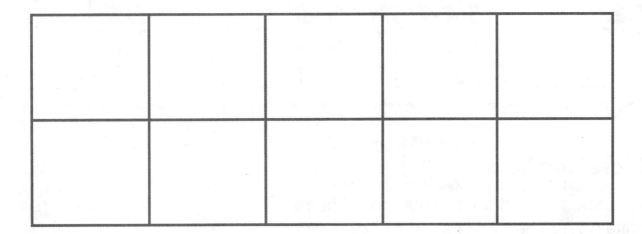 to show each number.

FOR THE TEACHER • Read the following problem. Beca has 8 toy cars. Can she arrange her cars in pairs on a shelf? Have children set pairs of cubes vertically on the ten frames. Continue the activity with other numbers, such as 7 and 13.

Math Talk
When you make pairs for 7 and for 10, how are these models different? **Explain.**

Chapter 1

Count out cubes for each number. Make pairs.
Even numbers show pairs with no cubes left over.
Odd numbers show pairs with one cube left over.

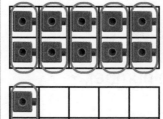
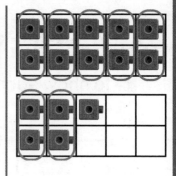

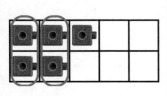

5 __odd__   8 __even__   12 _____   15 _____

Share and Show

Use cubes. Count out the number of cubes.
Make pairs. Then write **even** or **odd**.

1. 6 _____   2. 3 _____

3. 2 _____   4. 9 _____

5. 4 _____   6. 10 _____

7. 7 _____   8. 13 _____

9. 11 _____   10. 20 _____

Name _____

On Your Own

Shade in the ten frames to show the number.
Circle **even** or **odd**.

11. ### 17

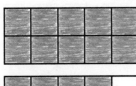

even   odd

12. ### 16

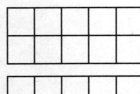

even   odd

13. ### 19

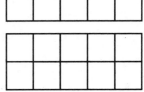

even   odd

14. ### 25

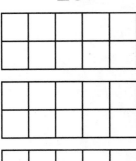

even   odd

15. ### 22

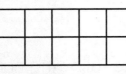

even   odd

16. ### 28

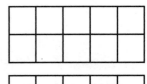

even   odd

17. **H.O.T.** Which two numbers in the box are even?

8   5

3   6

_____ and _____

How do you know that they are even?

_____

_____

_____

PROBLEM SOLVING

18. Fill in the blanks to describe the groups of numbers.
Write **even** or **odd**.

_____ numbers

_____ numbers

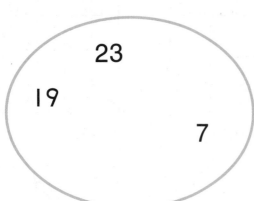

23

19

7

4

12

28

19. **H.O.T.** Write each of the following numbers
inside the loop that it belongs in.

5   6   10   21   32   49

20. ⭐ **Test Prep** There are an even number
of girls and an odd number of boys in
Gina's class. Which of these choices
could tell about her class?

○ 8 girls and 12 boys

○ 9 girls and 8 boys

○ 10 girls and 7 boys

○ 11 girls and 9 boys

TAKE HOME ACTIVITY • Have your child show you a number, such as 9,
using small objects and explain why the number is even or odd.

FOR MORE PRACTICE:
Standards Practice Book, pp. P13–P14

Name _____

Algebra: Compare and Order Numbers to 100

Essential Question How do you compare and order numbers?

Listen and Draw  REAL WORLD

Show each number in different ways.
Then answer the question.

45
____ tens ____ ones

54
____ tens ____ ones

_____ has more beads.

 FOR THE TEACHER • Read the following problem. For each number, have children draw a quick picture and record the number of tens and ones in the number. Christina and Ana each have some beads. Christina has 45 beads and Ana has 54 beads. Who has more beads?

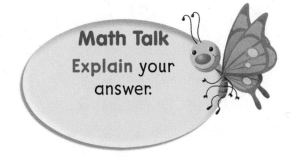 **Math Talk** **Explain** your answer.

Chapter I

Draw quick pictures to show the numbers.
Compare the numbers using place value.
If the tens are the same, compare the ones.

Start by comparing the tens digits first.

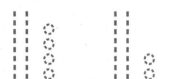

24 ⓥ 22

24 is greater than 22.

12 ⓦ 17

12 is less than 17.

34 ⓧ 34

34 is equal to 34.

Share and Show

Draw quick pictures.
Compare the numbers. Write >, <, or =.

1.   42 ◯ 42

2.   25 ◯ 27

✓ 3.   35 ◯ 45

✓ 4.   57 ◯ 51

On Your Own

Compare the numbers. Write >, <, or =.

5. 79 ◯ 97

6. 26 ◯ 26

7. 45 ◯ 51

8. 43 ◯ 34

9. 18 ◯ 48

10. 62 ◯ 61

11. 33 ◯ 33

12. 42 ◯ 14

Compare the numbers. Write > or <.
Then circle to show their order.

13. 43 ◯ 47 ◯ 52

least to greatest

greatest to least

14. 74 ◯ 67 ◯ 59

least to greatest

greatest to least

15. 26 ◯ 29 ◯ 33

least to greatest

greatest to least

Aubrey has number cards to place on a number line.

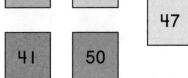

45   52   47
41   50

16. Circle the cards she should use. Write the missing numbers on the number line where they belong.

43   44   46   48   49   51

17.  **H.O.T.** Compare Aubrey's missing numbers. Write them in order from least to greatest.

___ < ___ < ___

Explain how you found your answer.

_____

_____

_____

18. ⭐ **Test Prep** Adam has 37 coins. Julia has fewer coins than Adam. Which could be the number of coins that Julia has?

- ○ 21
- ○ 37
- ○ 73
- ○ 39

TAKE HOME ACTIVITY · Ask your child how to compare numbers, such as 14 and 41.

FOR MORE PRACTICE:
Standards Practice Book, pp. P15–P16

✓ Chapter 1 Review/Test

Vocabulary

Use a word in the box to complete each sentence.

| even |
| odd |
| digits |

1. The numbers 3 and 7 are _____ numbers. (pp. 33–36)

2. 5 and 2 are _____ in the number 52. (pp. 13–16)

Concepts and Skills

Draw quick pictures to show the number.
Describe the number in two ways. (pp. 17–20)

3. 37

37 = ____ tens ____ ones

37 = ____ + ____

4. 73

73 = ____ tens ____ ones

73 = ____ + ____

Write the number another way. (pp. 21–23)

5. forty-seven

____ + ____

6. 6 tens 3 ones

_____

Shade in the ten frames to show the number.
Circle **even** or **odd**. (pp. 33–36)

7. 15

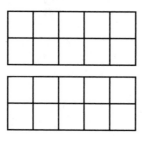

even   odd

8. 18

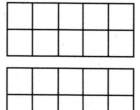

even   odd

Fill in the bubble for the correct answer choice.

9. Jamie wrote this riddle.

> My number has 4 tens.
> It has more ones than tens.

Which 2-digit number matches her clues? (pp. 13–16)

- ○ 24
- ○ 42
- ○ 48
- ○ 84

10. Emily wants to write 52 in different ways.
Which is another way to write 52? (pp. 21–23)

- ○ 50 + 20
- ○ 50 + 2
- ○ 5 ones 2 tens
- ○ 20 + 5

11. Aaron used blocks to show how many stickers he has.

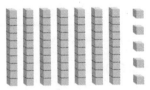

How many stickers does Aaron have? (pp. 25–28)

- ○ 12
- ○ 57
- ○ 70
- ○ 75

42 forty-two

Name _____

Fill in the bubble for the correct answer choice.

12. Which of the following numbers is less than 64? (pp. 37–40)

   ○ 46
   ○ 68
   ○ 64
   ○ 94

13. Mrs. Shaw is buying 26 markers. She can buy them in packs of 10 markers or as single markers. Which of these is a way that she can buy the markers? (pp. 29–32)

Packs of 10 markers	Single markers
2	6
0	26

   ○ 1 pack of 10 markers and 26 single markers

   ○ 6 packs of 10 markers and 2 single markers

   ○ 1 pack of 10 markers and 16 single markers

   ○ 3 packs of 10 markers and 6 single markers

14. Which is another way to describe 59? (pp. 17–20)

   ○ 90 + 5
   ○ 50 + 9
   ○ 9 + 5
   ○ 5 + 9

15. There are 56 books about football and
58 books about baseball in the store.
Compare these numbers of books.

____ ◯ ____

Explain how you compared the two numbers.

_____

_____

_____

Performance Task

16. Mrs. Payne is buying 42 pencils.
She can buy them in packs of
10 pencils or as single pencils.
What are the different ways
Mrs. Payne can buy the pencils?
Make a list to solve.

Packs of 10 pencils	Single pencils

Choose two of the ways from the list. Explain how
these two ways show the same total amount of pencils.

Numbers to 1,000

Curious About Math with
Curious George

The White House is the home of the President of the United States in Washington, D.C. The White House has 412 doors and 147 windows. What is the value of the digit 1 in the number 412?

Name _____

Identify Numbers to 30

Write how many.

1. 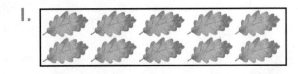   _____ leaves

2. 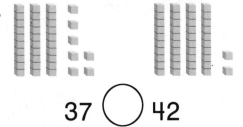   _____ bugs

Place Value: 2-Digit Numbers

Circle the value of the red digit.

3. **47**
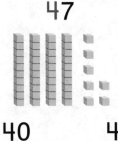

40   4

4. **84**
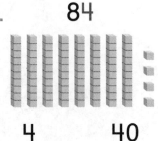

4   40

5. **65**
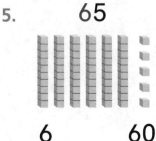

6   60

Compare 2-Digit Numbers

Compare. Write >, <, or =.

6.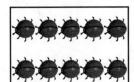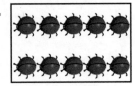

37 ◯ 42

7.

40 ◯ 33

Family note: This page checks your child's understanding of important skills needed for success in Chapter 2.

 GO Online   Assessment Options
Soar to Success Math

© Houghton Mifflin Harcourt Publishing Company

Name _____

Vocabulary Builder

Review Words
compare
more
fewer
digits
tens
ones

Visualize It
Fill in the boxes of the graphic organizer.
Show ways to **compare.**

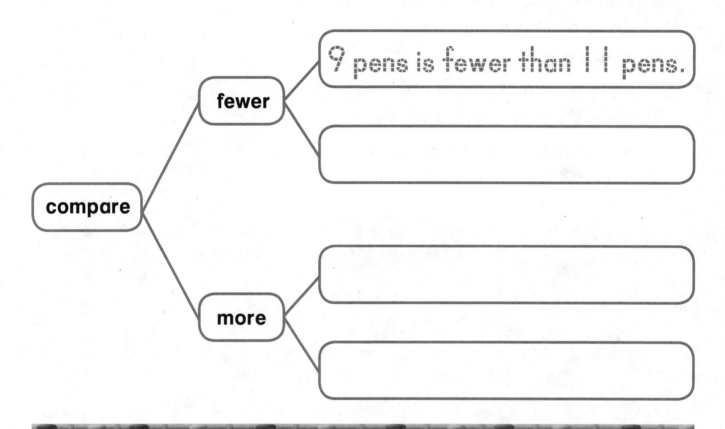

compare
fewer
9 pens is fewer than 11 pens.
more

Understand Vocabulary
Use the review words. Complete the sentences.

1. 2 is in the _____ place in 52.

2. 5 is in the _____ place in 52.

3. 3 and 9 are _____ in the number 39.

GO Online
• eStudent Edition
• Multimedia eGlossary

Game

Fish for Digits

Materials
- 12 ● • 12 ● • 1 🎲

Play with a partner.

1. Name a place value for a digit. You can say **tens** or **ones**. Toss the 🎲.

2. Match the number on the 🎲 and the place value that you named with a fish.

3. Put a ● on that fish. Take turns.

4. Match all the fish. The player with more ● wins.

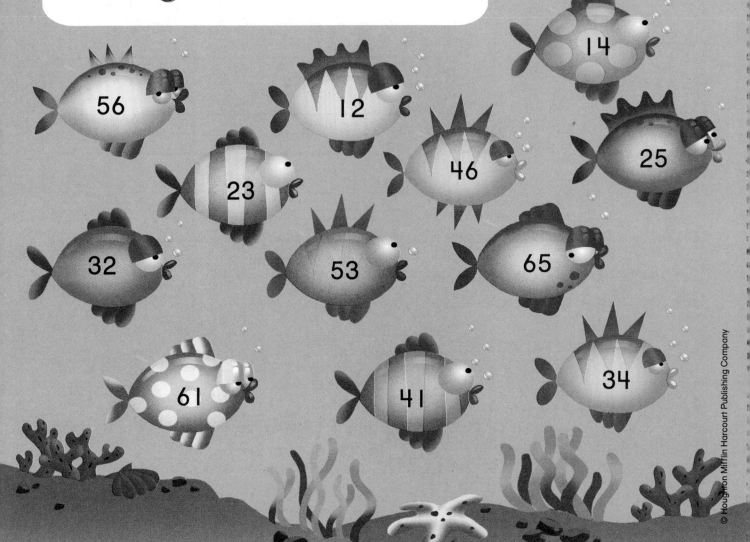

14

56

12

46

25

23

32

53

65

34

61

41

Name _____

Hundreds

Essential Question How are tens grouped as hundreds?

Listen and Draw REAL WORLD

Circle groups of ten. Count the tens.

FOR THE TEACHER • Read the following problem and have children group ones blocks to solve. Bernie dropped 100 pennies. How many groups of 10 pennies can he make as he picks up the pennies?

Math Talk
How many ones are in 3 tens? In 7 tens?

Chapter 2

10 tens is the same as 1 **hundred**.

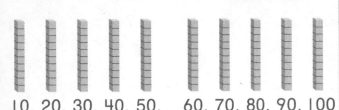

10, 20, 30, 40, 50,   60, 70, 80, 90, 100

_10_ tens = _1_ hundred

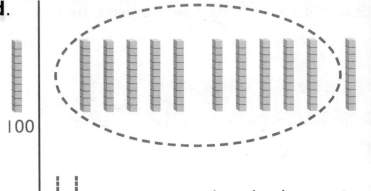

_11_ tens = ____ hundred ____ ten

Share and Show

Circle tens to make 1 hundred. Write the number in two ways.

1.

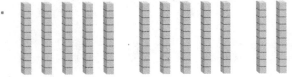

____ tens = ____ hundred ____ tens

✓2.

____ tens = ____ hundred ____ tens

✓3.

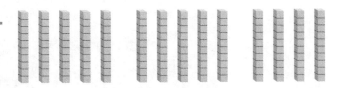

____ tens = ____ hundred ____ tens

On Your Own

Circle tens to make 1 hundred. Write the number in two ways.

4.

_____ tens = _____ hundred _____ tens

5.

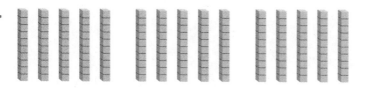

_____ tens = _____ hundred _____. tens

6.

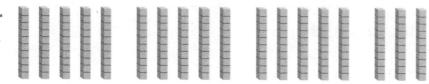

_____ tens = _____ hundred _____ tens

7.

_____ tens = _____ hundred _____ tens

H.O.T. Draw quick pictures of tens to show the number.
Then circle tens to show each hundred.

8. 1 hundred 9 tens

9. 2 hundreds 0 tens

Chapter 2 • Lesson 1

Solve. Write or draw to explain.

10. Kendra has 1 hundred stickers. 10 stickers fill a page. How many pages can she fill?

_____ pages

11. **H.O.T.** Riley has 30 bags of marbles. Each bag has 10 marbles. How many groups of 1 hundred marbles can he make?

_____ groups of 1 hundred

Write a number to make the story true.

12. Lisa sees boxes of crackers.
There are 10 crackers in each box.
Lisa sees 8 boxes. So, Lisa knows that

there are _____ crackers in all in the boxes.

13. ★ **Test Prep**   Which is the same number as 17 tens?

○ 17 ones

○ 17 hundreds

○ 1 ten 7 ones

○ 1 hundred 7 tens

TAKE HOME ACTIVITY · Have your child draw 100 Xs by drawing
10 groups of 10 Xs.

52 fifty-two

FOR MORE PRACTICE:
Standards Practice Book, pp. P21–P22

Name _____

Model 3-Digit Numbers

Essential Question How do you show a 3-digit number using blocks?

Listen and Draw REAL WORLD

Use ▭▭▭. Draw to show what you did.

FOR THE TEACHER • Read the following problem. Jack has 12 tens blocks. How many hundreds and tens does Jack have? Have children show Jack's blocks and then draw quick pictures. Then have children circle 10 tens and solve the problem. Show the hundreds block.

Math Talk
If Jack had 14 tens, how many hundreds and tens would he have? **Explain.**

Chapter 2

Model and Draw

In the number 348, the 3 is in the hundreds place, the 4 is in the tens place, and the 8 is in the ones place.

Write the digits in the chart.	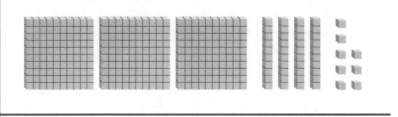
	Hundreds | **Tens** | **Ones**
	3 | 4 | 8

Write the digits in the chart.

Hundreds	Tens	Ones
3	4	8

Show the number 348 using blocks.

Draw quick pictures.

Share and Show

Write how many hundreds, tens, and ones.

Show with ▭ ▬▬▬ ▪. Then draw quick pictures.

☑ 1. 234

Hundreds	Tens	Ones

☑ 2. 107

Hundreds	Tens	Ones

Name _____

On Your Own

Write how many hundreds, tens, and ones.

Show with  _____ . Then draw quick pictures.

3. 125

Hundreds	Tens	Ones

4. 312

Hundreds	Tens	Ones

5. 245

Hundreds	Tens	Ones

6. 103

Hundreds	Tens	Ones

H.O.T. Look at the digits of the number. Draw quick pictures for the missing blocks.

7. 214

8. 130

Write the number that matches the clues.

9. My number has 2 hundreds.
   It has no tens.
   It has 3 ones.

Hundreds	Tens	Ones

My number is _____.

10. My number has 3 hundreds.
    It has 5 tens.
    It has no ones.

Hundreds	Tens	Ones

My number is _____.

11. **H.O.T.** How are the numbers 342 and 324 alike?
    How are they different?

    _____

    _____

    _____

12. ⭐ **Test Prep** Which shows
    101? You may wish to use the
    chart.

Hundreds	Tens	Ones

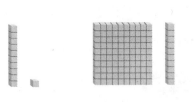 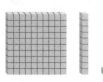

  ○   ○   ○   ○

TAKE HOME ACTIVITY • Write the number 438. Have your child
tell you the number of hundreds, tens, and ones for 438.

FOR MORE PRACTICE:
Standards Practice Book, pp. P23–P24

Hundreds, Tens, and Ones

Essential Question How do you write the 3-digit number that is shown by a set of blocks?

Listen and Draw REAL WORLD

Write the number of hundreds, tens, and ones.

Use ___ to model. Then draw quick pictures.

Hundreds	Tens	Ones

Hundreds	Tens	Ones

FOR THE TEACHER • Read the following sentence. Steven has 243 yellow beads. Write 243 on the board. Have children model 243 with base-ten blocks and draw quick pictures. Repeat using this sentence. Steven has 423 red beads.

Math Talk
Describe how the two numbers are alike. Describe how they are different.

Model and Draw

Write how many hundreds.
Then write how many tens
and ones. What is the number?

Hundreds	Tens	Ones

_____ is the number.

Share and Show

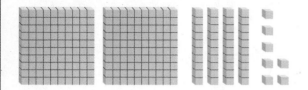

Write how many hundreds, tens, and ones.
Write the number.

1.

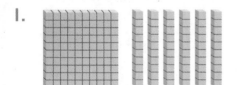

Hundreds	Tens	Ones

_____

2.

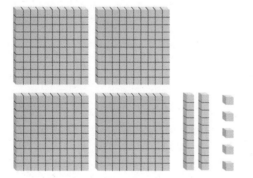

Hundreds	Tens	Ones

_____

3.

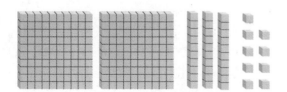

Hundreds	Tens	Ones

_____

Name _____

On Your Own

Write how many hundreds, tens, and ones.
Write the number.

4.
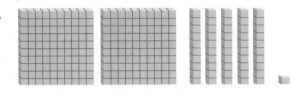

Hundreds	Tens	Ones

_____

5.
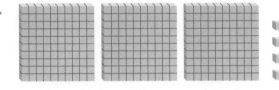

Hundreds	Tens	Ones

_____

6.
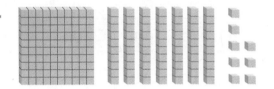

Hundreds	Tens	Ones

_____

7. Count the hundreds, tens, and ones.
   Write the number.

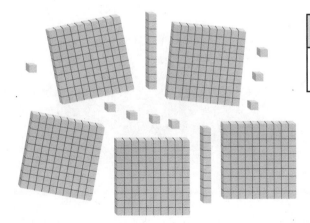

Hundreds	Tens	Ones

_____

Write the number that answers the riddle.
Use the chart.

8. I have 4 ones, 5 tens, and 1 hundred.
   What number am I?

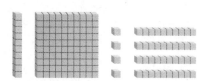

Hundreds	Tens	Ones

_____

9. Draw quick pictures of blocks you could use to model 315.

10. **H.O.T.** Write the greatest number you can make that has 3 digits.

Hundreds	Tens	Ones

_____

11. ★ **Test Prep** Karen has 279 pictures. How many hundreds are in this number?

○ 2 hundreds

○ 7 hundreds

○ 9 hundreds

○ 18 hundreds

TAKE HOME ACTIVITY · Say a 3-digit number, such as 546. Then have your child draw the hundreds, tens, and ones for that number.

FOR MORE PRACTICE:
Standards Practice Book, pp. P25–P26

Name _____

Place Value to 1,000

Essential Question How do you know the values of the digits in numbers?

Listen and Draw REAL WORLD

Write the numbers. Then draw quick pictures.

_____ sheets of colored paper

Hundreds	Tens	Ones

_____ sheets of plain paper

Hundreds	Tens	Ones

Math Talk
Describe how 5 tens is different from 5 hundreds.

FOR THE TEACHER • Read the following. There are 245 sheets of colored paper in the supply closet. There are 458 sheets of plain paper by the computer table. Have children write each number and draw quick pictures to show each number.

Chapter 2

Model and Draw

The place of a digit in a number tells its value.
What is the value of each digit in 327?

327
The 3 is in the hundreds place. The value of this digit is 300.

Hundreds	Tens	Ones
3	2	7

3 hundreds   2 tens   7 ones
300   20   7

There are 10 hundreds in 1 **thousand**.

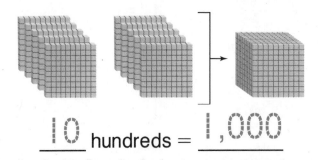

__10__ hundreds = __1,000__

Thousands	Hundreds	Tens	Ones
1	0	0	0

1 thousand   0 hundreds   0 tens   0 ones
1,000   0   0   0

Share and Show

Circle the value or the meaning of the red digit.

☑ 1. 459   500   50   5

☑ 2. 362   3 hundreds   3 tens   3 ones

On Your Own

Circle the value or the meaning of the red digit.

3. 362	600	60	6
4. 607	7 ones	7 tens	7 hundreds
5. 1,000	1	100	1,000
6. 914	9 tens	9 hundreds	9 thousands
7. 380	8	80	800
8. 692	6 ones	6 tens	6 hundreds

 Write the number that matches the clues.

9. Clues:

- The value of my hundreds digit is 300.
- The value of my tens digit is 0.
- The value of my ones digit is an even number greater than 7.

The number is _____.

10. Richard is making a Venn diagram. Where should he write the other numbers in the diagram?

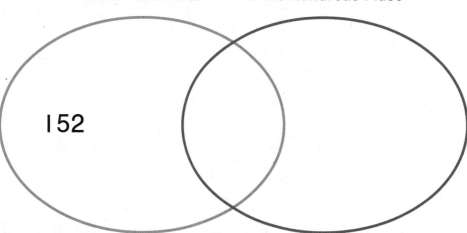

Numbers with a 5 in the Tens Place   Numbers with a 2 in the Hundreds Place

152

~~152~~
215
454
257
352
205
250

---

11. **H.O.T.** Describe where 752 should be written in the diagram. Explain your answer.

_____

_____

_____

---

12. ⭐ **Test Prep** Which of these numbers has the digit 4 in the tens place?

○ 64
○ 149
○ 437
○ 504

TAKE HOME ACTIVITY · Ask your child to write 3-digit numbers, such as "a number with 2 hundreds" and "a number with a 9 in the ones place."

FOR MORE PRACTICE:
Standards Practice Book, pp. P27–P28

Name _____

Different Forms of Numbers

Essential Question What are three ways to write a number?

Listen and Draw REAL WORLD

Write the number. Write how many hundreds, tens, and ones.

_____ hundreds _____ tens _____ ones

_____ hundreds _____ tens _____ ones

_____ hundreds _____ tens _____ ones

FOR THE TEACHER • Read the following problem.
Evan has 426 marbles. How many hundreds, tens, and
ones are in 426? Continue the activity for 204 and 341.

Math Talk
How many
hundreds are in
361? **Explain** how
you know.

© Houghton Mifflin Harcourt Publishing Company

Chapter 2

Model and Draw

You can use quick pictures to show a number.
You can write a number in different ways.

five hundred thirty-six

___5___ hundreds ___3___ tens ___6___ ones

___500___ + ___30___ + ___6___

_____

Share and Show

Read the number and draw quick pictures.
Then write the number in different ways.

1. four hundred seven

_____ hundreds _____ tens _____ ones

_____ + _____ + _____

_____

2. three hundred twenty-five

_____ hundreds _____ tens _____ ones

_____ + _____ + _____

_____

3. two hundred fifty-three

_____ hundreds _____ tens _____ ones

_____ + _____ + _____

_____

On Your Own

Read the number and draw quick pictures.
Then write the number in different ways.

4. one hundred seventy-three

_____ hundred _____ tens _____ ones

_____ + _____ + _____

_____

5. three hundred forty-seven

_____ hundreds _____ tens _____ ones

_____ + _____ + _____

_____

Write the number another way.

6. 500 + 30 + 2

_____

7. 641

_____

8. 8 hundreds 7 ones

_____

© Houghton Mifflin Harcourt Publishing Company

PROBLEM SOLVING

Write the 3-digit number that matches the clues.

9. My number has twice as many ones as tens. It has more hundreds than tens. Two of the digits are 5 and 8. What is my number? _____

---

10. **H.O.T.** Mark one point that is between the two points shown on the number line. Write the number for your point in three different ways.

250   260

_____ hundreds _____ tens _____ ones

_____ + _____ + _____

_____

---

11. ⭐ **Test Prep**   Daniel counts the number of chairs in the lunch room. The number has 5 hundreds, 0 tens, and 7 ones. What is the number?

- ○ 57
- ○ 507
- ○ 570
- ○ 517

TAKE HOME ACTIVITY · Ask your child to write the number 948 in different ways.

FOR MORE PRACTICE:
Standards Practice Book, pp. P29–P30

Name _____

Different Ways to Show Numbers

Essential Question How can you use blocks or quick pictures to show a number in different ways?

Listen and Draw REAL WORLD

Use ▭▭▭ to show the number of books. Then draw quick pictures and write the number.

_____ books

FOR THE TEACHER • Read the following two sentences. Mrs. Lee packed 14 boxes of books. She put 10 books in each box. Have children use tens blocks to show the books and then draw quick pictures. Have them circle enough tens to make 1 hundred and write the number.

Math Talk
Describe how you knew how to write the number.

Model and Draw

Here are two ways to show 148.

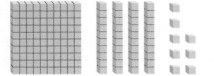

Hundreds	Tens	Ones

Hundreds	Tens	Ones

Share and Show

Write how many hundreds, tens, and ones.

1. 213

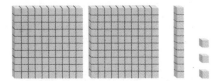

Hundreds	Tens	Ones

Hundreds	Tens	Ones

2. 132

Hundreds	Tens	Ones

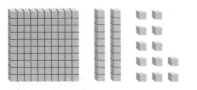

Hundreds	Tens	Ones

Name _____

On Your Own

Write how many hundreds, tens, and ones.

3. 144

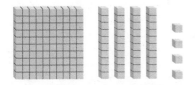

Hundreds	Tens	Ones

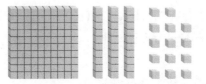

Hundreds	Tens	Ones

4. 204

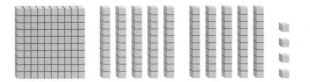

Hundreds	Tens	Ones

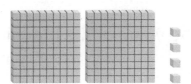

Hundreds	Tens	Ones

5. **H.O.T.** Write the number that these blocks show.

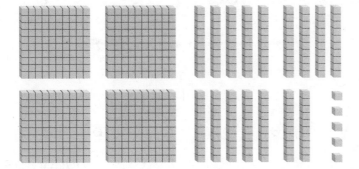

_____

TAKE HOME ACTIVITY • Write the number 156. Have your child draw quick pictures of two ways to show this number.

Chapter 2 • Lesson 6

FOR MORE PRACTICE:
Standards Practice Book, pp. P31–P32

Mid-Chapter Checkpoint

Concepts and Skills

Write how many hundreds, tens,
and ones. Write the number. (pp. 57–60)

1.

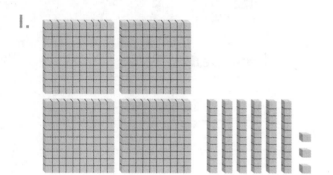

Hundreds	Tens	Ones

_____

Circle the value or the meaning of the red digit. (pp. 61–64)

2. 528	5	50	500
3. 674	4 ones	4 tens	4 hundreds
4. 367	600	60	6

⭐ Test Prep

5. Which is another way to write
the number 630? (pp. 65–68)

○ 60 + 3

○ 6 hundreds 3 tens

○ 600 + 3

○ 6 hundreds 3 ones

Name _____

Count by 10s and 100s

Essential Question How can you use place value to count by 10s or count by 100s?

Listen and Draw REAL WORLD

Draw quick pictures for the numbers.

Girls

Hundreds	Tens	Ones

Boys

Hundreds	Tens	Ones

Math Talk
Describe how the two numbers are different.

FOR THE TEACHER • Read the following sentence to the children. There are 342 girls at Center School. Have the children draw a quick picture for 342. Then tell them that there are 352 boys. Have them draw a quick picture for the number of boys.

Chapter 2

Model and Draw

You can show 10 less or 10 more than a number by changing the tens digit.

10 less than 264

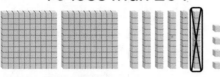

Hundreds	Tens	Ones
2	5	4

10 more than 264

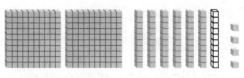

Hundreds	Tens	Ones
2	7	4

You can show 100 less or 100 more than a number by changing the hundreds digit.

100 less than 264

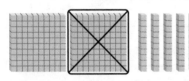

Hundreds	Tens	Ones
1	6	4

100 more than 264

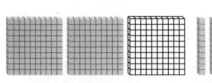

Hundreds	Tens	Ones
3	6	4

Share and Show

Write the number.

1. 10 more than 648

   _____

☑ 2. 100 less than 263

   _____

☑ 3. Count on by 10s.

   253, _____, _____, _____, 293

Name _____

On Your Own

Write the number.

4. 10 more than 471

   _____

5. 10 less than 143

   _____

6. 100 more than 555

   _____

7. 100 less than 364

   _____

8. 100 more than 900

   _____

9. 10 less than 163

   _____

10. Count on by 10s.

    329, _____, _____, _____, 369

11. Count back by 10s.

    897, _____, _____, _____, 857

12. Count on by 100s.

    105, _____, _____, _____, 505

13. Count back by 100s.

    622, _____, _____, _____, 222

14. **H.O.T.** Write the number that is 10 more than 193.

    _____

15. **H.O.T.** Write the number that is 100 less than 105.

    _____

PROBLEM SOLVING

REAL WORLD

Write Math

Solve. Write or draw to explain.

16. A number has 2 digits. It has 6 ones and 4 tens. What is the number?

_____

17. Juan's book has 248 pages. This is 10 more pages than there are in Kevin's book. How many pages are in Kevin's book?

_____ pages

18. **H.O.T.** Use the clues to answer the question.

Clues:

- Shawn reads 213 pages.

- Maria reads 100 more pages than Shawn.

- Gavin reads 10 fewer pages than Maria.

How many pages does Gavin read?

_____ pages

19. ⭐ **Test Prep** Cara begins at 456 and counts on by 100s. Which could be a number that she says?

- ○ 466
- ○ 486
- ○ 856
- ○ 886

TAKE HOME ACTIVITY • Write the number 596. Have your child name the number that is 100 more than 596.

76 seventy-six

© Houghton Mifflin Harcourt Publishing Company

FOR MORE PRACTICE:
Standards Practice Book, pp. P33–P34

Name _____

Algebra: Number Patterns

Essential Question How does place value help you identify counting patterns?

Listen and Draw REAL WORLD

Shade the numbers in the counting pattern.

801	802	803	804	805	806	807	808	809	810
811	812	813	814	815	816	817	818	819	820
821	822	823	824	825	826	827	828	829	830
831	832	833	834	835	836	837	838	839	840
841	842	843	844	845	846	847	848	849	850
851	852	853	854	855	856	857	858	859	860
861	862	863	864	865	866	867	868	869	870
871	872	873	874	875	876	877	878	879	880
881	882	883	884	885	886	887	888	889	890
891	892	893	894	895	896	897	898	899	900

FOR THE TEACHER • Read the following problem and discuss the counting pattern. Blossom Bakery sold 823 muffins in the morning. In the afternoon it sold four more packages, each with 10 muffins. How many muffins did the bakery sell in all?

Math Talk
What number will follow 863 in this pattern? **Explain.**

Chapter 2

Model and Draw

Compare the digits of the numbers.
What two numbers are next in the pattern?

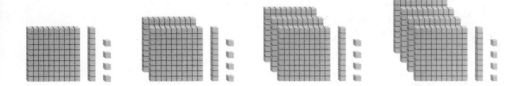

114,   214,   314,   414,   ,   ⬛

The _____ digit changes by one each time.

The next two numbers are _____ and _____.

Share and Show

Compare the digits to find the next two numbers.

1. 37, 47, 57, 67, ⬛, ⬛

   The next two numbers are _____ and _____.

2. 245, 345, 445, 545, ⬛, ⬛

   The next two numbers are _____ and _____.

3. 421, 431, 441, 451, ⬛, ⬛

   The next two numbers are _____ and _____.

4. 389, 489, 589, 689, ⬛, ⬛

   The next two numbers are _____ and _____.

Name _____

Make a Model • Compare Numbers

Essential Question How can you make a model to solve a problem?

Children bought 217 cartons of chocolate milk and 188 cartons of plain milk. Did they buy more cartons of chocolate milk or plain milk?

Unlock the Problem REAL WORLD

What do I need to find?

if the children bought **more** cartons of chocolate milk or plain milk

What information do I need to use?

_____ cartons of chocolate milk

_____ cartons of plain milk

Show how to solve the problem.

Make a model. Then draw quick pictures of your models.

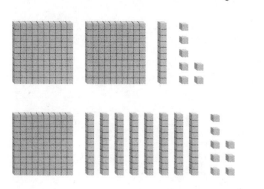

more cartons of _____ milk

HOME CONNECTION • Your child used base-ten blocks to represent the numbers in the problem. These models were used as a tool for comparing numbers to solve the problem.

Try Another Problem

Make a model to solve.
Then draw quick pictures.

- What do I need to find?
- What information do I need to use?

1. At the zoo, there are 137 birds and 142 reptiles. Are there more birds or more reptiles at the zoo?

more _____

2. Tom's book has 105 pages.
Delia's book has 109 pages.
Whose book has fewer pages?

_____ book

Math Talk

Explain what you did to solve the second problem.

Name _____

Share and Show

Make a model to solve.
Then draw quick pictures.

---

3. Mary's puzzle has
164 pieces. Jake's puzzle
has 180 pieces. Whose
puzzle has more pieces?

_____ puzzle

---

4. There are 246 children at
Dan's school. There are
251 children at Karen's
school. At which school are
there fewer children?

_____ school

---

5. There are 131 crayons in a
box. There are 128 crayons in
a bag. Are there more crayons
in the box or in the bag?

in the _____

---

6. There are 308 books in
the first room. There are
273 books in the second
room. In which room are
there fewer books?

in the _____ room

Chapter 2 • Lesson 9

On Your Own

Choose a way to solve.
Write or draw to explain.

7. Ms. Tyler sold 115 small cards and 108 large cards. Did she sell fewer small cards or fewer large cards?

fewer _____ cards

8. A number has a 1 in the tens place. Which of these could be the number?

    three hundred fifty-one
    one hundred fifty
    three hundred fifteen

9. **H.O.T.** Which is another way to write 257?

    2 hundreds 57 tens
    25 tens 7 ones
    25 hundreds 7 ones

10. ⭐ **Test Prep** Which number is greater than 456?

    ○ 265
    ○ 356
    ○ 654
    ○ 426

TAKE HOME ACTIVITY • Ask your child to explain how he or she solved two of the problems on this page.

FOR MORE PRACTICE:
Standards Practice Book, pp. P37–P38

Name _____

Algebra: Compare Numbers

Essential Question How do you compare numbers?

Listen and Draw REAL WORLD

Use models. Then draw quick pictures.

Rory scored _____ points.

Hundreds	Tens	Ones

Claire scored _____ points.

Hundreds	Tens	Ones

_____ is greater than _____.

_____ scored more points

than _____.

Math Talk

Use **is greater than** or **is less than** to tell about 137 and 215.

FOR THE TEACHER • Read the following problem and have children complete the activity. Rory scored 179 points in a video game. Claire scored 213 points in the same game. Who scored more points?

Chapter 2

Model and Draw

Compare numbers by looking at the greatest place value first.

If the hundreds are the same, compare the tens.	If the hundreds and tens are the same, compare the ones.	If the hundreds, tens, and ones are the same, then the numbers are equal.

241 is greater than 234.

241 > 234

123 is less than 128.

123 < 128

247 is equal to 247.

247 = 247

Share and Show

Write **is greater than**, **is less than**, or **is equal to**.
Then write >, <, or =.

1.
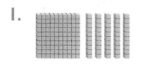

150 _____ 250.

150 ◯ 250

2.
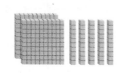

212 _____ 218.

212 ◯ 218

 3.
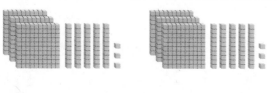

353 _____ 353.

353 ◯ 353

 4.
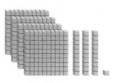 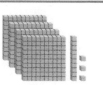

431 _____ 413.

431 ◯ 413

On Your Own

Compare. Write >, <, or =.

5.

315 ◯ 215

6.

231 ◯ 231

7.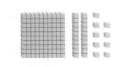

129 ◯ 140

8.

202 ◯ 107

9.

323 ◯ 323

10.

227 ◯ 1,000

H.O.T. When you compare the numbers, which is the last place value position that you need to look at? Write **hundreds place, tens place,** or **ones place.**

11. 256 and 314

_____

12. 548 and 539

_____

13. Explain your answer for Exercise 11.

_____

_____

_____

PROBLEM SOLVING REAL WORLD

Solve. Write or draw to explain.

14. There are 256 pages in Keisha's notebook. There are 258 pages in Jack's notebook. Whose notebook has more pages?

_____ notebook

15. **H.O.T.** Ms. Dixon sees more than 119 birds but fewer than 132 birds. How many birds might she have seen?

_____ birds

16. ⭐ **Test Prep** Mr. Kirby has 246 stickers. Ms. Hayes has fewer stickers. Which number tells how many stickers Ms. Hayes could have?

○ 198
○ 250
○ 426
○ 247

TAKE HOME ACTIVITY · Ask your child how he or she compares numbers, such as 185 and 178.

FOR MORE PRACTICE:
Standards Practice Book, pp. P39–P40

Name _____

Algebra: Order Numbers

Essential Question How do you order numbers?

Listen and Draw REAL WORLD

Write the numbers. Then draw quick pictures.

_____ red stars

Hundreds	Tens	Ones

_____ blue stars

Hundreds	Tens	Ones

_____ green stars

Hundreds	Tens	Ones

Math Talk
Describe how the numbers are different.

FOR THE TEACHER • Read the following sentences. Kwan has three groups of stars. He has 251 red stars, 97 blue stars, and 236 green stars. Have children write the numbers and then draw quick pictures.

Chapter 2

You can compare digits to order numbers from least to greatest or from greatest to least.

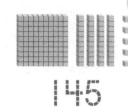

The hundreds and tens are the same. So, compare the ones.

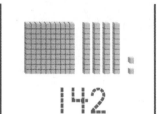 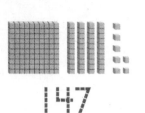

147   142   145

2 < 5 < 7

7 > 5 > 2

142 < 145 < 147
least   greatest

____ ◯ ____ ◯ ____
greatest   least

Share and Show

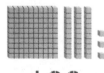 Math Board

Compare the numbers. Write them in order from least to greatest. Write > or <.

Write the number for each model first.

1.

133   ____   ____

____ ◯ ____ ◯ ____
least   greatest

2.

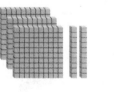 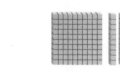 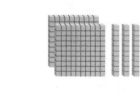

____   ____   ____

____ ◯ ____ ◯ ____
least   greatest

90 ninety

On Your Own

Compare the numbers. Write them in order
from greatest to least. Write > or <.

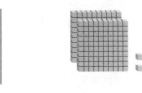
Write the number
for each model first.

3.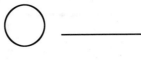

_____   _____   _____

_____ ◯ _____ ◯ _____
greatest   least

4.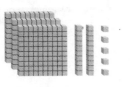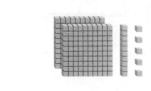

_____   _____   _____

_____ ◯ _____ ◯ _____
greatest   least

 Compare the numbers to solve.

5.   865   6.   390
      705   89
      895   376
      645   412

Which is greatest? _____   Which is greatest? _____

Which is least? _____   Which is least? _____

Write Math

Solve.

7. There are 3 trucks carrying oranges. One truck has 450 oranges. Another truck has 540 oranges in it, and the other truck has 514 oranges in it.

Label the trucks in order of greatest number to least number of oranges.

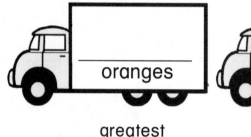

      greatest   least

8. **H.O.T.** Paul has fewer than 205 stamps. He has more than 137 stamps. How many stamps might he have?

Write that number in the box.

205 > ☐ > 137

9. ⭐ **Test Prep** Jenna has 152 paper clips. Zachary has 149 paper clips. Shelby has 161 paper clips.

Which of the following is true?

- ○ 149 < 161 < 152
- ○ 161 < 149 < 152
- ○ 152 > 149 > 161
- ○ 161 > 152 > 149

TAKE HOME ACTIVITY · Write three 3-digit numbers. Then have your child write the numbers in order from least to greatest.

FOR MORE PRACTICE:
Standards Practice Book, pp. P41–P42

 Chapter 2 Review/Test

Vocabulary

Use a word in the box to complete each sentence.

| hundred |
| thousand |
| least |
| greatest |

1. When you put 136, 132, and 138 in order,

   132 is the _____ number. (pp. 89-92)

2. 10 hundreds is the same as 1 _____. (pp. 61-64)

3. 10 tens is the same as 1 _____. (pp. 49-52)

Concepts and Skills

Read the number and draw quick pictures.
Then write the number in different ways. (pp. 65-68)

4. two hundred thirty-five

   _____ hundreds _____ tens _____ ones

   _____ + _____ + _____

   _____

Compare. Write >, <, or =. (pp. 85-88)

5.

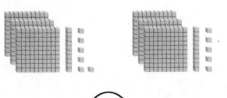

316 ◯ 315

6.

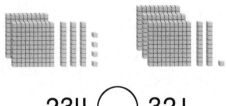

234 ◯ 321

Fill in the bubble for the correct answer choice.

7. Which is another way to show 14 tens? (pp. 49-52)

   ○ 1 ten 4 ones

   ○ 1 hundred 4 tens

   ○ 1 thousand 4 hundreds

   ○ 14 ones

8. Jenna is thinking of a number that has
   3 ones, 2 tens, and 4 hundreds.
   What is the number? (pp. 53-60)

   ○ 324

   ○ 342

   ○ 423

   ○ 432

9. Dylan has 324 baseball cards.
   Malia has 342 baseball cards.

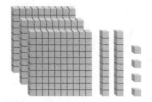 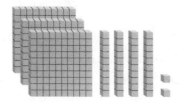

   Which of the following is true? (pp. 85-88)

   ○ 324 > 342

   ○ 324 < 342

   ○ 324 > 432

   ○ 342 < 243

Fill in the bubble for the correct answer choice.

10. Emma collected 127 shells at the beach.
What is the value of the digit 2 in 127? (pp. 61-64)

- ○   2
- ○   12
- ○   20
- ○ 200

11. There are 3 boxes of crayons on the table.
One box has 142 crayons. Another box has
163 crayons. The third box has 134 crayons.

Which of the following is true? (pp. 89-92)

- ○ 134 < 142 < 163
- ○ 142 < 163 < 134
- ○ 134 > 163 > 142
- ○ 163 > 134 > 142

12. Juan wants to write this number in a different way.

582

Which is another way to write this number? (pp. 65-68)

- ○ 50 + 82
- ○ 500 + 8 + 2
- ○ 500 + 80 + 2
- ○ 50 + 80 + 2

Short Answer

13. Compare the digits to find the next two numbers.

507,   517,   527,   537,   ,   ▮

The next two numbers are _____ and _____.

Describe how the numbers in the pattern change.

_____

_____

Performance Task

14. There are many people at a baseball game.
The number of people is greater than 346,
but less than 370. Complete the sentence below.

The number of people could be _____ people.

Explain how you chose your number.

_____

_____

Draw quick pictures to show how you know that your
number is greater than 346 but less than 370.

All About Animals

by John Hudson

Focal POINT

Developing quick recall of addition facts and related subtraction facts and fluency with multidigit addition and subtraction

The giraffe is the tallest land animal in the world. Adult giraffes are 13 to 17 feet tall. Newborn giraffes are about 6 feet tall.

A group of 5 giraffes drinks water at a watering hole. A group of 5 giraffes eats leaves from trees. How many giraffes are there in all?

_____ giraffes

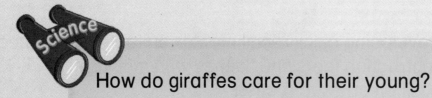

How do giraffes care for their young?

The ostrich is the largest bird in the world.
Ostriches cannot fly, but they can run fast.
Ostrich eggs weigh about 3 pounds each!
Several ostriches will lay eggs in a shared nest.

There are 6 eggs in a nest. Then 5 more eggs
are put in that nest. How many eggs are in the
nest now?

_____ eggs

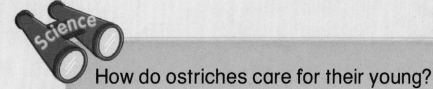

How do ostriches care for their young?

Kangaroos can move quickly by jumping with their two back feet. When they are moving slowly, they use all four legs.

Western gray kangaroos live in groups called mobs. There are 8 kangaroos in a mob. 4 more kangaroos join the mob. How many kangaroos are in the mob in all?

_____ kangaroos

How do kangaroos care for their young?

Wild boars like to eat roots. They use their tough snouts to dig. Wild boars can be up to 6 feet long.

Wild boars live in groups called sounders. There is one sounder of 14 boars. If 7 of the boars are eating, how many boars are not eating?

____ boars

How do wild boars care for their young?

Moose are the largest kind of deer. Male moose have antlers that may be 5 to 6 feet wide. Moose can trot and gallop. They are also good swimmers!

A ranger saw 7 moose in the morning and 6 moose in the afternoon. How many moose did the ranger see that day?

_____ moose

© Houghton Mifflin Harcourt Publishing Company

How do moose care for their young?

Name _____

Write About the Story

Choose one kind of animal.
Draw a picture and write your own
story about that kind of animal.
Use addition in your story.

Vocabulary Review

add   in all

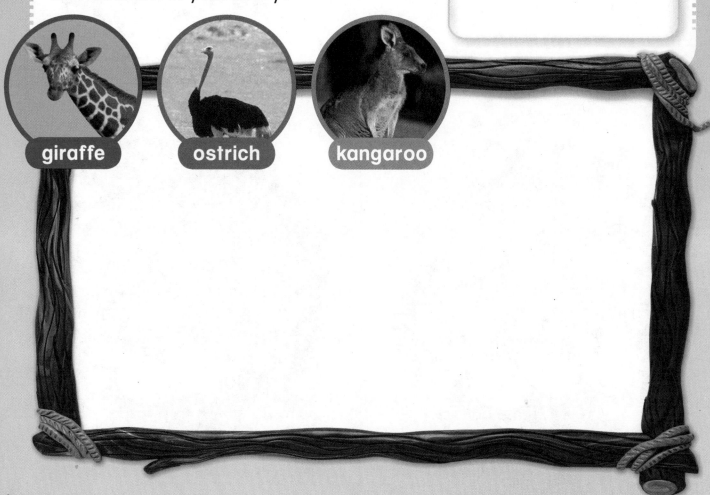

giraffe   ostrich   kangaroo

Write Math

_____

_____

_____

_____

How many eggs are there?

Draw more ostrich eggs in each nest. Write an addition sentence below each nest to show how many eggs are in each nest now.

_____

_____

 Choose a different animal from the story. Write another story that uses addition.

Chapter 3 Basic Facts and Relationships

Curious About Math with Curious George

Parrot fish live near coral reefs in tropical ocean waters. These brightly colored fish have sharp teeth that they use to scrape food off the coral.

Suppose 15 parrot fish are eating around a coral reef. 8 of the fish swim away. How many fish are still eating?

Name _____

Use a Number Line to Count On

Use the number line to count on. Write the sum.

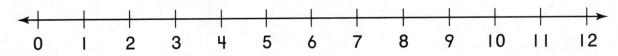

0 1 2 3 4 5 6 7 8 9 10 11 12

1. $8 + 2 =$ _____   2. $5 + 1 =$ _____   3. $6 + 3 =$ _____

Sums to 10

Write the sum.

4. $\begin{array}{r} 4 \\ +\,3 \\ \hline \end{array}$ 5. $\begin{array}{r} 5 \\ +\,0 \\ \hline \end{array}$ 6. $\begin{array}{r} 2 \\ +\,7 \\ \hline \end{array}$ 7. $\begin{array}{r} 2 \\ +\,3 \\ \hline \end{array}$ 8. $\begin{array}{r} 9 \\ +\,1 \\ \hline \end{array}$

Doubles and Doubles Plus One

Write the addition sentence.

9.

____ ◯ ____ ◯ ____

10.

____ ◯ ____ ◯ ____

11.

____ ◯ ____ ◯ ____

12.

____ ◯ ____ ◯ ____

 Family note: This page checks your child's understanding of important skills needed for success in Chapter 3.

 Online  Assessment Options
Soar to Success Math

Name _____

Vocabulary Builder

Review Words
addition
subtraction
plus
minus
equals
count on
count back

Visualize It

Sort the review words in the graphic organizer.

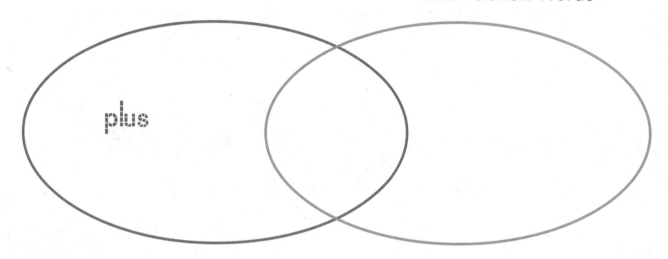

Addition Words   **Subtraction** Words

plus

Understand Vocabulary

1. Circle the **addition** sentence. $3 + 6 = 9$ $9 - 6 = 3$

2. Circle the **subtraction** sentence. $8 + 2 = 10$ $10 - 2 = 8$

3. Circle the **count on** fact. $5 - 1 = 4$ $4 + 1 = 5$

4. Circle the **count back** fact. $8 - 2 = 6$ $6 + 2 = 8$

GO Online
• eStudent Edition
• Multimedia eGlossary

Game Caterpillar Chase

Materials

- 1 ⬛ • 1 ⬛ • 1 🎲

Play with a partner.

1. Put your ⬛ on START.
2. Toss the 🎲, and move that many spaces.

3. Say the sum or difference. Your partner checks your answer.
4. Take turns. The first person to get to FINISH wins.

FINISH

$$7 + 3$$ $$1 - 1$$ $$3 + 4$$ $$6 - 0$$ $$9 + 0$$

$$2 + 4$$

$$1 + 6$$ $$4 - 1$$ $$3 + 0$$ $$9 - 8$$ $$5 - 2$$

$$5 - 5$$

$$7 - 4$$ $$3 + 5$$ $$0 + 4$$ $$7 - 5$$ $$2 + 3$$ $$9 - 7$$

START

$$4 + 4$$ $$6 - 1$$ $$8 + 2$$ $$5 + 3$$

$$8 - 2$$

Name _____

Addition Facts

Essential Question What are some ways to remember sums?

Listen and Draw REAL WORLD

Draw pictures to show the problems.

FOR THE TEACHER • Read the following two problems. Have children draw a picture and write a number sentence for each. On Monday, Tony recycled 3 cans and 6 bottles. How many containers did he recycle? On Tuesday, Tony recycled 6 cans and 3 bottles. How many containers did he recycle?

Math Talk
Explain how the two problems are alike. **Explain** how they are different.

Model and Draw

These are some ways to remember **sums**.

> Any number plus zero equals that number.

$9 + 0 = \underline{9}$

$7 + 0 = \underline{7}$

> Use doubles for doubles-plus-one and doubles-minus-one facts.

$5 + 5 = \underline{10}$

$5 + 6 = \underline{11}$

$5 + 4 = \underline{9}$

> Changing the order of the **addends** does not change the sum.

$\underline{8} = 2 + 6$

$\underline{8} = 6 + 2$

Share and Show

Write the sums.

1. $2 + 2 = \underline{\hspace{1.5em}}$

   $2 + 3 = \underline{\hspace{1.5em}}$

2. $5 + 0 = \underline{\hspace{1.5em}}$

   $2 + 0 = \underline{\hspace{1.5em}}$

3. $3 + 8 = \underline{\hspace{1.5em}}$

   $8 + 3 = \underline{\hspace{1.5em}}$

4. $\underline{\hspace{1.5em}} = 4 + 4$

   $\underline{\hspace{1.5em}} = 4 + 3$

5. $5 + 7 = \underline{\hspace{1.5em}}$

   $7 + 5 = \underline{\hspace{1.5em}}$

6. $\underline{\hspace{1.5em}} = 7 + 7$

   $\underline{\hspace{1.5em}} = 7 + 8$

7. $\underline{\hspace{1.5em}} = 9 + 9$

   $\underline{\hspace{1.5em}} = 9 + 10$

8. $4 + 2 = \underline{\hspace{1.5em}}$

   $2 + 4 = \underline{\hspace{1.5em}}$

9. $\underline{\hspace{1.5em}} = 6 + 6$

   $\underline{\hspace{1.5em}} = 6 + 7$

On Your Own

Write the sums.

10. 7 + 1 = ____

1 + 7 = ____

11. ____ = 4 + 0

____ = 9 + 0

12. 5 + 5 = ____

5 + 4 = ____

13. 8 + 2 = ____

2 + 8 = ____

14. 10 + 9 = ____

9 + 10 = ____

15. 7 + 8 = ____

8 + 7 = ____

16. ____ = 4 + 1

____ = 1 + 4

17. 7 + 0 = ____

6 + 0 = ____

18. 8 + 8 = ____

8 + 9 = ____

19. 5 + 3 = ____

3 + 5 = ____

20. ____ = 9 + 5

____ = 5 + 9

21. 6 + 7 = ____

7 + 6 = ____

H.O.T. Find the addends for each shaded box in the addition table. Write the facts for the shaded boxes.

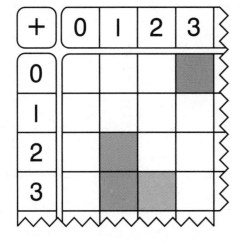

+	0	1	2	3
0				
1				
2				
3				

22. ☐ + ☐ = ☐

23. ☐ + ☐ = ☐

24. ☐ + ☐ = ☐

25. ☐ + ☐ = ☐

PROBLEM SOLVING

REAL WORLD

Write Math

Solve. Write or draw to explain.

26. Roger builds 4 toy airplanes. Then he builds 3 more toy airplanes. How many toy airplanes does he build altogether?

_____ toy airplanes

27. Joanne made 10 clay bowls last week. She made the same number of clay bowls this week. How many clay bowls did she make in all?

_____ clay bowls

28. **H.O.T.** Sam painted 3 pictures. Ellie painted twice as many pictures as Sam. How many pictures did they paint altogether?

_____ pictures

29. ⭐ **Test Prep** Chloe draws 8 pictures. Reggie draws 1 more picture than Chloe. How many pictures do they draw in all?

- ○ 7
- ○ 9
- ○ 15
- ○ 17

TAKE HOME ACTIVITY · Ask your child to write three different doubles facts.

FOR MORE PRACTICE:
Standards Practice Book, pp. P47–P48

Name _____

Make-a-Ten Facts

Essential Question How is the make-a-ten strategy used to find sums?

Listen and Draw REAL WORLD

Write the fact below the ten frame when you hear the problem that matches the model.

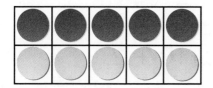

_____

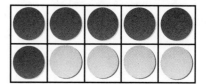

_____

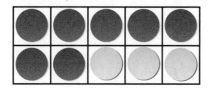

_____

_____

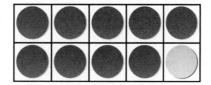

_____

FOR THE TEACHER • Read the following problem. There are 6 dog bones and 4 dog biscuits. How many dog treats are there in all? Have children find the ten frame for the problem and write the addition sentence. Repeat by revising the story for each addition fact represented on the other ten frames.

Math Talk
Describe a pattern you see in these make-a-ten facts.

Chapter 3

Model and Draw

$7 + 5 = ?$

Start with 7 and 5.

You need to add 3 to 7 to make a ten. Break apart 5 as 3 and 2.

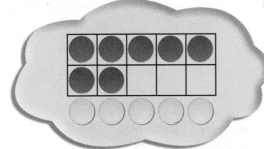

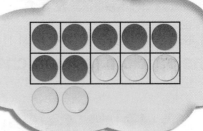

Now you have $10 + 2$.

$10 + 2 = 12$, so $7 + 5 =$ _____.

Share and Show

Write the sum. Show the make-a-ten fact you used.

1. $8 + 3 =$ _____

2 1

$10 +$ ____ $=$ ____

2. $2 + 9 =$ _____

$10 +$ ____ $=$ ____

3. $8 + 5 =$ _____

$10 +$ ____ $=$ ____

4. $4 + 7 =$ _____

$10 +$ ____ $=$ ____

5. $3 + 9 =$ _____

$10 +$ ____ $=$ ____

6. $7 + 6 =$ _____

$10 +$ ____ $=$ ____

Name _____

On Your Own

Write the sum. Show the make-a-ten fact you used.

7. $4 + 9 =$ _____

$10 +$ ____ $=$ ____

8. $9 + 8 =$ _____

$10 +$ ____ $=$ ____

9. $8 + 6 =$ _____

$10 +$ ____ $=$ ____

10. $5 + 9 =$ _____

$10 +$ ____ $=$ ____

11. $7 + 9 =$ _____

$10 +$ ____ $=$ ____

12. $8 + 4 =$ _____

$10 +$ ____ $=$ ____

13. $9 + 9 =$ _____

$10 +$ ____ $=$ ____

14. $8 + 7 =$ _____

$10 +$ ____ $=$ ____

 Write the missing addend.

15. $9 + 6 =$ ____ $+ 5$

16. $8 + 5 = 10 +$ ____

17. $7 +$ ____ $= 10 + 2$

18. ____ $+ 6 = 10 + 4$

Solve. Write or draw to explain.

19. There are 9 yellow bicycles at the store. There are 6 red bicycles at the store. How many bicycles are there in all?

_____ bicycles

20. There are 5 bees in a hive. Then 9 more bees go into the hive. How many bees are in the hive altogether?

_____ bees

21. **H.O.T.** Max is thinking of a doubles fact. It has a sum that is greater than the sum of 6 + 4 but less than the sum of 8 + 5. What fact is Max thinking of?

____ + ____ = ____

22. ⭐ **Test Prep** Natasha had 8 shells. Then she found 5 more shells. How many shells does she have now?

○ 3
○ 12
○ 13
○ 14

 TAKE HOME ACTIVITY · Ask your child to name pairs of numbers that have a sum of 10. Then have him or her write the addition sentences.

FOR MORE PRACTICE:
Standards Practice Book, pp. P49–P50

Add 3 Addends

Essential Question How can you add three numbers?

Listen and Draw REAL WORLD

Model with counters. Then draw to show the problem.

_____ marbles

_____ marbles

FOR THE TEACHER • Read the following problem. Have children model and then draw to show the problem. Kara put 4 marbles in a blue bag, 2 marbles in a red bag, and 6 marbles in a green bag. How many marbles did she put in the bags in all? Repeat for a second problem with sum of 11.

Math Talk
Explain how you decided which two numbers to add first in the first problem.

Chapter 3

Model and Draw

You can group numbers in different ways to add.

Choose two numbers.
Look for facts you know.

Changing the way the numbers are grouped does not change the sum.

$3 + 2 + 7 = ?$

$5 + 7 = \underline{12}$

$3 + 2 + 7 = ?$

$3 + 9 = \underline{}$

$3 + 2 + 7 = ?$

$10 + 2 = \underline{}$

Share and Show

Solve two ways. Circle the two addends you add first.

1. $1 + 8 + 2 = \underline{}$ $1 + 8 + 2 = \underline{}$

2. $7 + 3 + 3 = \underline{}$ $7 + 3 + 3 = \underline{}$

3. $4 + 2 + 4 = \underline{}$ $4 + 2 + 4 = \underline{}$

☑ 4. $2 + 8 + 2 = \underline{}$ $2 + 8 + 2 = \underline{}$

☑ 5.
$$\begin{array}{r} 3 \\ 2 \\ +\,6 \\ \hline \end{array} \qquad \begin{array}{r} 3 \\ 2 \\ +\,6 \\ \hline \end{array}$$

6.
$$\begin{array}{r} 7 \\ 0 \\ +\,2 \\ \hline \end{array} \qquad \begin{array}{r} 7 \\ 0 \\ +\,2 \\ \hline \end{array}$$

Name _____

On Your Own

Solve two ways. Circle the two addends you add first.

7. 4 + 1 + 6 = ____   4 + 1 + 6 = ____

8. 4 + 3 + 3 = ____   4 + 3 + 3 = ____

9. 1 + 5 + 3 = ____   1 + 5 + 3 = ____

10. 6 + 4 + 4 = ____   6 + 4 + 4 = ____

11. 5 + 5 + 5 = ____   5 + 5 + 5 = ____

12. 7 + 0 + 6 = ____   7 + 0 + 6 = ____

13.
```
    5          5
    3          3
  + 4        + 4
  ___        ___
```

14.
```
    4          4
    2          2
  + 7        + 7
  ___        ___
```

 H.O.T. Write the missing addend.

15.
```
    5
    5
  + □
  ___
   14
```

16.
```
    4
    □
  + 4
  ___
   12
```

17.
```
    3
    □
  + 7
  ___
   11
```

18.
```
    5
    3
  + □
  ___
   13
```

Choose a way to solve.
Write or draw to explain.

19. Beth eats 4 green grapes.
Lin eats 3 red grapes and
6 purple grapes. How many
grapes do they eat in all?

_____ grapes

20. Eli eats 5 green grapes and
4 red grapes. Tyler eats
4 purple grapes. How many
grapes do they eat in all?

_____ grapes

21. **H.O.T.** Nick, Alex, and
Sophia eat 17 raisins in all.
Nick and Alex each eat
5 raisins. How many raisins
does Sophia eat?

_____ raisins

22. ⭐ **Test Prep** Morgan has
2 red apples, 7 yellow apples,
and 2 green apples. How many
apples does she have in all?

○ 4
○ 9
○ 10
○ 11

 TAKE HOME ACTIVITY • Have your child explain two ways to add 3, 6, and 4.

120 one hundred twenty

FOR MORE PRACTICE:
Standards Practice Book, pp. P51–P52

Name _____

Relate Addition and Subtraction

Essential Question How are addition and subtraction related?

Listen and Draw REAL WORLD

Use cubes to model the problem.
Then complete the bar model to show the problem.

8 red balls	7 yellow balls

_____ balls in all

_____ soccer balls

_____ balls left inside	7 balls outdoors

15 balls in all

_____ soccer balls

FOR THE TEACHER • Read the following problems. Have children model and complete the bar model for each. The soccer team has 8 red balls and 7 yellow balls. How many balls does the team have in all? The soccer team has 15 balls inside the locker room. The children took the 7 yellow balls outdoors. How many soccer balls were left inside?

Math Talk
Explain how the bar models for the two problems are alike and how they are different.

Chapter 3

one hundred twenty-one **121**

Model and Draw

You can use addition facts to remember **differences**. Related facts have the same whole and parts.

> Think of the addends in an addition fact to find the difference for a related subtraction fact.

6	7

13

$6 + 7 = \underline{13}$

	7

13

$13 - 7 = \underline{\hspace{1.5cm}}$

Share and Show

Write the sum and difference for the related facts.

1. $5 + 4 = \underline{\hspace{1cm}}$

   $9 - 4 = \underline{\hspace{1cm}}$

2. $2 + 7 = \underline{\hspace{1cm}}$

   $9 - 2 = \underline{\hspace{1cm}}$

3. $3 + 8 = \underline{\hspace{1cm}}$

   $11 - 8 = \underline{\hspace{1cm}}$

4. $5 + 8 = \underline{\hspace{1cm}}$

   $13 - 5 = \underline{\hspace{1cm}}$

5. $5 + 4 = \underline{\hspace{1cm}}$

   $9 - 4 = \underline{\hspace{1cm}}$

6. $10 + 10 = \underline{\hspace{1cm}}$

   $20 - 10 = \underline{\hspace{1cm}}$

7. $8 + 7 = \underline{\hspace{1cm}}$

   $15 - 7 = \underline{\hspace{1cm}}$

8. $4 + 7 = \underline{\hspace{1cm}}$

   $11 - 7 = \underline{\hspace{1cm}}$

9. $7 + 5 = \underline{\hspace{1cm}}$

   $12 - 7 = \underline{\hspace{1cm}}$

Name _____

On Your Own

Write the sum and difference for the related facts.

10. $4 + 3 =$ _____

$7 - 3 =$ _____

11. $2 + 6 =$ _____

$8 - 6 =$ _____

12. $9 + 10 =$ _____

$19 - 10 =$ _____

13. $7 + 3 =$ _____

$10 - 7 =$ _____

14. $8 + 6 =$ _____

$14 - 6 =$ _____

15. $3 + 9 =$ _____

$12 - 9 =$ _____

16. $6 + 5 =$ _____

$11 - 5 =$ _____

17. $7 + 7 =$ _____

$14 - 7 =$ _____

18. $9 + 6 =$ _____

$15 - 9 =$ _____

19. $5 + 9 =$ _____

$14 - 9 =$ _____

20. $4 + 8 =$ _____

$12 - 4 =$ _____

21. $9 + 7 =$ _____

$16 - 7 =$ _____

H.O.T. Write a related subtraction fact for each addition fact.

22. $7 + 8 = 15$

_____

23. $5 + 7 = 12$

_____

24. $6 + 7 = 13$

_____

25. $9 + 8 = 17$

_____

Solve. Write or draw to explain.

26. Trevor has 7 kites. Pam has 4 kites. How many more kites does Trevor have?

_____ more kites

27. Mr. Simon has a bag of 7 pears and a bag of 6 pears. His family eats 5 pears. How many pears are left?

_____ pears

28. **H.O.T.** Describe how you solved Exercise 27.

_____

_____

_____

29. ★ **Test Prep** Carmen has 11 balloons. She gives 6 balloons to Mark. How many balloons does Carmen have now?

○ 5
○ 6
○ 7
○ 17

TAKE HOME ACTIVITY · Ask your child to name some subtraction facts that he or she knows well.

FOR MORE PRACTICE:
Standards Practice Book, pp. P53–P54

Name _____

Fact Families

Essential Question How does knowing fact families help you find sums and differences?

Listen and Draw REAL WORLD

Use cubes to model the problem.
Then complete the bar model to show the problem.

5 red beads	6 blue beads

_____ beads in all

_____ beads

6 blue beads	5 red beads

_____ beads in all

_____ beads

6 blue beads	_____ red beads

11 beads in all

_____ beads

_____ blue beads	5 red beads

11 beads in all

_____ beads

Math Talk

Explain how these four problems are related.

FOR THE TEACHER • Read the following problem. Have children model and complete the bar model for the problem. Bethany uses 5 red beads and 6 blue beads to make a bracelet. How many beads does she use in all? Repeat the activity with problems about the beads for 6 + 5, 11 − 6, and 11 − 5.

Chapter 3

one hundred twenty-five **125**

Model and Draw

You can build a **fact family** for these numbers.

| 4 | 8 | 12 |

Write addition sentences.
Add in any order.

$$4 + 8 = \underline{12}$$

$$\underline{} + \underline{} = \underline{}$$

Write subtraction sentences.
Subtract by undoing the addition.

$$12 - 8 = \underline{4}$$

$$\underline{} - \underline{} = \underline{}$$

Share and Show

Complete the fact family.

1.   13 6 7

$$6 + 7 = \underline{}$$

$$\underline{} + \underline{} = \underline{}$$

$$13 - 7 = \underline{}$$

$$\underline{} - \underline{} = \underline{}$$

2. 8 0 8

$$0 + 8 = \underline{}$$

$$\underline{} + \underline{} = \underline{}$$

$$8 - \underline{} = 0$$

$$\underline{} - \underline{} = \underline{}$$

3.   14 9 5

$$9 + 5 = \underline{}$$

$$\underline{} + \underline{} = \underline{}$$

$$14 - \underline{} = 9$$

$$\underline{} - \underline{} = \underline{}$$

4.   12 7 5

$$7 + 5 = \underline{}$$

$$\underline{} + \underline{} = \underline{}$$

$$12 - 5 = \underline{}$$

$$\underline{} - \underline{} = \underline{}$$

Name _____

On Your Own

Complete the fact family.

5.

(14
  6   8)

6 + 8 = ___   14 − ___ = 6

___ + ___ = ___   ___ − ___ = ___

6.

(11
  3   8)

3 + 8 = ___   11 − 8 = ___

___ + ___ = ___   ___ − ___ = ___

7.

(15
  9   6)

9 + 6 = ___   15 − ___ = 9

___ + ___ = ___   ___ − ___ = ___

8.

(16
  7   9)

7 + 9 = ___   16 − ___ = 7

___ + ___ = ___   ___ − ___ = ___

9.

(9
  9   0)

9 + 0 = ___   9 − 0 = ___

___ + ___ = ___   ___ − ___ = ___

 H.O.T. Cross out the fact that does not belong
in the fact family. Then write the correct fact.

10. 7 + 8 = 15   15 − 8 = 7

   8 + 7 = 15   8 − 7 = 1   ___ ◯ ___ ◯ ___

11. 5 + 8 = 13   13 − 8 = 5

   8 + 3 = 11   13 − 5 = 8   ___ ◯ ___ ◯ ___

PROBLEM SOLVING

REAL WORLD

Write Math

Circle 3 numbers that can be used to build a fact family. Then write the facts.

12. 5   6   ___ + ___ = ___ | ___ − ___ = ___

    7   12   ___ + ___ = ___ | ___ − ___ = ___

13. 7   8   ___ + ___ = ___ | ___ − ___ = ___

    13   15   ___ + ___ = ___ | ___ − ___ = ___

14. 8   16   ___ + ___ = ___ | ___ − ___ = ___

    8   14

15. **H.O.T.** Write one more fact family that has only two facts. Explain why this fact family has only two facts.

    _____

    _____

    _____

16. ⭐ **Test Prep** Which fact is needed to complete the fact family?

    4 + 6 = 10

    6 + 4 = 10

    10 − 4 = 6

    ○ 4 + 2 = 6
    ○ 10 − 6 = 4
    ○ 8 − 6 = 2
    ○ 6 − 2 = 4

TAKE HOME ACTIVITY • Ask your child to write a fact family for 2, 9, and 11.

FOR MORE PRACTICE:
Standards Practice Book, pp. P55–P56

Name _____

Subtraction Facts

Essential Question What are some ways to remember differences?

Listen and Draw REAL WORLD

Draw a picture to show the problem.

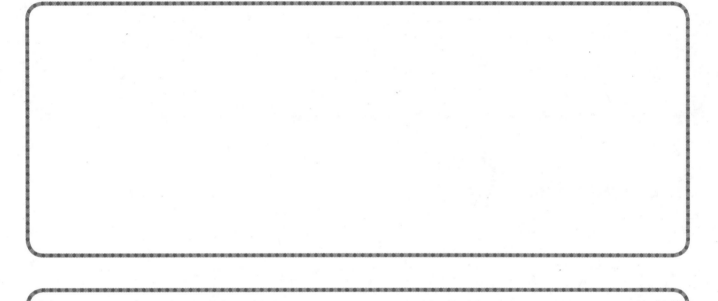

FOR THE TEACHER • Read the following problem, and have children draw a picture and write a number sentence for it. Sarika made 5 glasses of lemonade to sell at her lemonade stand. It rained all morning, so she sold none. How many glasses of lemonade did she have left? Repeat the activity for this problem. The next day, Sarika made 5 glasses of lemonade and sold all of them. How many glasses were left?

Math Talk
Describe a related addition fact for one of these problems.

Chapter 3

Model and Draw

These are some ways to remember differences.

> You can count back by 1, 2, or 3.
>
> $7 - 1 =$ ____
>
> $7 - 2 =$ ____
>
> $7 - 3 =$ ____

> You can think about a missing addend to subtract.
>
> $8 - 5 = \blacksquare$
>
> $5 + 3 = 8$
>
> So, $8 - 5 =$ ____.

> You can think of related facts in a fact family.
>
> $2 + 1 = 3$
>
> $1 + 2 = 3$
>
> $3 - 2 =$ ____
>
> $3 - 1 =$ ____

Share and Show

Write the difference.

1. $6 - 4 =$ ____

2. $10 - 7 =$ ____

3. ____ $= 5 - 2$

4. $14 - 6 =$ ____

5. $8 - 4 =$ ____

6. $11 - 3 =$ ____

7. ____ $= 7 - 5$

8. $17 - 10 =$ ____

9. $5 - 0 =$ ____

10. $13 - 9 =$ ____

11. $9 - 3 =$ ____

12. ____ $= 7 - 6$

13. $12 - 3 =$ ____

14. $15 - 5 =$ ____

15. $9 - 5 =$ ____

16. $10 - 4 =$ ____

17. ____ $= 8 - 3$

18. $13 - 5 =$ ____

19. $11 - 2 =$ ____

20. ____ $= 14 - 4$

21. $12 - 8 =$ ____

Name _____

On Your Own

Write the difference.

22. $11 - 2 =$ _____   23. $9 - 7 =$ _____   24. _____ $= 7 - 4$

25. $12 - 5 =$ _____   26. $13 - 3 =$ _____   27. $7 - 0 =$ _____

28. _____ $= 16 - 10$ 29. $15 - 8 =$ _____   30. $13 - 7 =$ _____

31. $10 - 8 =$ _____   32. $13 - 4 =$ _____   33. _____ $= 9 - 6$

34. _____ $= 9 - 4$ 35. $11 - 8 =$ _____   36. $12 - 7 =$ _____

37. $13 - 8 =$ _____   38. $17 - 9 =$ _____   39. $16 - 8 =$ _____

H.O.T. Write the differences. Then write
the next fact in the pattern.

40. $10 - 1 =$ _____ | 41. $12 - 9 =$ _____ | 42. $18 - 9 =$ _____

$8 - 1 =$ _____ | $13 - 9 =$ _____ | $17 - 8 =$ _____

$6 - 1 =$ _____ | $14 - 9 =$ _____ | $16 - 7 =$ _____

$4 - 1 =$ _____ | $15 - 9 =$ _____ | $15 - 6 =$ _____

_____ | _____ | _____

TAKE HOME ACTIVITY • With your child, practice
saying subtraction facts from this lesson.

Chapter 3 · Lesson 6   FOR MORE PRACTICE:
Standards Practice Book, pp. P57–P58

Name _____

✓ Mid-Chapter Checkpoint

Concepts and Skills

Write the sum. (pp. 109–120)

1. 3 + 6 = ____
2. 8 + 0 = ____
3. 7 + 7 = ____

4. 9 + 4 = ____
5. 5 + 6 = ____
6. 2 + 8 = ____

7. 3 + 7 + 2 = ____
8. 4 + 4 + 6 = ____

Write the sum and difference for the related facts. (pp. 121–124)

9. 5 + 0 = ____
10. 3 + 9 = ____
11. 8 + 7 = ____

  5 − 0 = ____
  12 − 9 = ____
  15 − 8 = ____

Complete the fact family. (pp. 125–128)

12.
13
4 9

4 + 9 = ____

13 − ____ = 4

____ + ____ = ____

____ − ____ = ____

 Test Prep (pp. 129–131)

13. There are 12 flute players in the band. There are 4 trumpet players in the band.

How many more flute players than trumpet players are in the band?

○ 16
○ 14
○ 8
○ 6

Represent Addition and Subtraction

Essential Question What are some different ways you can model addition and subtraction problems?

Listen and Draw REAL WORLD

Complete the bar model to show the problem.

_____ pennies

_____ pennies

FOR THE TEACHER • Read each problem and have children complete the bar models. Hailey has 5 pennies in her pocket and 7 pennies in her wallet. How many pennies does she have in all? Blake has 12 pennies in his bank. He gives 5 pennies to his sister. How many pennies does he have now?

Math Talk
Explain how the sum compares with the addends. **Explain** how the difference compares with the number you are subtracting from.

You can use bar models to help you subtract.

Ben eats 14 crackers.
Ron eats 6 crackers.
How many more crackers does Ben eat than Ron?

Ben	14 crackers	
Ron	6 crackers	

_____ crackers

Suzy bakes 14 cookies.
She gives 6 cookies to Grace.
How many cookies does Suzy have left?

6 cookies	_____ cookies left

14 cookies in all

You can use bar models to help you add.

Lin makes 8 muffins.
Alex makes 6 muffins.
How many muffins do they make in all?

8 muffins	6 muffins

_____ muffins in all

Share and Show

Complete the bar model to solve.

✓ 1. James bought 15 plain bagels and 9 raisin bagels. How many more plain bagels than raisin bagels did he buy?

15 plain bagels

9 raisin bagels	

 _____ more plain bagels

Name _____

On Your Own

Complete the bar model to solve.

---

2. Ali has 5 books about dogs and 6 books about cats. How many books does Ali have?

| 5 dog books | 6 cat books |

_____ books in all

_____ books

---

3. The teacher had 18 pencils. She gave 9 pencils to Erin. How many pencils does the teacher have left?

| _____ pencils left | 9 pencils to Erin |

18 pencils in all

_____ pencils

---

4. Anne has 16 red clips and 9 blue clips. How many more red clips than blue clips does she have?

| 16 red clips |

| 9 blue clips |

_____ more red clips

---

5. **H.O.T.** Jon has 12 crayons. Ali has 7 fewer crayons than Jon. How many crayons does Ali have?

| 12 crayons |

| _____ crayons |

7 crayons

_____ crayons

PROBLEM SOLVING

 REAL WORLD

Use the information in the table to solve. Write or draw to explain.

Flowers Jenna Picked	
Flowers	**Number**
roses	6
tulips	8
daisies	11

6. Jenna put the roses and the tulips in a vase. How many flowers did she put in the vase?

_____ flowers

7. **H.O.T.** Four of the daisies are white. The other daisies are yellow. How many daisies are yellow?

_____ yellow daisies

8. ⭐**Test Prep** Mrs. Johnson wants to put 18 roses in a vase. She put 9 roses in the vase. How many more roses does she need to put in the vase?

- ○ 6
- ○ 8
- ○ 9
- ○ 15

 TAKE HOME ACTIVITY · Ask your child to describe one way to solve this problem. There are 7 pennies in one pocket and 9 pennies in another pocket. How many pennies are there in all?

FOR MORE PRACTICE:
Standards Practice Book, pp. P59–P60

Name _____

Write a Number Sentence • Basic Facts

Essential Question How can writing a number sentence help you solve a problem?

There were 13 boys and 8 girls at the playground. How many more boys than girls were at the playground?

🔑 Unlock the Problem

What do I need to find?

how many more boys
_____
than girls
_____ were at the playground

What information do I need to use?

There were ___13 boys___ and ___8 girls___ at the playground.

Show how to solve the problem.

Complete the bar model.
Then write a number sentence to solve the problem.

_____ ◯ _____ ◯ _____   _____ more boys

© Houghton Mifflin Harcourt Publishing Company

HOME CONNECTION · Your child wrote number sentences to solve problems. Writing number sentences is one way to represent and solve a problem.

Chapter 3   one hundred thirty-seven **137**

Try Another Problem

Write a number sentence to show the problem.

- What do I need to find?
- What information do I need to use?

1. There were 7 girls playing ball. Some more girls joined them. Then there were 16 girls playing ball. How many girls joined them?

_____ girls

_____ ○ _____ ○ _____

2. There were 15 boys at the park. Then 6 boys went home. How many boys were still at the park?

_____ boys

_____ ○ _____ ○ _____

Math Talk
Did you write an addition sentence or a subtraction sentence for Exercise 1? **Explain.**

Share and Show

Write a number sentence to show the problem.

☑ 3. There were 9 big dogs and 8 little dogs at the dog park. How many dogs were at the dog park?

___ ◯ ___ ◯ ___

____ dogs

☑ 4. There were 14 girls flying kites. Some of the girls went home. Then there were 7 girls flying kites. How many girls went home?

___ ◯ ___ ◯ ___

____ girls

5. There were some ducks in a pond. Four more ducks joined them. Then there were 12 ducks in the pond. How many ducks were in the pond at first?

___ ◯ ___ ◯ ___

____ ducks

6. There were 13 red ants and 4 black ants on the sidewalk. How many more red ants than black ants were on the sidewalk?

___ ◯ ___ ◯ ___

____ more red ants

On Your Own

Choose a way to solve.
Write or draw to explain.

7. Joel picked 6 red peppers
and some green peppers.
He picked 11 peppers in all.
How many green peppers
did Joel pick?

_____ green peppers

8. Heather and Jason have
18 pennies in all. They each
have the same number of
pennies. How many
pennies do they
each have?

_____ pennies

9. **H.O.T.** Greg found 4 acorns.
Ben found 5 more acorns than
Greg found. How many acorns
did they find in all?

_____ acorns

10. ⭐ **Test Prep** Jon counted 12 butterflies
and Jessie counted 7 butterflies. How many
fewer butterflies did Jessie count than Jon?

- ○ 5
- ○ 7
- ○ 12
- ○ 19

TAKE HOME ACTIVITY · Ask your child to explain
how he or she solved one of the problems above.

FOR MORE PRACTICE:
Standards Practice Book, pp. P61–P62

Name _____

Algebra: Balance Number Sentences

Essential Question How can you find missing addends?

Listen and Draw REAL WORLD

Draw to show the problem.

_____ books

_____ books

FOR THE TEACHER • Read this problem and have children draw a diagram to represent it. Claire had some books. She bought 5 more. Now she has 11 books. How many books did she have to start? Repeat activity for this problem. Craig had some books. He gave 6 books to friends. Now he has 5 books left. How many books did he have before he gave books to friends?

Math Talk

Describe what you drew to show the first problem.

Chapter 3

Model and Draw

What number will complete the number sentence?

$3 + 5 = 6 + \boxed{?}$

$\underline{8} = 6 + \boxed{?}$

So, $3 + 5 = 6 + \boxed{}$.

THINK:
Both sides of the equal sign must have the same value.

$3 + 5 \quad 6 + 2$

Share and Show

Write the number that will complete the number sentence.

1. $4 + 3 = \boxed{} + 2$

7

2. $3 + \boxed{} = 4 + 2$

6

3. $\boxed{} + 4 = 6 + 2$

4. $4 + \boxed{} = 6 + 5$

✓ 5. $\boxed{} + 8 = 9 + 4$

✓ 6. $7 + 5 = \boxed{} + 8$

Name _____

On Your Own

Write the number that will complete
the number sentence.

7. $1 + 6 = 3 + \boxed{}$

8. $7 + \boxed{} = 0 + 9$

9. $\boxed{} + 7 = 4 + 6$

10. $6 + 7 = \boxed{} + 5$

11. $8 + 3 = 5 + \boxed{}$

12. $\boxed{} + 5 = 9 + 1$

13. $5 + 9 = 7 + \boxed{}$

14. $6 + \boxed{} = 3 + 9$

15. $7 + \boxed{} = 8 + 8$

16. $8 + 7 = \boxed{} + 9$

H.O.T. Write two numbers that will
complete the number sentence.

17. $5 + \boxed{} = \boxed{} + 7$

18. $6 + \boxed{} = 1 + \boxed{}$

19. $\boxed{} + \boxed{} = 8 + 4$

20. $\boxed{} + 3 = \boxed{} + 6$

21. $\boxed{} + 2 = 7 + \boxed{}$

22. $9 + \boxed{} = \boxed{} + 4$

PROBLEM SOLVING

H.O.T. Write number sentences that use both addition and subtraction. Use each choice only once.

23. $9 - 2 = 3 + 4$

    $7 = 7$

$$\cancel{9 - 2}$$
$$\cancel{3 + 4}$$
$$1 + 4$$
$$14 - 6$$
$$5 + 4$$
$$15 - 6$$
$$10 - 5$$
$$4 + 4$$

24. _____ = _____

25. _____ = _____

26. _____ = _____

27. ⭐ **Test Prep** Which number will make this number sentence true?

    $5 + 8 = \boxed{} + 7$

    ○ 20
    ○ 13
    ○ 9
    ○ 6

TAKE HOME ACTIVITY · Write two number sentences similar to those in this lesson. Have your child solve for the missing numbers.

144 one hundred forty-four

© Houghton Mifflin Harcourt Publishing Company

FOR MORE PRACTICE:
Standards Practice Book, pp. P63–P64

Name _____

Equal and Not Equal

Essential Question How do you know if both sides of a number sentence are equal or not equal?

Listen and Draw REAL WORLD

Use cubes to model the problem.
Then draw to show your work.

FOR THE TEACHER • Read the following problems. Have children solve and explain their answers. Alana has 6 red buttons and 4 blue buttons. Teresa has 8 green buttons and 2 black buttons. Do Alana and Teresa have the same number of buttons? Explain. Ross has 8 red buttons and 5 blue buttons. Grant has 6 green buttons and 5 black buttons. Do Ross and Grant have the same number of buttons? Explain.

Math Talk
Explain how you can compare the number of buttons that the boys in the second problem have.

Chapter 3

Use = to show that two amounts are equal. 5 = 5
Use ≠ to show that two amounts are **not equal**. 5 ≠ 4

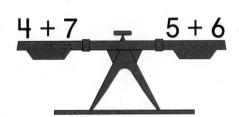

4 + 7   5 + 6

11   (=)   11

So, 4 + 7 = 5 + 6.

is equal to

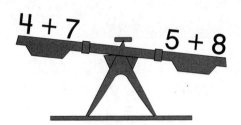

4 + 7   5 + 8

11   (≠)   13

So, 4 + 7 ≠ 5 + 8.

is not
equal to

Share and Show

Write = or ≠ to make the number sentence true.

1. 8 + 5 ◯ 6 + 7

2. 5 + 8 ◯ 9 + 6

3. 11 − 4 ◯ 14 − 6

4. 10 − 5 ◯ 12 − 7

✓ 5. 9 + 0 ◯ 4 + 5

✓ 6. 15 − 6 ◯ 9 − 3

Name _____

On Your Own

Write $=$ or $\neq$ to make the number sentence true.

7. $6 + 8 \bigcirc 7 + 5$

8. $5 + 7 \bigcirc 8 + 4$

9. $9 + 5 \bigcirc 7 + 7$

10. $16 - 7 \bigcirc 17 - 9$

11. $6 + 6 \bigcirc 6 + 5$

12. $9 + 5 \bigcirc 5 + 9$

13. $6 + 4 \bigcirc 10 + 0$

14. $12 - 5 \bigcirc 14 - 7$

15. $9 + 4 \bigcirc 6 + 7$

16. $12 - 8 \bigcirc 11 - 7$

 Write a number to make the number sentence true.

17. $4 + 7 \neq 5 + \boxed{}$

18. $4 + 5 < 12 - \boxed{}$

19. $14 - 6 > 4 + \boxed{}$

20. $8 + 2 \neq 6 + \boxed{}$

21. $16 - 7 < 6 + \boxed{}$

22. $13 - 5 > 14 - \boxed{}$

Circle all the cards that make the number sentence true.

23.

☐ = 12

| 5 + 2 + 5 | 6 + 5 |

| 8 + 4 | 7 + 3 + 3 |

24. H.O.T.

☐ ≠ 9

| 18 − 9 | 13 − 5 |

| 3 + 3 + 6 | 16 − 7 |

25.

☐ = 15

| 9 + 6 | 7 + 8 |

| 8 + 9 | 4 + 2 + 5 |

26. ⭐ **Test Prep**   Marisa wrote a number sentence on the board.

13 − 6 ≠ ◯

Which makes this number sentence true?

○ 3 + 4

○ 14 − 8

○ 7 + 0

○ 16 − 9

TAKE HOME ACTIVITY · Ask your child to tell you what the symbol ≠ means and then complete this number sentence. 3 + 8 ≠ _____.

FOR MORE PRACTICE:
Standards Practice Book, pp. P65–P66

Fill in the bubble for the correct answer choice.

15. It rained on 14 days in January. It rained on
8 days in February. On how many more days
did it rain in January than in February? (pp. 121–124)

○ 6

○ 8

○ 14

○ 22

16. Chase saw 4 ladybugs and 9 ants
on a rock. How many more ants than
ladybugs did he see? (pp. 133–136)

○ 5

○ 6

○ 13

○ 15

17. Grace and Amber each have the same number
of school shirts. Grace has 1 red shirt and 3 blue
shirts. Amber has 2 red shirts and some blue shirts.
How many blue shirts does Amber have? (pp. 141–144)

○ 1

○ 2

○ 3

○ 4

Short Answer

18. Kyle and Luis together have the same number of fish as Mary. How many fish does Luis have?

Kyle	Luis	Mary
5 fish	? fish	11 fish

Write a number sentence to show the problem.
Explain how the number sentence shows the problem.

_____

_____

_____

Performance Task

19. Morgan counts 6 ducks in a pond and some ducks on the grass. There are 14 ducks in all. How many ducks are on the grass? Draw or write to show how you found your answer.

How many more ducks are on the grass than in the pond?
Draw or write to show how you found your answer.

2-Digit Addition

Curious About Math with

Curious George

The keys of a modern piano are made from wood or plastic, but older pianos had keys made from ebony and ivory. Playing a piano is sometimes called "tickling the ivories."

A modern piano has 36 black keys and 52 white keys. How many keys is this in all?

Name _____

Show What You Know

Addition Patterns

Add 2. Complete each addition sentence.

1. 1 + __2__ = __3__   4. 4 + ____ = ____

2. 2 + ____ = ____   5. 5 + ____ = ____

3. 3 + ____ = ____   6. 6 + ____ = ____

Addition Facts

Write the sum.

7.   7
  + 3

8.   8
  + 8

9.   6
  + 7

10.   4
  + 4

11.   9
  + 5

12.   8
  + 7

Tens and Ones

Write the number. Then write the number
of tens and ones.

13.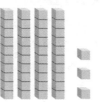

____ = ____ tens ____ ones

14.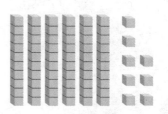

____ = ____ tens ____ ones

Family note: This page checks your child's understanding
of important skills needed for success in Chapter 4.

 Assessment Options
Online **Soar to Success Math**

© Houghton Mifflin Harcourt Publishing Company

Name _____

Vocabulary Builder

Review Words
sum
addend
digit
tens
ones

Visualize It

Use review words to fill in the graphic organizer.

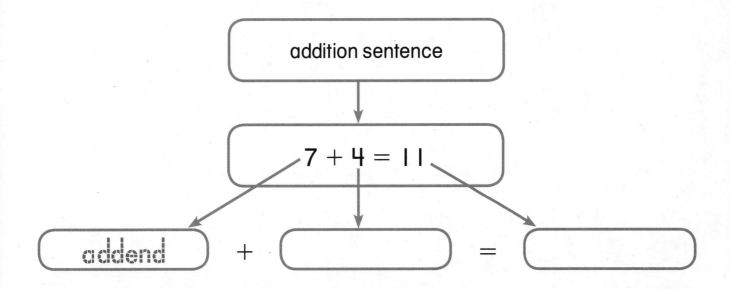

addition sentence

7 + 4 = 11

addend + ⬚ = ⬚

Understand Vocabulary

1. Write a number with the **digit** 3 in
   the **tens** place.   _____

2. Write a number with the **digit** 5 in
   the **ones** place.   _____

3. Write a number that has the same **digit**
   in the **tens** place and the **ones** place.   _____

4. Write a number with **digits** that have
   a **sum** of 8.   _____

Game · What is the Sum?

Materials

- 12
- 12 ●
- 1 🎲

Play with a partner.

1. Put your ● on START.
2. Toss the 🎲. Move that many spaces.
3. Say the sum. Your partner checks your answer.

4. If your answer is correct, find that number on a square. Put one of your ● on that square.
5. Take turns until both players reach FINISH. The player with more ● on the board wins.

START

$$\begin{array}{r} 2 \\ +7 \\ \hline \end{array}$$
$$\begin{array}{r} 6 \\ +5 \\ \hline \end{array}$$
$$\begin{array}{r} 3 \\ +9 \\ \hline \end{array}$$
$$\begin{array}{r} 0 \\ +7 \\ \hline \end{array}$$
$$\begin{array}{r} 8 \\ +6 \\ \hline \end{array}$$

FINISH

$$\begin{array}{r} 9 \\ +8 \\ \hline \end{array}$$

7	18	9	11	15
13	6	17	8	10
16	4	12	14	5

$$\begin{array}{r} 6 \\ +2 \\ \hline \end{array}$$

$$\begin{array}{r} 1 \\ +4 \\ \hline \end{array}$$

$$\begin{array}{r} 8 \\ +7 \\ \hline \end{array}$$

$$\begin{array}{r} 5 \\ +8 \\ \hline \end{array}$$
$$\begin{array}{r} 9 \\ +9 \\ \hline \end{array}$$
$$\begin{array}{r} 7 \\ +9 \\ \hline \end{array}$$
$$\begin{array}{r} 2 \\ +2 \\ \hline \end{array}$$
$$\begin{array}{r} 4 \\ +6 \\ \hline \end{array}$$
$$\begin{array}{r} 5 \\ +1 \\ \hline \end{array}$$

Name _____

Break Apart Ones to Add

Essential Question How does breaking apart a number make adding easier?

Listen and Draw REAL WORLD

Use ▭▭▭▭▭ ▪. Draw to show what you did.

FOR THE TEACHER • Read the following problem. Have children use blocks to solve. Griffin read 27 books about animals and 6 books about space. How many books did he read in all?

Math Talk
Describe what you did with the blocks.

Break apart ones to make a ten.
Use this as a way to add.

$27 + 8 = \underline{}$

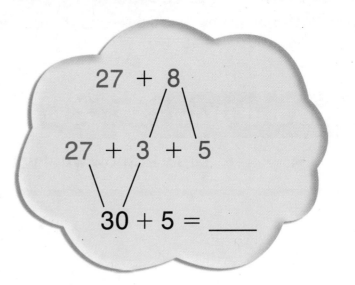

$27 + 8$

$27 + 3 + 5$

$30 + 5 = \underline{}$

$27 + 8 = \underline{}$

Share and Show

Math Board

Draw quick pictures. Break apart ones
to make a ten. Then add and write the sum.

1. $15 + 7 = \underline{}$

2. $26 + 5 = \underline{}$

☑3. $37 + 8 = \underline{}$

☑4. $28 + 6 = \underline{}$

On Your Own

Break apart ones to make a ten. Then add and write the sum.

5. 23 + 9 = ____

6. 48 + 5 = ____

7. 18 + 5 = ____

8. 33 + 9 = ____

9. 27 + 6 = ____

10. 49 + 4 = ____

11. 24 + 8 = ____

12. 58 + 7 = ____

13. 36 + 8 = ____

14. 47 + 9 = ____

 Write the missing digit.

15. 49 + 7 = ☐6

16. 35 + ☐ = 44

17. ☐5 + 7 = 62

18. 2☐ + 8 = 35

19. 74 + 9 = 8☐

20. ☐6 + 3 = 79

Solve. Write or draw to explain.

21. Megan has 38 animal pictures and 8 people pictures. How many pictures does she have in all?

_____ pictures

22. Bruce counts 25 trees at the park and 7 trees on the way home. How many trees does he count in all?

_____ trees

H.O.T. Use the model. Write the missing numbers.

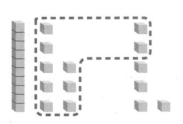

23. Jamal had _____ toy cars. Then his friend gave him _____ more toy cars. How many toy cars does he have now?

_____ toy cars

24. ⭐ **Test Prep** Alicia puts 25 books on the shelf. Trenton puts 8 books on the shelf. How many books in all do they put on the shelf?

○ 17
○ 23
○ 33
○ 37

TAKE HOME ACTIVITY · Tell your child a number from 0 to 10. Have your child name a number to add to yours that would make a sum of 10.

FOR MORE PRACTICE:
Standards Practice Book, pp. P71–P72

Name _____

Use Compensation

Essential Question How can you make an addend a ten to help solve an addition problem?

Listen and Draw REAL WORLD

Use ▭▭▭▭ ▪ to model the problem.
Draw to show what you did.

FOR THE TEACHER • Read the following problem and have children use blocks to solve. The children voted for their favorite field trip. 17 children voted for the zoo and 26 children voted for the museum. How many children voted altogether?

Math Talk

Explain how you decided which addend to make a ten.

Chapter 4

one hundred sixty-one **161**

Take ones from an addend to make the other addend the next ten.

Adding can be easier when one of the addends is a ten.

$25 + 48 = ?$

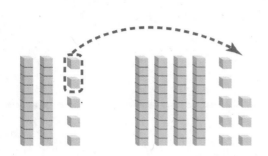

$\underline{23} + \underline{50} = \underline{}$

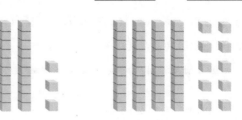

Share and Show

Math Board

Show how to make one addend the next ten.
Complete the new addition sentence.

1. $37 + 25 = ?$

$\underline{40} + \underline{} = \underline{}$

2. $27 + 46 = ?$

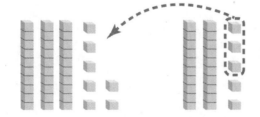

$\underline{} + \underline{} = \underline{}$

3. $14 + 29 = ?$

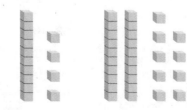

$\underline{} + \underline{} = \underline{}$

On Your Own

Show how to make one addend the next ten.
Complete the new addition sentence.

4. $18 + 13 = ?$

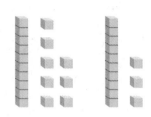

_____ + _____ = _____

5. $24 + 18 = ?$

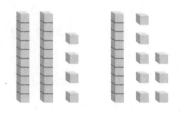

_____ + _____ = _____

6. $39 + 19 = ?$

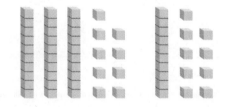

_____ + _____ = _____

7. $27 + 24 = ?$

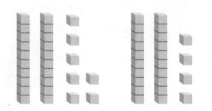

_____ + _____ = _____

8. $19 + 32 = ?$

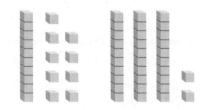

_____ + _____ = _____

Solve. Write or draw to explain.

9. Zach finds 38 twigs. Kelly finds 27 twigs. How many twigs do they find in all?

_____ twigs

10. **H.O.T.** The chart shows the leaves that Philip collected. He wants a collection of 52 leaves, using only two colors. Which two colors of leaves should he use?

Leaves Collected	
Color	Number
green	27
brown	29
yellow	25

_____ and _____

11. ⭐ **Test Prep** Keisha sees 25 small trees at the park. She sees 14 tall trees at the park. How many trees does she see altogether?

○ 49

○ 39

○ 38

○ 31

TAKE HOME ACTIVITY · Have your child choose one problem on this page and explain how to solve it in another way.

FOR MORE PRACTICE:
Standards Practice Book, pp. P73–P74

Name _____

Break Apart Addends as Tens and Ones

Essential Question How do you break apart addends to add tens and then add ones?

Listen and Draw

Write the number. Then write the number as tens plus ones.

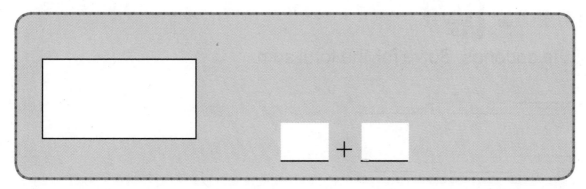

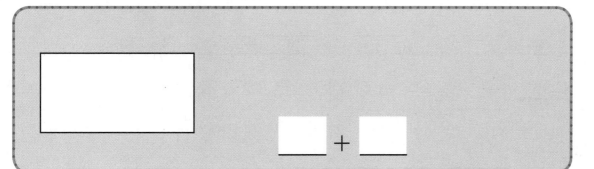

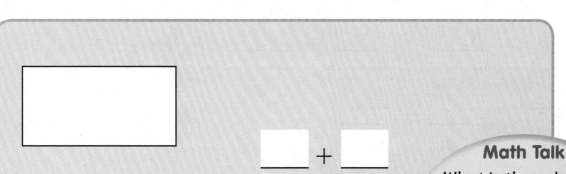

Math Talk

What is the value of the 6 in the number 63? **Explain** how you know.

FOR THE TEACHER • Direct children's attention to the orange box. Have children write 25 inside the white rectangle. Then ask children to write 25 as tens plus ones. Repeat the activity for 36 and 42.

Chapter 4

Break apart the addends.
Add the tens and add the ones.
Then find the total sum.

27 ⟶ 20 + 7
+48 ⟶ 40 + 8

_____ + _____ = _____

60 + 15
      /\
    10 5

70 + 5 = 75

Share and Show

Break apart the addends. Solve for the total sum.

1.   35 ⟶ _____ + _____

    +54 ⟶ _____ + _____
    _____

                _____ + _____ = _____

2.   43 ⟶ _____ + _____

    +29 ⟶ _____ + _____
    _____

                _____ + _____ = _____

3.   56 ⟶ _____ + _____

    +38 ⟶ _____ + _____
    _____

                _____ + _____ = _____

Name _____

On Your Own

Break apart the addends. Solve for the total sum.

4. 14 ⟶ ____ + ____

    +23 ⟶ ____ + ____
    _____

    ____ + ____ = ____

---

5. 37 ⟶ ____ + ____

    +45 ⟶ ____ + ____
    _____

    ____ + ____ = ____

---

6. 54 ⟶ ____ + ____

    +16 ⟶ ____ + ____
    _____

    ____ + ____ = ____

7. **H.O.T.** Write the missing numbers in the problem.

    4 3 ⟶ ____ + ____

    + ⟶ 30 + 7
    _____

    ____ + ____ = ____

Choose a way to solve.
Write or draw to explain.

8. Julie read 18 pages of her book in the morning. She read 17 more pages in the afternoon. How many pages did she read altogether?

_____ pages

9. **H.O.T.** Christopher has 35 baseball cards. The rest of his cards are basketball cards. He has 58 cards in all. How many basketball cards does he have?

_____ basketball cards

10. ⭐ **Test Prep** Tomás has 17 art pencils. His sister has 26 art pencils. How many art pencils do they have in all?

- ○ 31
- ○ 33
- ○ 41
- ○ 43

TAKE HOME ACTIVITY · Write 32 + 48 on a sheet of paper. Have your child break apart the numbers and find the sum.

FOR MORE PRACTICE:
Standards Practice Book, pp. P75–P76

Name _____

Model Regrouping for Addition

Essential Question When do you regroup in addition?

Listen and Draw REAL WORLD

Use ▭▭▭▭ ▫ to model the problem.
Draw quick pictures to show what you did.

Tens	Ones

Math Talk
Describe how you made a ten in your model.

 FOR THE TEACHER • Read the following problem. Brandon has 24 action figures. His friend Mario has 8 action figures. How many figures do they have in all?

Chapter 4

one hundred sixty-nine **169**

Model and Draw

Add 37 and 25.

Step 1 Look at the ones. Can you make a ten?

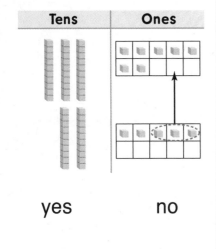

Tens	Ones

yes   no

Step 2 If you can make a ten, **regroup**.

Tens	Ones

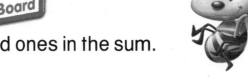

Trade 10 ones for 1 ten to regroup.

Step 3 Write how many tens and ones. Write the sum.

Tens	Ones

____ tens ____ ones

____

Share and Show

Write how many tens and ones in the sum. Write the sum.

1. Add 47 and 15.

Tens	Ones

____ tens ____ ones

____

✓ 2. Add 48 and 8.

Tens	Ones

____ tens ____ ones

____

✓ 3. Add 26 and 38.

Tens	Ones

____ tens ____ ones

____

170 one hundred seventy

On Your Own

Write how many tens and ones in the sum.
Write the sum.

4. Add 79 and 6.

Tens	Ones

_____ tens _____ ones

_____

5. Add 18 and 64.

Tens	Ones

_____ tens _____ ones

_____

6. Add 23 and 39.

Tens	Ones

_____ tens _____ ones

_____

7. Add 54 and 25.

Tens	Ones

_____ tens _____ ones

_____

8. Add 33 and 7.

Tens	Ones

_____ tens _____ ones

_____

9. Add 27 and 68.

Tens	Ones

_____ tens _____ ones

_____

10. **H.O.T.** Draw quick pictures for the missing addend.

Tens	Ones

__8__ tens __0__ ones

__80__

Choose a way to solve.
Write or draw to explain.

11. Taylor has 25 toy animals and 12 books. Jorge has 8 more toy animals than Taylor has. How many toy animals does Jorge have?

_____ toy animals

12. **H.O.T.** Ellen has 36 animal stickers. Jeff has 44 stickers. How many more stickers would they need to have 100 stickers altogether?

_____ more stickers

13. ⭐ **Test Prep** Mrs. Sanders has two fish tanks. There are 14 fish in the small tank. There are 27 fish in the large tank. How many fish are in the two tanks?

○ 47
○ 41
○ 33
○ 31

TAKE HOME ACTIVITY · Ask your child to write a word problem about adding two groups of stamps.

FOR MORE PRACTICE:
Standards Practice Book, pp. P77–P78

Name _____

Model and Record 2-Digit Addition

Essential Question How do you record
2-digit addition?

Listen and Draw REAL WORLD

Use ▭▭▭▭ ▪ to model the problem.
Draw quick pictures to show what you did.

Tens	Ones

Math Talk
Did you trade blocks in your model? **Explain** why or why not.

FOR THE TEACHER • Read the following problem. Mr. Riley's class collected 54 cans for the food drive. Miss Bright's class collected 35 cans. How many cans did they collect altogether?

Chapter 4

Model and Draw

Trace over the quick pictures in the steps.

Step 1 Model 37 + 26. Are there 10 ones to regroup?

Tens	Ones

Tens	Ones
	3	7
+	2	6

Step 2 Write the regrouped ten. Write how many ones are in the ones place now.

Tens	Ones

Tens	Ones
	3	7
+	2	6
		3

Step 3 How many tens are there? Write how many tens are in the tens place.

Tens	Ones

Tens	Ones
1	3	7
+	2	6
	6	3

Share and Show

Draw quick pictures to help you solve. Write the sum.

✓ 1.

Tens	Ones
	2	6
+	3	2

Tens	Ones

✓ 2.

Tens	Ones
	5	8
+	2	4

Tens	Ones

On Your Own

Draw quick pictures to help you solve. Write the sum.

3.

Tens	Ones
☐	
3	4
+	9

Tens	Ones

4.

Tens	Ones
☐	
2	7
+ 2	4

Tens	Ones

5.

Tens	Ones
☐	
3	5
+ 2	3

Tens	Ones

6.

Tens	Ones
☐	
5	9
+	6

Tens	Ones

7.

Tens	Ones
☐	
2	8
+ 6	2

Tens	Ones

8.

Tens	Ones
☐	
4	9
+ 4	8

Tens	Ones

PROBLEM SOLVING

Draw a quick picture or write an addition problem to solve.

9. Christina got 34 points in the spelling contest. Brian got 46 points in the spelling contest. Did they get 82 points in all?

Circle your answer.

yes   no

Tens	Ones

Tens	Ones
☐	
+	

10. **H.O.T.** Edna has 35 colored pencils. If Manny gives her 18 colored pencils, will she have more than 54 colored pencils?

Circle your answer.

yes   no

Tens	Ones

Tens	Ones
☐	
+	

11. ⭐**Test Prep** Ms. Green's students painted 19 pictures. Mr. Lee's students painted 23 pictures. How many pictures did the students paint altogether?

- ○ 32
- ○ 36
- ○ 40
- ○ 42

 TAKE HOME ACTIVITY · Write two 2-digit numbers and ask your child if he or she would regroup to find the sum.

FOR MORE PRACTICE:
Standards Practice Book, pp. P79–P80

Name _____

2-Digit Addition

Essential Question How do you record the steps when adding 2-digit numbers?

Listen and Draw *REAL WORLD*

Draw quick pictures to model each problem.

Tens	Ones

Tens	Ones

FOR THE TEACHER • Read the following problem and have children draw quick pictures to solve. The animal shelter has 35 dogs and 47 cats for adoption. How many pets are there in all? Repeat the activity with this problem. After a pet fair, there are only 18 dogs and 21 cats at the shelter. How many pets are at the shelter now?

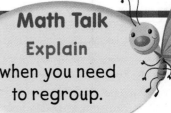

Math Talk
Explain when you need to regroup.

Chapter 4

one hundred seventy-seven **177**

Model and Draw

Add 59 and 24.

Step 1 Add the ones.
$9 + 4 = 13$

Step 2 Regroup.
13 ones is the same as 1 ten 3 ones.

Step 3 Add the tens.
$1 + 5 + 2 = 8$

Tens	Ones
||||	o o o / o o o / o o o / o o o
||	o o o

Tens	Ones
5	9
+ 2	4

Tens	Ones
||||	o o o / o o o / o o o / o o o
||	o o o

Tens	Ones
5	9
+ 2	4
	3

Tens	Ones
||||	o o o

Tens	Ones
1	
5	9
+ 2	4
8	3

Share and Show

Regroup if you need to. Write the sum.

1.

Tens	Ones
4	2
+ 2	9

 2.

Tens	Ones
3	1
+ 1	4

3.

Tens	Ones
2	7
+ 4	5

On Your Own

Regroup if you need to. Write the sum.

4.

Tens	Ones
☐	
4	8
+	7

5.

Tens	Ones
☐	
3	5
+ 4	2

6.

Tens	Ones
☐	
7	3
+ 2	0

7.

3	3
+ 2	7

8.

5	2
+	5

9.

3	6
+ 5	8

10.

6	4
+ 2	5

11.

3	5
+ 3	8

12.

3	8
+ 5	2

 H.O.T. Write the missing digits.

13.

5	3
+ ☐	☐
7	8

14.

☐	☐
+ 4	7
9	3

15.

3	☐
+ 1	9
☐	0

PROBLEM SOLVING

16. **H.O.T.** Abby used a different way to add.

$$\begin{array}{r} 35 \\ +\ 48 \\ \hline 13 \\ +\ 70 \\ \hline 83 \end{array}$$

Find the sum, using Abby's way.

$$\begin{array}{r} 5\ 7 \\ +\ 2\ 9 \\ \hline \end{array}$$

17. Describe Abby's way of adding 2-digit numbers.

_____

_____

_____

18. ⭐ **Test Prep** Philip had 68 stamps in his collection. He bought 14 more stamps. How many stamps does he have now?

○ 82
○ 74
○ 72
○ 56

 TAKE HOME ACTIVITY · Ask your child to show you two ways to add 45 and 38.

FOR MORE PRACTICE:
Standards Practice Book, pp. P81–P82

Practice 2-Digit Addition

Essential Question How do you record the steps when adding 2-digit numbers?

Listen and Draw REAL WORLD

Choose one way to solve the problem.
Draw or write to show what you did.

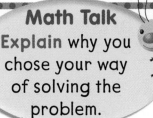

Math Talk
Explain why you chose your way of solving the problem.

FOR THE TEACHER • Read the following problem. There were 45 boys and 63 girls who ran in the race. How many children ran altogether?

Chapter 4

Model and Draw

Mrs. Meyers sold 47 snacks before the game. Then she sold 85 snacks during the game. How many snacks did she sell in all?

Step 1 Add the ones.	**Step 2** Add the tens.	**Step 3** 13 tens can be regrouped as 1 hundred 3 tens. Write the hundreds digit and the tens digit in the sum.
$7 + 5 = 12$	$1 + 4 + 8 = 13$	
Regroup 12 ones as 1 ten 2 ones.		

Step 1:
```
   1
   4 7
 + 8 5
 ------
     2
```

Step 2:
```
   1
   4 7
 + 8 5
 ------
     2
```

Step 3:
```
   1
   4 7
 + 8 5
 ------
 1 3 2
```

Share and Show

Write the sum.

1.
```
   3 8
 + 9 4
 ------
```

2.
```
   4 5
 + 5 2
 ------
```

3.
```
   8 3
 + 7 6
 ------
```

4.
```
   5 6
 + 3 5
 ------
```

☑ 5.
```
   6 3
 + 5 1
 ------
```

☑ 6.
```
   7 4
 + 4 9
 ------
```

Name _____

On Your Own

Write the sum.

7.

```
  5 2
+ 3 7
```

8.

```
  8 8
+ 2 1
```

9.

```
  7 4
+ 6 7
```

10.

```
  9 3
+ 5 4
```

11.

```
  2 5
+ 4 9
```

12.

```
  9 2
+ 7 8
```

13.

```
  5 6
+ 1 6
```

14.

```
  3 1
+ 4 5
```

15.

```
  4 3
+ 7 2
```

16. **H.O.T.** Without finding the sums, circle the pairs of addends for which the sum will be greater than 100.

Explain how you decided which pairs to circle.

```
73
18
```

```
54
71
```

```
47
62
```

```
36
59
```

_____

_____

_____

TAKE HOME ACTIVITY · Tell your child two 2-digit numbers. Have him or her rewrite the numbers and find their sum.

Name _____

 **Mid-Chapter Checkpoint**

Concepts and Skills

Break apart ones to make a ten. Then add and write the sum. (pp.157–160)

1. $37 + 8 =$ _____

2. $55 + 7 =$ _____

Break apart the addends. Solve for the total sum. (pp.165–168)

3. $\begin{array}{r} 27 \\ +36 \\ \hline \end{array}$ ⟶ _____ + _____

⟶ _____ + _____

_____ + _____ = _____

4. $\begin{array}{r} 48 \\ +23 \\ \hline \end{array}$ ⟶ _____ + _____

⟶ _____ + _____

_____ + _____ = _____

⭐ Test Prep

5. Julia collected 25 cans to recycle. Dan collected 14 cans. How many cans did they collect in all? (pp.177–180)

○ 39
○ 29
○ 15
○ 11

Name _____

Rewrite 2-Digit Addition

Essential Question What are two different ways to write addition problems?

Listen and Draw REAL WORLD

Write the numbers for each addition problem.

+ _____

+ _____

+ _____

+ _____

FOR THE TEACHER • Read the following problem and have children write the addends in vertical format. Juan's family drove 32 miles to his grandmother's house. Then they drove 14 miles to his aunt's house. How far did they drive in all? Repeat for three more problems.

Math Talk
Explain why it is important to line up the digits of the addends in columns.

Chapter 4

Model and Draw

Add. 28 + 45 = ?

Step 1 For 28, write the tens digit in the tens column.

Write the ones digit in the ones column.

Repeat for 45.

```
  2  8
+ 4  5
```

Step 2 Add the ones.

Regroup if you need to.

Add the tens.

```
  2  8
+ 4  5
```

Share and Show

Rewrite the numbers. Then add.

1. 25 + 8

    +_____

2. 37 + 17

    +_____

3. 25 + 45

    +_____

4. 38 + 29

    +_____

5. 42 + 45

    +_____

6. 63 + 9

    +_____

7. 15 + 36

    +_____

8. 74 + 18

    +_____

Name _____

On Your Own

Rewrite the numbers. Then add.

9. $27 + 54$

$+$ _____

10. $34 + 3$

$+$ _____

11. $26 + 17$

$+$ _____

12. $48 + 38$

$+$ _____

13. $50 + 32$

$+$ _____

14. $61 + 38$

$+$ _____

15. $37 + 43$

$+$ _____

16. $79 + 17$

$+$ _____

H.O.T. Choose two numbers. Write them in the problem. Then solve.

17. After school, there are two clubs.

There are _____ children in the singing club.

There are _____ children in the sports club.
How many children are in the two clubs?

_____ children

| 25 |
| 14 |
| 17 |
| 32 |
| 28 |

PROBLEM SOLVING

 REAL WORLD

 Write Math

Use the table. Write or draw to show how you solved the problems.

Points Scored This Season	
Player	Number of Points
Anna	26
Lou	37
Becky	23
Kevin	19

18. How many points did Lou and Becky score in all?

_____ points

19. **H.O.T.** Which two players scored 56 points in all? Add to check your answer.

_____ and _____

20. ⭐ **Test Prep** John has 29 markers. Claire has 36 markers. How many markers do they have in all?

- ○ 53
- ○ 56
- ○ 65
- ○ 68

TAKE HOME ACTIVITY · Have your child write and solve another problem, using the table above.

FOR MORE PRACTICE:
Standards Practice Book, pp. P85–P86

Name _____

Draw a Diagram • Addition

Essential Question How can drawing
a diagram help you solve a problem?

Kendra had 13 crayons. Her dad gave her
some more crayons. Then she had 19 crayons.
How many crayons did Kendra's dad give her?

🔑 Unlock the Problem

What do I need to find?

how many crayons
_____

Kendra's dad gave her

What information do I need to use?

She had _____ crayons.
After he gave her more
crayons, she had

_____ crayons.

Complete the bar model. Show how to solve the problem.

There are
19 crayons
in all.

13	_____

19

_____ crayons

HOME CONNECTION • Your child used a bar model to
represent the problem. The bar model helps show what
the missing amount is in order to solve the problem.

Try Another Problem

Complete the bar model to solve.

- What do I need to find?
- What information do I need to use?

1. Mr. Stivers has 24 red pens. He buys 19 blue pens. How many pens does he have now?

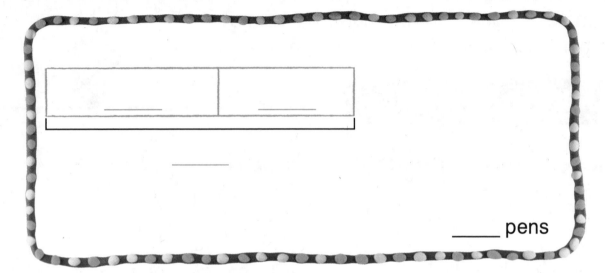

_____ pens

2. Hannah has 10 pencils. Jim and Hannah have 17 pencils altogether. How many pencils does Jim have?

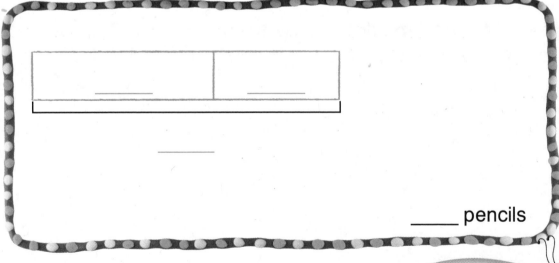

_____ pencils

Math Talk

Explain how you know if an amount is a part or the whole in a problem.

Share and Show

Complete the bar model to solve.

3. There are 8 owls flying in the forest. There are 15 owls resting in trees. How many owls are there in all?

_____	_____

_____

_____ owls

4. Aimee and Matthew catch 17 crickets in all. Aimee catches 9 crickets. How many crickets does Matthew catch?

_____	_____

_____

_____ crickets

5. There are 17 moths near a tree. 25 moths join them. How many moths are near the tree now?

_____	_____

_____

_____ moths

6. Percy sees a grasshopper jumping in the grass. He counts 16 jumps. Then he counts 15 more jumps. How many total jumps does he count?

_____	_____

_____

_____ jumps

On Your Own

Choose a way to solve.
Write or draw to explain.

7. Rita put 5 paper clips in each cup. There are 3 cups in all. How many paper clips are in the cups?

_____ paper clips

8. Jeff has 19 postcards and 2 pens. He buys 20 more postcards. How many postcards does he have now?

_____ postcards

9. **H.O.T.** Alicia drew 15 flowers. Marie drew 4 more flowers than Alicia drew. How many flowers did they draw in all?

_____ flowers

10. ⭐ **Test Prep** There are 23 books in a box. There are 29 books on a shelf. How many books are there in all?

○ 42
○ 52
○ 56
○ 61

TAKE HOME ACTIVITY · Ask your child to explain how to solve one of the problems above.

FOR MORE PRACTICE:
Standards Practice Book, pp. P87–P88

Name _____

Estimate Sums

Essential Question How can you estimate sums?

Listen and Draw REAL WORLD

Draw quick pictures for the numbers.

Matt   Beth

Matt and Beth have _____ than 20 crayons.

FOR THE TEACHER • Read the following problem. Have children draw quick pictures to represent the numbers and then answer the question. Matt has 9 crayons and Beth has 7 crayons. Together, do they have more or less than 20 crayons?

Math Talk
Explain how you answered the question without finding the total number of crayons.

Model and Draw

When you **estimate**, you tell about how many.

Estimate. Is the sum greater or less than 50?

$$52 + 38 = \blacksquare$$

THINK:
Since 52 is greater than 50, 52 + 38 is greater than 50.

Estimate. Is the sum greater or less than 100?

$$23 + 51 = \blacksquare$$

THINK:
2 tens + 5 tens = 7 tens
70 is less than 100.
23 + 51 is less than 100.

Share and Show

Estimate the sum.
Circle the better choice.

1. $19 + 18 = \blacksquare$

   greater than 20

   less than 20

2. $27 + 4 = \blacksquare$

   greater than 50

   less than 50

3. $47 + 32 = \blacksquare$

   greater than 50

   less than 50

4. $84 + 43 = \blacksquare$

   greater than 100

   less than 100

On Your Own

Estimate the sum.
Circle the better choice.

5. $11 + 0 = \blacksquare$

greater than 20

less than 20

6. $50 + 43 = \blacksquare$

greater than 50

less than 50

7. $35 + 33 = \blacksquare$

greater than 50

less than 50

8. $21 + 65 = \blacksquare$

greater than 100

less than 100

9. $16 + 32 = \blacksquare$

greater than 20

less than 20

10. $3 + 7 = \blacksquare$

greater than 20

less than 20

11. $48 + 40 = \blacksquare$

greater than 100

less than 100

12. $71 + 36 = \blacksquare$

greater than 100

less than 100

PROBLEM SOLVING

REAL WORLD

Estimate to solve.

13. **H.O.T.** Vanessa says she has more than 100 stickers. She has 30 bird stickers, 20 puppy stickers, and 25 kitten stickers. Do you agree that Vanessa has more than 100 stickers? Explain.

_____

_____

_____

Estimate to solve.

14. Which is greater, the number of roses in the garden, or the total number of daisies and violets? Circle.

roses   daisies and violets

Flowers in the Garden	
Flowers	**Number of Flowers**
daisies	37
roses	50
violets	21

15. ⭐ **Test Prep** Mr. Ortega has some paper clips. He has 47 large paper clips and 36 small paper clips. About how many paper clips does he have in all? Choose the best estimate.

- ○ less than 20
- ○ less than 50
- ○ more than 50
- ○ more than 100

TAKE HOME ACTIVITY · Have your child explain how he or she solved Exercise 14.

FOR MORE PRACTICE:
Standards Practice Book, pp. P89–P90

Name _____

Find Sums for 3 Addends

Essential Question What are some ways to add 3 numbers?

Listen and Draw REAL WORLD

Draw to show the problem.

FOR THE TEACHER • Read the following problem and have children draw to show it. Mr. Kim went to the party supply store and bought 5 blue balloons, 4 red balloons, and 5 yellow balloons. How many balloons did Mr. Kim buy in all? Repeat for another problem.

Math Talk

Explain how you decided which two numbers to add first.

Chapter 4

one hundred ninety-seven **197**

Model and Draw

There are different ways to add.

How can you add 23, 41, and 17?

Think of a strategy you know to choose which digits in the ones column to add first.

> You can make a ten first. Then add the other ones digit. Then add the tens.

> Add from top to bottom. First add the top two digits in the ones column, then add the next digit. Then add the tens.

```
  2 3
  4 1
+ 1 7
```

$3 + 7 = 10$
$10 + 1 = 11$

```
  2 3
  4 1
+ 1 7
```

$3 + 1 = 4$
$4 + 7 = 11$

Share and Show

Add.

1.
```
   33
   34
+  32
```

2.
```
   47
   21
+   7
```

3.
```
   65
   13
+  15
```

4.
```
   58
   27
+   2
```

5.
```
   12
   29
+  35
```

6.
```
   10
   42
+  36
```

✓7.
```
   71
   21
+   6
```

✓8.
```
   30
   29
+  48
```

Name _____

On Your Own

Add.

9.
```
   22
   27
+  18
```

10.
```
   26
   31
+  19
```

11.
```
   24
   11
+  53
```

12.
```
   33
   48
+   6
```

13.
```
   40
   17
+  32
```

14.
```
   25
   25
+  25
```

15.
```
   19
   65
+  24
```

16.
```
    4
   73
+  16
```

17.
```
   35
   24
+  58
```

18.
```
   32
   18
+  28
```

19.
```
   42
   31
+  12
```

20.
```
   70
   18
+  17
```

21. **H.O.T.** Circle the 3 numbers that you can add to get the sum. Use the clues below.

- One number is the sum of 8 + 8.
- One number is between 20 and 30.

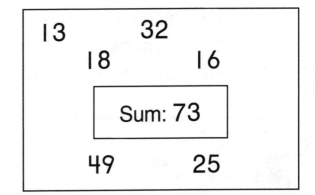

13   32
    18   16

Sum: 73

49   25

22. **H.O.T.** Garrett, Aaron, and Karine bought 64 marbles. Garrett bought 19 marbles. Karine bought 6 more marbles than Garrett. How many marbles did Aaron buy?

First, find how many marbles Karine bought.

Garrett	19	
Karine	19	6

Karine bought _____ marbles.

Next, find how many marbles Garrett and Karine have together.

Garrett: 19	Karine: _____

Together they have _____ marbles.

Then, find how many marbles Aaron bought.

Garrett and Karine: _____	Aaron: _____

64 marbles bought altogether

Aaron bought _____ marbles.

23. ⭐ **Test Prep** Mrs. Paul has 23 red notebooks, 15 green notebooks, and 27 blue notebooks. How many notebooks does Mrs. Paul have in all?

○ 38
○ 42
○ 55
○ 65

TAKE HOME ACTIVITY · Ask your child to show you two ways to add 17, 13, and 24.

© Houghton Mifflin Harcourt Publishing Company

FOR MORE PRACTICE:
Standards Practice Book, pp. P91–P92

Name _____

Represent Addition Problems

Essential Question How can you write a number sentence to represent a problem?

Listen and Draw REAL WORLD

Write the numbers for each problem. Then solve.

+ _____

+ _____

FOR THE TEACHER • Read the following problem and have children write the addends in vertical format. Ed's puppy played outside for 15 minutes. Then she played inside for 9 minutes. How many minutes did Ed's puppy play in all? Repeat with another problem.

Math Talk
Explain how you found the sum for the first problem.

Model and Draw

You can write a number sentence to show a problem.

Sandy has 16 pencils. Nancy has 13 pencils. How many pencils do they have altogether?

$$16 + 13 = 29$$

THINK:
$$
\begin{array}{r}
16 \text{ pencils} \\
+ \ 13 \text{ pencils} \\
\hline
29 \text{ pencils}
\end{array}
$$

They have _____ pencils altogether.

Share and Show

Write a number sentence for the problem. Solve.

☑1. Lily has 18 carrots and 24 potatoes growing in her garden. How many vegetables does Lily have in all?

_____

_____ vegetables

☑2. 83 people went to a movie on Thursday. 53 of them were children and the rest were adults. How many adults were at the movie?

_____

_____ adults

On Your Own

Write a number sentence for the problem. Solve.

3. Chris and his friends went to the zoo. In the Reptile House, they saw 9 snakes and 14 lizards. How many reptiles did they see in all?

_____

_____ reptiles

4. Jake had a stamp collection. Then he bought 20 more stamps. Now he has 56 stamps. How many stamps did Jake have in his collection to start?

_____

_____ stamps

5. **H.O.T.** Joe has 19 daisies in a bunch. Donald has 12 more daisies than Joe. How many daisies do Donald and Joe have altogether?

_____

_____ daisies

PROBLEM SOLVING

Read about the field trip. Then write number sentences to answer the questions.

> Last week our class went to the park. We counted the plants and animals. We saw 26 oak trees, 19 pine trees, and 12 maple trees. We also saw 13 cardinals and 35 blue jays.

6. How many birds did the class see in all?

_____   _____ birds

7. What is the total number of trees the class saw?

_____   _____ trees

8. ⭐ **Test Prep** Mr. Downey baked 54 cookies last week. He baked 38 cookies this week. How many cookies did Mr. Downey bake altogether?

- ○ 92
- ○ 82
- ○ 26
- ○ 16

 TAKE HOME ACTIVITY · Have your child explain how he or she solved Exercise 8.

FOR MORE PRACTICE:
Standards Practice Book, pp. P93–P94

Name _____

✓ Chapter 4 Review/Test

Vocabulary

Use a word in the box to complete each sentence.

| estimate |
| regroup |
| addend |

1. When finding the sum for 37 + 14,

   _____ 10 ones to make 1 ten. (pp. 169–172)

2. When you find about how many, you _____ . (pp. 193–196)

Concepts and Skills

Draw quick pictures to solve. Write the sum. (pp. 173–176)

3.

Tens	Ones
□	
2	6
+ 3	2

Tens	Ones

4.

Tens	Ones
□	
5	3
+ 2	7

Tens	Ones

Estimate the sum.
Circle the better choice. (pp. 193–196)

5.   18 + 23 = ■

   greater than 50

   less than 50

6.   91 + 28 = ■

   greater than 100

   less than 100

Fill in the bubble for the correct answer choice.

7. Lauren's family drove to the beach.
They saw 14 gulls the first day.
The next day they saw 7 more gulls.

How many gulls did they see
in all? (pp. 157–160)

- ○ 7
- ○ 20
- ○ 21
- ○ 31

8. Mr. O'Brien visited a lighthouse. He climbed
26 stairs. Then he climbed 64 more stairs
to the top. How many stairs did he climb
in all? (pp. 169–172)

- ○ 90
- ○ 82
- ○ 80
- ○ 42

Tens	Ones

9. Nicole made a necklace. She used
13 red beads. She used 28 blue beads.
How many beads did she use altogether? (pp. 161–164)

- ○ 15
- ○ 31
- ○ 35
- ○ 41

Name _____

Fill in the bubble for the correct answer choice.

10. Scott baked 24 muffins. He placed 15 muffins on the plate. How many muffins are not on the plate? (pp. 201–204)

- ○ 6
- ○ 8
- ○ 9
- ○ 19

11. Carlos is visiting a museum. There are 23 people in his group. There are 36 people in a second group. There are 42 people in a third group.

How many people are in the three groups in all? (pp. 197–200)

- ○ 911
- ○ 101
- ○ 78
- ○ 59

12. Amy picked 57 strawberries. Her mother picked 34 strawberries. How many strawberries did they pick in all? (pp. 181–183)

- ○ 91
- ○ 90
- ○ 83
- ○ 81

Short Answer

13. Ling saw these two signs at the theater. How many seats are there altogether in the two sections?

Section A	Section B
35 seats	43 seats

_____ seats

Did you regroup to find the sum? Explain.

_____

_____

Performance Task

14. Mike visited the train museum. He saw 17 blue passenger cars, 32 freight cars, and 25 black passenger cars. How many passenger cars did Mike see in all?

_____ passenger cars

How did you choose which numbers to add? Explain how you found your answer.

_____

_____

_____

2-Digit Subtraction

Curious About Math with

Curious George

There are hundreds of different kinds of dragonflies. If 52 dragonflies are in a garden and 10 fly away, how many dragonflies are left? How many are left if 10 more fly away?

Name _____

Show What You Know

Subtraction Patterns

Subtract 2. Complete each subtraction sentence.

1. $7 - \underline{2} = \underline{5}$

4. $4 - \underline{} = \underline{}$

2. $6 - \underline{} = \underline{}$

5. $3 - \underline{} = \underline{}$

3. $5 - \underline{} = \underline{}$

6. $2 - \underline{} = \underline{}$

Subtraction Facts

Write the difference.

7. $\begin{array}{r} 8 \\ -5 \\ \hline \end{array}$

8. $\begin{array}{r} 14 \\ -6 \\ \hline \end{array}$

9. $\begin{array}{r} 13 \\ -9 \\ \hline \end{array}$

10. $\begin{array}{r} 16 \\ -7 \\ \hline \end{array}$

11. $\begin{array}{r} 12 \\ -6 \\ \hline \end{array}$

12. $\begin{array}{r} 15 \\ -8 \\ \hline \end{array}$

Tens and Ones

Write the number. Then write the number of tens and ones.

13.

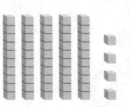

____ = ____ tens ____ ones

14.

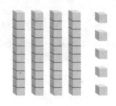

____ = ____ tens ____ ones

Family note: This page checks your child's understanding of important skills needed for success in Chapter 5.

GO Online

Assessment Options
Soar to Success Math

© Houghton Mifflin Harcourt Publishing Company

Vocabulary Builder

Visualize It

Fill in the boxes of the graphic organizer.

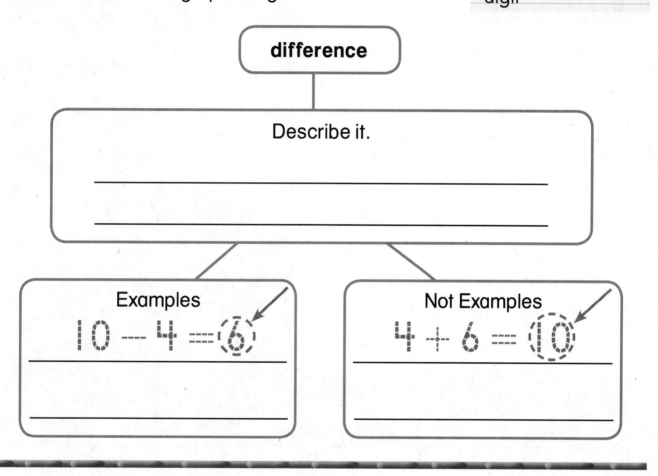

Understand Vocabulary

Draw a line to complete the sentence.

1. A **digit** can be •   • as 2 **tens**.

2. You can **regroup** •   • 0, 1, 2, 3, 4, 5, 6, 7, 8, or 9.

3. 20 **ones** are the same •   • to trade 10 ones for 1 ten.

GO Online • eStudent Edition
• Multimedia eGlossary

Game

Subtraction Search

Materials

- 3 sets of number cards 4–9 • 18 ●

Play with a partner.

1. Shuffle all the cards. Place them face down in one stack.

2. Take one card. Find a square with a subtraction problem with this number as the difference. Your partner checks your answer.

3. If you are correct, place a ● on that square. If there is no match, skip your turn.

4. Take turns. The first player to have ● on all the squares wins.

Player 1

12 − 5	9 − 2	10 − 5
16 − 7	13 − 7	17 − 9
7 − 3	11 − 5	18 − 9

Player 2

8 − 3	15 − 7	11 − 6
17 − 8	9 − 3	16 − 8
13 − 9	6 − 2	14 − 7

Name _____

Break Apart Ones to Subtract

Essential Question How does breaking apart
a number make subtracting easier?

Listen and Draw

Write two addends for each sum.

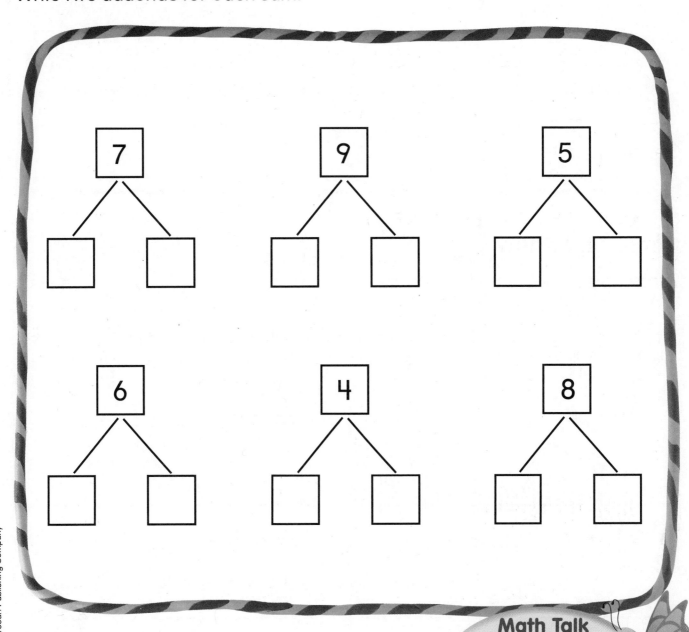

FOR THE TEACHER • After children have
recorded addends for each sum, have a class
discussion on the different facts that children
represented on their papers.

Math Talk
Describe how
you chose addends
for each sum.

Chapter 5

two hundred thirteen **213**

Model and Draw

Break apart ones. Subtract in two steps.

$63 - 7 = \blacksquare$

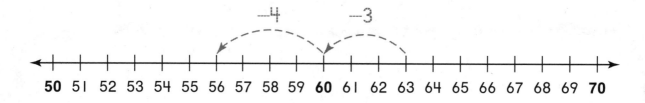

Start at 63.
Subtract 3 to get
to 60. Then subtract
4 more.

So, $63 - 7 =$ _____.

Share and Show

Break apart ones to subtract. Write the difference.

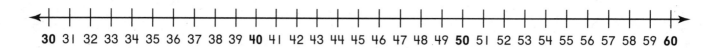

1. $55 - 8 =$ _____

2. $42 - 5 =$ _____

3. $41 - 9 =$ _____

4. $54 - 6 =$ _____

5. $44 - 7 =$ _____

6. $52 - 8 =$ _____

On Your Own

Break apart ones to subtract. Write the difference.

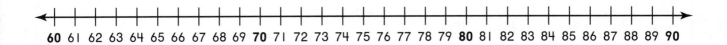

60 61 62 63 64 65 66 67 68 69 **70** 71 72 73 74 75 76 77 78 79 **80** 81 82 83 84 85 86 87 88 89 **90**

7. $75 - 7 =$ _____

8. $86 - 8 =$ _____

9. $82 - 5 =$ _____

10. $83 - 7 =$ _____

11. $72 - 7 =$ _____

12. $76 - 9 =$ _____

13. $85 - 8 =$ _____

14. $71 - 6 =$ _____

H.O.T. Write the differences. Then write the next fact in the pattern.

15. $54 - 5 = \underline{\quad 49 \quad}$

$54 - 6 =$ _____

$54 - 7 =$ _____

_____

16. $81 - 4 = \underline{\quad 77 \quad}$

$71 - 4 =$ _____

$61 - 4 =$ _____

_____

PROBLEM SOLVING

Choose a way to solve.
Write or draw to explain.

17. Cheryl built a toy train with 27 train cars. Then she added 18 more train cars to the train. How many train cars are on the toy train now?

_____ train cars

18.  Samuel had 46 marbles. He gave some marbles to a friend and has 9 marbles left. How many marbles did he give his friend?

_____ marbles

19.  **Test Prep** Matthew had 73 blocks. He gave 8 blocks to his sister. How many blocks does Matthew have now?

- ○ 81
- ○ 70
- ○ 68
- ○ 65

 TAKE HOME ACTIVITY · Ask your child to describe how to find the difference for 34 − 6.

FOR MORE PRACTICE:
Standards Practice Book, pp. P99–P100

Name _____

Break Apart Numbers to Subtract

Essential Question How does breaking apart a number make subtracting easier?

Listen and Draw REAL WORLD

Draw jumps on the number line to show how you broke apart the number to subtract.

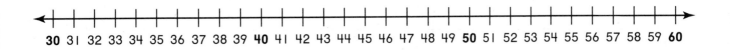

30 31 32 33 34 35 36 37 38 39 **40** 41 42 43 44 45 46 47 48 49 **50** 51 52 53 54 55 56 57 58 59 **60**

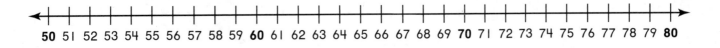

50 51 52 53 54 55 56 57 58 59 **60** 61 62 63 64 65 66 67 68 69 **70** 71 72 73 74 75 76 77 78 79 **80**

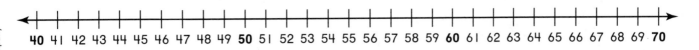

40 41 42 43 44 45 46 47 48 49 **50** 51 52 53 54 55 56 57 58 59 **60** 61 62 63 64 65 66 67 68 69 **70**

FOR THE TEACHER • Read the following problem. Have children draw jumps on the number line to solve. Mrs. Hill had 45 paintbrushes. She gave 9 paintbrushes to students in her art class. How many paintbrushes does Mrs. Hill have now? Repeat the same problem situation for 72 − 7 and 53 − 6.

Math Talk
For one of the problems, **describe** what you did.

Chapter 5

Break apart the number you are subtracting into tens and ones.

Subtract 10.
Next, subtract 2 to get to 60.
Then subtract 5 more.

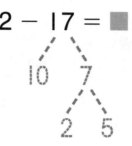

$$72 - 17 = \blacksquare$$

10   7

2   5

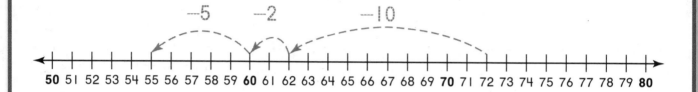

–5   –2   –10

50 51 52 53 54 55 56 57 58 59 **60** 61 62 63 64 65 66 67 68 69 **70** 71 72 73 74 75 76 77 78 79 **80**

So, $72 - 17 = $ ____.

Share and Show

Break apart the number you are subtracting.
Write the difference.

20 21 22 23 24 25 26 27 28 29 **30** 31 32 33 34 35 36 37 38 39 **40** 41 42 43 44 45 46 47 48 49 **50**

1. $43 - 18 = $ ____

10   8

3   5

2. $45 - 14 = $ ____

10   4

✓ 3. $46 - 17 = $ ____

✓ 4. $44 - 16 = $ ____

Name _____

On Your Own

Break apart the number you are subtracting.
Write the difference.

40 41 42 43 44 45 46 47 48 49 **50** 51 52 53 54 55 56 57 58 59 **60** 61 62 63 64 65 66 67 68 69 **70**

5. $57 - 15 = $ ___

6. $63 - 17 = $ ___

7. $68 - 19 = $ ___

8. $61 - 18 = $ ___

9. $65 - 13 = $ ___

10. $59 - 14 = $ ___

11. $62 - 11 = $ ___

12. $67 - 18 = $ ___

13. Look at Tom's steps to solve a problem.
Solve this problem in the same way.

$$42 - 15 = ?$$

Tom
$35 - 18 = ?$
$35 - 10 = 25$
$25 - 5 = 20$
$20 - 3 = \text{(17)}$

Solve. Write or draw to explain.

14. 38 people went to the library in the morning. 33 people went to the library in the afternoon. How many people in all went to the library?

_____ people

15. **H.O.T.** Jane saw 53 books on a shelf. She moved some of the books to a table. Then there were 36 books still on the shelf. How many books did she move to the table?

_____ books

16. ⭐ **Test Prep**   There are 32 newspapers in the first stack. There are 19 newspapers in the second stack. How many more newspapers are in the first stack than in the second stack?

○ 51
○ 27
○ 23
○ 13

TAKE HOME ACTIVITY · Ask your child to write a subtraction story that uses 2-digit numbers.

FOR MORE PRACTICE:
Standards Practice Book, pp. P101–P102

Name _____

Model Regrouping for Subtraction

Essential Question When do you regroup in subtraction?

Listen and Draw REAL WORLD

Use ▭▭▭▭ ▭ to model the problem.
Draw quick pictures to show your model.

Tens	Ones

© Houghton Mifflin Harcourt Publishing Company

Math Talk
Describe why you traded a tens block for 10 ones blocks.

FOR THE TEACHER • Read the following problem. Michelle counted 21 butterflies in her garden. Then 7 butterflies flew away. How many butterflies were still in the garden?

Chapter 5

Model and Draw

How do you subtract 26 from 53?

Step 1 Show 53. Are there enough ones to subtract 6?

Tens	Ones

yes   (no)

Step 2 If there are not enough ones, regroup 1 ten as 10 ones.

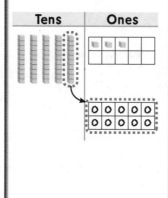

Step 3 Subtract 6 ones from 13 ones.

Tens	Ones

Step 4 Subtract the tens. Write the tens and ones. Write the difference.

Tens	Ones

____ tens ____ ones

____

Share and Show

Draw to show the regrouping.
Write how many tens and ones. Write the difference.

1. Subtract 13 from 41.

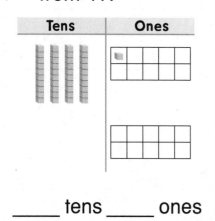

____ tens ____ ones

____

2. Subtract 9 from 48.

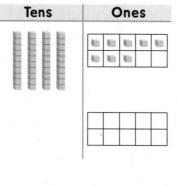

____ tens ____ ones

____

3. Subtract 28 from 52.

Tens	Ones

____ tens ____ ones

____

Name _____

On Your Own

Write how many tens and ones. Write the difference.

4. Subtract 8 from 23.

Tens	Ones

_____ ten _____ ones

_____

5. Subtract 36 from 45.

Tens	Ones

_____ tens _____ ones

_____

6. Subtract 6 from 43.

Tens	Ones

_____ tens _____ ones

_____

7. Subtract 39 from 67.

Tens	Ones

_____ tens _____ ones

_____

8. Subtract 21 from 50.

Tens	Ones

_____ tens _____ ones

_____

9. Subtract 29 from 56.

Tens	Ones

_____ tens _____ ones

_____

10. **H.O.T.** Write the missing numbers to make your own problem.

Subtract _____ from 53.

Tens	Ones

__2__ tens _____ ones

_____

PROBLEM SOLVING

REAL WORLD

Write Math

Choose a way to solve.
Write or draw to explain.

11. Claire's puzzle has 85 pieces.
She has used 46 pieces
so far. How many puzzle
pieces have not been
used yet?

_____ puzzle pieces

12. **H.O.T.** Billy has 16 marbles.
Sara has 9 more marbles
than Billy. Kim has 18 fewer
marbles than Sara. How many
marbles does Kim have?

- First find how many
  marbles Sara has.
- Then find how many
  marbles Kim has.

_____ marbles

13. ⭐ **Test Prep** There were 65 toy
animals in the store. Then the
clerk sold 17 toy animals. How many
toy animals are in the store now?

○ 48
○ 52
○ 72
○ 82

TAKE HOME ACTIVITY · Ask your child to write a subtraction
story and then explain how to solve it.

224 two hundred twenty-four

FOR MORE PRACTICE:
Standards Practice Book, pp. P103–P104

Name _____

Model and Record 2-Digit Subtraction

Essential Question How do you record 2-digit subtraction?

Listen and Draw REAL WORLD

Use ▭▭▭▭ ▪ to model the problem.
Draw quick pictures to show your model.

Tens	Ones

Math Talk
Did you trade blocks in your model? **Explain** why or why not.

FOR THE TEACHER • Read the following problem. Mr. Kelly made 47 muffins. His students ate 23 of the muffins. How many muffins were not eaten?

Chapter 5

© Houghton Mifflin Harcourt Publishing Company

Model and Draw

Trace over the quick pictures in the steps.

Subtract.   56
           − 19

Step 1 Show 56. Are there enough ones to subtract 9?

Tens	Ones

Tens	Ones
5	6
− 1	9

Step 2 If there are not enough ones, regroup 1 ten as 10 ones.

Tens	Ones

Tens	Ones
4	16
5̷	6̷
− 1	9

Step 3 Subtract the ones.

$$16 − 9 = 7$$

Tens	Ones

Tens	Ones
4	16
5̷	6̷
− 1	9
	7

Step 4 Subtract the tens.

$$4 − 1 = 3$$

Tens	Ones

Tens	Ones
4	16
5̷	6̷
− 1	9
3	7

Share and Show

Draw a quick picture to solve. Write the difference.

1.

Tens	Ones		Tens	Ones
4	7			
− 1	5			

2.

Tens	Ones		Tens	Ones
3	2			
− 1	8			

On Your Own

Draw a quick picture to solve. Write the difference.

3.

Tens	Ones
☐	☐
3	5
2	9

Tens	Ones

4.

Tens	Ones
☐	☐
2	8
	5

Tens	Ones

5.

Tens	Ones
☐	☐
5	3
2	6

Tens	Ones

6.

Tens	Ones
☐	☐
3	2
1	3

Tens	Ones

7.

Tens	Ones
☐	☐
4	4
1	7

Tens	Ones

8.

Tens	Ones
☐	☐
3	8
1	8

Tens	Ones

PROBLEM SOLVING

Draw a quick picture or write a subtraction problem to solve.

9. Sophie has 63 points in the math contest. Dave has 46 points. Does Sophie have 18 more points than Dave?

Tens	Ones

Tens	Ones
□	□
−	

Circle your answer.

yes   no

10. Jamie had some markers. She gave 13 markers to George and had 29 markers left. Did she have 46 markers to start with?

Tens	Ones

Tens	Ones
□	□
−	

Circle your answer.

yes   no

11. ⭐ **Test Prep** Mr. Sims has a box of 44 erasers. He gives 18 erasers to his students. How many erasers does Mr. Sims have now?

- ○ 22
- ○ 26
- ○ 36
- ○ 62

 TAKE HOME ACTIVITY · Write 73 − 28 on a sheet of paper. Ask your child if he or she would regroup to find the difference.

228 two hundred twenty-eight

© Houghton Mifflin Harcourt Publishing Company

FOR MORE PRACTICE:
Standards Practice Book, pp. P105–P106

Name _____

2-Digit Subtraction

Essential Question How do you record the steps when subtracting with 2-digit numbers?

Listen and Draw REAL WORLD

Draw a quick picture to model each problem.

Tens	Ones

Tens	Ones

Math Talk
Explain how you know when to regroup.

FOR THE TEACHER • Read the following problem. Devin had 36 toy robots on his shelf. He moved 12 of the robots to his closet. How many robots are on the shelf now? Repeat the activity with this problem: Devin had 54 toy cars. He gave 9 of them to his brother. How many cars does Devin have now?

Model and Draw

Subtract.

$$\begin{array}{r} 42 \\ -15 \end{array}$$

Step 1 Are there enough ones to subtract 5?

Tens	Ones
||||	o o

Tens	Ones
☐	☐
4	2
− 1	5

Step 2 Regroup 1 ten as 10 ones.

Tens	Ones
|||	o o o / o o o / o o o o

Tens	Ones
3	12
4̸	2̸
− 1	5

Step 3 Subtract the ones.
$$12 - 5 = 7$$

Tens	Ones
|||	o o o / o o o / o o o

Tens	Ones
3	12
4̸	2̸
− 1	5
	7

Step 4 Subtract the tens.
$$3 - 1 = 2$$

Tens	Ones
||Ⅹ	o o o / o o o / o o o

Tens	Ones
3	12
4̸	2̸
− 1	5
2	7

Share and Show

Regroup if you need to. Write the difference.

1.

Tens	Ones
☐	☐
3	1
− 1	4

2.

Tens	Ones
☐	☐
5	6
− 2	1

3.

Tens	Ones
☐	☐
7	2
− 3	5

On Your Own

Regroup if you need to. Write the difference.

4.

Tens	Ones
☐	☐
2	3
− 1	4

5.

Tens	Ones
☐	☐
8	7
− 5	7

6.

Tens	Ones
☐	☐
3	4
− 1	8

7.

Tens	Ones
☐	☐
6	1
− 1	3

8.

4	5
− 1	8

9.

5	2
− 3	6

10.

3	2
− 1	3

11.

7	5
− 4	3

12.

5	6
− 2	7

13.

9	4
− 2	9

14.

8	7
− 3	9

15.

8	3
− 4	6

H.O.T. Write the missing numbers.

16.

6	14
☐	☐
− 2	6
4	8

17.

3	9
☐	☐
− ☐	☐
2	7

18.

8	11
☐	☐
− 5	8
☐	3

19. **H.O.T.** This is how Scott found the difference for 83 − 27.

```
   83
 −20
 ───
   63
 − 3
 ───
   60
 − 4
 ───
   56
```

Find the difference for 92 − 68 using Scott's way.

20. Describe Scott's way of subtracting 2-digit numbers.

_____

_____

_____

_____

21. ⭐ **Test Prep**   There are 34 chickens in the barn. If 16 chickens go outside, into the yard, how many chickens will still be in the barn?

○ 18
○ 22
○ 42
○ 50

 TAKE HOME ACTIVITY · Ask your child to write a 2-digit subtraction problem with no regrouping. Have your child explain why he or she chose those numbers.

FOR MORE PRACTICE:
Standards Practice Book, pp. P107–P108

Name _____

Practice 2-Digit Subtraction

Essential Question How do you record the steps when subtracting 2-digit numbers?

Listen and Draw REAL WORLD

Choose one way to solve the problem.
Draw or write to show what you did.

FOR THE TEACHER • Read the following problem and have children choose their own methods for solving it. There are 74 books in Mr. Barron's classroom. 19 of the books are about computers. How many books are not about computers?

Math Talk

Describe a different way that you could have solved the problem.

Carmen had 50 game cards. Then she gave 16 game cards to Theo. How many game cards does Carmen have now?

Step 1 Look at the ones. There are not enough ones to subtract 6 from 0. So, regroup.

$$
\begin{array}{r}
^4\!\!\!/\;10 \\
\cancel{5}\;\cancel{0} \\
-\;1\;6 \\
\hline
\end{array}
$$

Step 2 Subtract the ones.

$$10 - 6 = 4$$

$$
\begin{array}{r}
4\;10 \\
\cancel{5}\;\cancel{0} \\
-\;1\;6 \\
\hline
4
\end{array}
$$

Step 3 Subtract the tens.

$$4 - 1 = 3$$

$$
\begin{array}{r}
4\;10 \\
\cancel{5}\;\cancel{0} \\
-\;1\;6 \\
\hline
3\;4
\end{array}
$$

Share and Show

Write the difference.

1.
$$
\begin{array}{r}
3\;8 \\
-\;1\;9 \\
\hline
\end{array}
$$

2.
$$
\begin{array}{r}
6\;5 \\
-\;3\;2 \\
\hline
\end{array}
$$

3.
$$
\begin{array}{r}
8\;3 \\
-\;7\;6 \\
\hline
\end{array}
$$

4.
$$
\begin{array}{r}
5\;2 \\
-\;1\;7 \\
\hline
\end{array}
$$

✓ 5.
$$
\begin{array}{r}
7\;0 \\
-\;3\;8 \\
\hline
\end{array}
$$

✓ 6.
$$
\begin{array}{r}
2\;3 \\
-\;\;\;4 \\
\hline
\end{array}
$$

Name _____

On Your Own

Write the difference.

7.

$$\begin{array}{r} 4\ 1 \\ -\ 2\ 4 \\ \hline \end{array}$$

8.

$$\begin{array}{r} 5\ 8 \\ -\ 1\ 6 \\ \hline \end{array}$$

9.

$$\begin{array}{r} 6\ 0 \\ -\ 1\ 3 \\ \hline \end{array}$$

10.

$$\begin{array}{r} 5\ 2 \\ -\ 4\ 7 \\ \hline \end{array}$$

11.

$$\begin{array}{r} 7\ 2 \\ -\ 4\ 6 \\ \hline \end{array}$$

12.

$$\begin{array}{r} 3\ 7 \\ -\ \ 6 \\ \hline \end{array}$$

13.

$$\begin{array}{r} 7\ 4 \\ -\ 4\ 6 \\ \hline \end{array}$$

14.

$$\begin{array}{r} 9\ 0 \\ -\ 1\ 8 \\ \hline \end{array}$$

15.

$$\begin{array}{r} 4\ 0 \\ -\ \ 7 \\ \hline \end{array}$$

16. Write the missing numbers in the subtraction problems.

$$\begin{array}{r} 6\ \ 15 \\ -\ \quad\ \\ \hline 4\ \ 7 \end{array}$$

$$\begin{array}{r} 7\ \ 13 \\ -\ \quad\ \\ \hline 2\ \ 5 \end{array}$$

TAKE HOME ACTIVITY • Ask your child to show you one way to find the difference for 80 − 34.

FOR MORE PRACTICE:
Standards Practice Book, pp. P109–P110

Mid-Chapter Checkpoint

Concepts and Skills

Break apart the number you are subtracting. Use the
number line to help. Write the difference. (pp. 213–220)

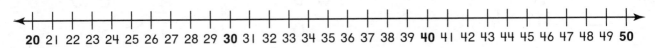

1. $34 - 8 =$ _____

2. $45 - 17 =$ _____

Draw a quick picture to solve. Write the
difference. (pp. 225–228)

3.

Tens	Ones		Tens	Ones
☐	☐			
4	2			
− 2	9			

4.

Tens	Ones		Tens	Ones
☐	☐			
5	4			
− 2	3			

Write the difference. (pp. 233–235)

5.
$$\begin{array}{r} 7\ 3 \\ -4\ 8 \\ \hline \end{array}$$

6.
$$\begin{array}{r} 6\ 0 \\ -2\ 6 \\ \hline \end{array}$$

7.
$$\begin{array}{r} 8\ 5 \\ -3\ 7 \\ \hline \end{array}$$

 **Test Prep** (pp. 229–232)

8. Marissa had 51 toy dinosaurs.
   She gave 14 toy dinosaurs to her
   brother. How many toy dinosaurs
   does she have now?

   ○ 33
   ○ 37
   ○ 47
   ○ 65

Name _____

Rewrite 2-Digit Subtraction

Essential Question What are two different ways to write subtraction problems?

Listen and Draw REAL WORLD

Write the numbers for each subtraction problem.

```
    —
  _____
```

```
    —
  _____
```

```
    —
  _____
```

```
    —
  _____
```

Math Talk Why is it important to line up the digits of the numbers in columns? **Explain.**

FOR THE TEACHER • Read the following problem. Have children write the numbers in vertical format. There were 45 children at a party. Then 23 children left the party. How many children were still at the party? Repeat for three more problems.

Chapter 5

Model and Draw

Subtract. $81 - 36 = ?$

Step 1 For 81, write the tens digit in the tens column.

Write the ones digit in the ones column.

Repeat for 36.

$$\begin{array}{r} 8\ 1 \\ -\ 3\ 6 \\ \hline \end{array}$$

Step 2 Look at the ones. Regroup if you need to.

Subtract the ones. Subtract the tens.

$$\begin{array}{r} 7\ 11 \\ \cancel{8}\ \cancel{1} \\ -\ 3\ 6 \\ \hline \end{array}$$

Share and Show

Rewrite the numbers. Then subtract.

1. $34 - 8$ ___

2. $48 - 24$ ___

3. $85 - 37$ ___

4. $63 - 19$ ___

5. $62 - 37$ ___

6. $51 - 27$ ___

✓7. $76 - 18$ ___

✓8. $95 - 48$ ___

On Your Own

Rewrite the numbers. Then subtract.

9. $42 - 15$	10. $85 - 47$	11. $63 - 23$	12. $51 - 23$
$-$ _____	$-$ _____	$-$ _____	$-$ _____
13. $78 - 53$	14. $54 - 38$	15. $92 - 39$	16. $87 - 28$
$-$ _____	$-$ _____	_____	_____

H.O.T. Choose a number.
Write it in the problem and solve.

17. There are 52 children riding on two buses for a field trip.

There are _____ children riding on the first bus.

How many children are riding on the second bus?

_____ children

Read about the class trip. Then answer the questions.

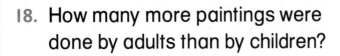

> Pablo's class went to the art museum. They
> saw 26 paintings done by children. They saw
> 53 paintings done by adults. They also saw
> 18 sculptures and 31 photographs.

18. How many more paintings were
done by adults than by children?

_____ more paintings

19. **H.O.T.** How many more paintings
than sculptures did they see?

_____ more paintings

20. ⭐ **Test Prep** Tom drew 23 pictures last year.
Beth drew 14 pictures. How many more pictures
did Tom draw than Beth?

○ 37

○ 19

○ 11

○ 9

TAKE HOME ACTIVITY · Ask your child to write and solve
a subtraction problem about a family trip.

FOR MORE PRACTICE:
Standards Practice Book, pp. P111–P112

Draw a Diagram • Subtraction

Essential Question How does drawing a diagram help you solve a problem?

Jane and her mom made 33 puppets for the craft fair. They sold 14 puppets. How many puppets did they have left?

🔑 Unlock the Problem

What do I need to find?

_____
they have left

What information do I need to use?

They made _____ puppets.

They sold _____ puppets.

**Complete the bar model.
Show how to solve the problem.**

_____	_____

_____

_____ puppets

HOME CONNECTION • Your child used a bar model to represent the problem. The bar model helps show what the missing amount is in order to solve the problem.

Try Another Problem

Complete the bar model. Then solve.

• What do I need to find?
• What information do I need to use?

1. Carlette had a box of 46 craft sticks. She used 28 craft sticks to make a sailboat. How many craft sticks were not used?

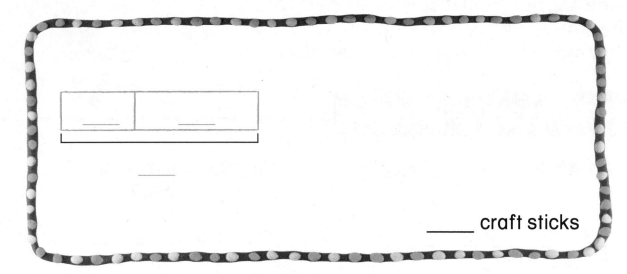

_____ craft sticks

2. Robbie's class made 31 clay figures. Sarah's class made 15 clay figures. How many more clay figures did Robbie's class make than Sarah's class?

_____ more clay figures

Math Talk
How do you know that Exercise 1 is a take-away problem? **Explain.**

Name _____

Share and Show

Complete the bar model. Then solve.

☑ 3. Mr. Hayes makes 32 wooden frames. He gives away 15 frames as gifts. How many frames does he have left?

_____ frames

☑ 4. Wesley has 21 ribbons in a box. He has 15 ribbons on the wall. How many more ribbons does he have in the box?

_____ more ribbons

---

5. Lynn wrote 22 poems. Some of her poems are in her notebook. 7 poems are not in her notebook. How many poems are in her notebook?

_____ poems

On Your Own

Choose a way to solve.
Write or draw to explain.

Write Math

6. Fred had 34 rocks in his collection. Then he got 11 more rocks. How many rocks does Fred have now?

_____ rocks

7. **H.O.T.** Jean has 19 flowers in her basket. She wants to have 32 flowers in all. How many more flowers does she need?

_____ more flowers

8. There are 154 tulip plants, 162 daisy plants, and 147 rose plants at the store. Are there more tulip plants or more daisy plants?

more _____ plants

9. ⭐**Test Prep** There are 48 crackers in the bag. The children eat 25 crackers. How many crackers are still in the bag?

○ 13
○ 17
○ 23
○ 63

TAKE HOME ACTIVITY • Ask your child to explain how he or she solved one of the problems above.

FOR MORE PRACTICE:
Standards Practice Book, pp. P113–P114

Name _____

Represent Subtraction Problems

Essential Question How can you write a number sentence to represent a problem?

Listen and Draw REAL WORLD

Draw to show the problem. Write a number sentence. Then solve.

 FOR THE TEACHER • Read this problem to children. Riley had 53 crayons. He gives some crayons to Courtney. Now Riley has 38 crayons. How many crayons did Riley give to Courtney?

 **Math Talk**
Describe how your drawing shows the problem.

Chapter 5

Model and Draw

You can write a number sentence to show a problem.

Liza has 65 postcards. She gives 24 postcards to Wesley. How many postcards does Liza have now?

$$65 - 24 = \underline{}$$

THINK:
$$\begin{array}{r} 65 \text{ postcards} \\ -24 \text{ postcards} \\ \hline 41 \text{ postcards} \end{array}$$

Liza has <u>41</u> postcards now.

Share and Show

Write a number sentence for the problem. Solve.

1. There were 32 birds in the trees. Then 18 birds flew away. How many birds were left in the trees?

_____

_____ birds

2. Carla read 43 pages in her book. Joe read 32 pages in his book. How many more pages did Carla read than Joe?

_____

_____ more pages

On Your Own .

Write a number sentence for the problem. Solve.

3. There were 40 ants on a rock. Some ants moved to the grass. Now there are 26 ants on the rock. How many ants moved to the grass?

_____

_____ ants

4. Keisha had a box of ribbons. She took 29 ribbons out of the box. Then there were 17 ribbons still in the box. How many ribbons were in the box to start with?

_____

_____ ribbons

5. **H.O.T.** There are 50 bees in a hive. Some bees fly out. If fewer than 20 bees are still in the hive, how many bees could have flown out?

Use subtraction to prove your answer.

_____ bees

PROBLEM SOLVING REAL WORLD

Solve. Write or draw to explain.

6. Haley had some stickers. John gave her 15 more stickers. Now Haley has 44 stickers. How many stickers did she have to start with?

_____ stickers

7. **H.O.T.** Brendan made this number line to find a difference. What was he subtracting from 100? Explain your answer.

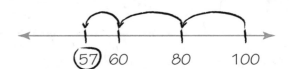

_____

_____

_____

8. ⭐ **Test Prep** There are 48 pictures on the zoo wall. Of these, 25 are wild cats and the rest are birds. How many of the pictures are birds?

- ○ 63
- ○ 37
- ○ 23
- ○ 13

TAKE HOME ACTIVITY · Have your child explain how he or she solved one problem in this lesson.

FOR MORE PRACTICE:
Standards Practice Book, pp. P115–P116

Name _____

Solve Multistep Problems

Essential Question How do you know what steps to do to solve a problem?

Listen and Draw REAL WORLD

Label the bar model to show each problem. Then solve.

_____

_____

_____

FOR THE TEACHER • Read this 1st problem for children. Cassie has 32 sheets of paper. She gives Jeff 9 sheets of paper. How many sheets of paper does Cassie have now? After children solve, read this 2nd problem. Cassie draws 18 pictures. Jeff draws 16 pictures. How many pictures did they draw altogether?

Math Talk
Explain how the two bar models are different.

Model and Draw

Bar models help you know what to do to solve a problem.

Alicia has 27 stamps. Matt has 38 stamps. How many more stamps do they need to get so they will have 91 stamps in all?

27	38

_____

They have _____ stamps in all.

First, find how many stamps they have in all.

_____	_____

_____

They need _____ more stamps.

Next, find how many more stamps they need.

Share and Show

Complete the bar models for the steps you do to solve the problem.

THINK: What do you need to find first?

☑ 1. Jackie has 93 beads. Ana has 46 small beads and 29 large beads. How many more beads would Ana need in order to have the same number of beads as Jackie?

_____	_____

_____

_____

_____	

_____ more beads

On Your Own

Complete the bar models for the steps you do
to solve the problem.

2. Ted has 35 trading cards. He
buys 22 more cards. Then he
gives 14 cards to Rudy. How
many cards does Ted have now?

_____ cards

3. Drew has 32 toy cars.
He trades 7 of those
cars for 11 other toy cars.
How many toy cars does
Drew have now?

_____ toy cars

4. Marta and Debbie each
have 17 ribbons. They
buy a package with
8 ribbons in it. How
many ribbons in all do
they have now?

_____ ribbons

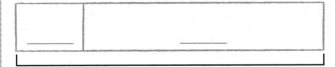

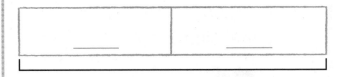

Write Math

Solve. Write or draw to explain.

5. Shelby and George find 65 rocks in all at the park. If Shelby found 28 of those rocks, how many rocks did George find?

_____ rocks

6. **H.O.T.** Benjamin finds 31 pinecones at the park. Together, Jenna and Ellen find the same number of pinecones as Benjamin. How many pinecones could each girl have found?

Jenna: _____ pinecones

Ellen: _____ pinecones

7. ⭐ **Test Prep** Tanya finds 22 leaves. Maurice finds 5 more leaves than Tanya finds. How many leaves did they find in all?

- ○ 59
- ○ 49
- ○ 27
- ○ 17

TAKE HOME ACTIVITY · Have your child explain how he or she would solve Exercise 6 if the number 31 was changed to 42.

FOR MORE PRACTICE:
Standards Practice Book, pp. P117–P118

✓ Chapter 5 Review/Test

Vocabulary

Use a word from the box to complete the sentence.

| ones |
| tens |
| regroup |

1. In 64 − 8, you could break apart _____ in the number 8 before you subtract. (pp. 213–216)

2. You can trade 1 ten for 10 ones when you _____. (pp. 221–224)

Concepts and Skills

Break apart the number you are subtracting. Use the number line to help. Write the difference. (pp. 213–220)

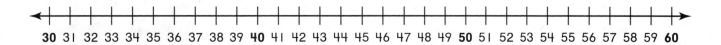

30 31 32 33 34 35 36 37 38 39 **40** 41 42 43 44 45 46 47 48 49 **50** 51 52 53 54 55 56 57 58 59 **60**

3. 43 − 7 = ___

4. 48 − 9 = ___

5. 51 − 16 = ___

6. 55 − 18 = ___

Draw a quick picture to solve. Write the difference. (pp. 225–228)

7.
Tens	Ones
□	□
4	2
− 1	5

Tens	Ones

8.
Tens	Ones
□	□
5	4
− 3	1

Tens	Ones

Fill in the bubble for the correct answer choice.

9. Amanda bought 43 stickers. She gave 16 stickers to her sister. How many stickers does Amanda have left? (pp. 241–244)

○ 17
○ 27
○ 39
○ 59

10. This year there were 34 sailboats in a race. Last year there were 19 sailboats in the race. How many more sailboats were in the race this year than last year? (pp. 229–232)

○ 15
○ 25
○ 33
○ 53

11. Jorge had 40 favorite games saved on his computer. He erased 12 of the games. How many favorite games does he have saved now? (pp. 221–224)

○ 28
○ 32
○ 48
○ 52

Tens	Ones

Name _____

Fill in the bubble for the correct answer choice.

12. Caleb baked 36 muffins. He brought them to school to share with his class. 25 muffins were eaten. How many muffins were left? (pp. 233–240)

○ 61
○ 51
○ 21
○ 11

13. The second grade children play games at recess. On Monday, 52 children played basketball. On Friday, 19 children played baseball and 27 children played basketball.

How many more children played games on Monday than on Friday? (pp. 249–252)

○ 46
○ 32
○ 25
○ 6

14. Tim needs 30 objects for a treasure hunt. He has collected some objects, but still needs 11 more objects. How many objects has he collected so far? (pp. 233–235)

○ 9
○ 19
○ 21
○ 41

Short Answer

15. Linda had 63 shells. She gave 34 shells to Joe.
How many shells does she have now? Write
a number sentence to show this problem. Explain
how the number sentence shows the problem.

_____

_____

_____

_____

Performance Task

16. At the bike store, there are 42 bikes in all. There
are large bikes and small bikes. 18 bikes are small.

How many bikes are large?
Draw or write to show how you found your answer.

How many more large bikes than small bikes are there?
Draw or write to show how you found your answer.

Curious About Math with

Curious George

Look at all the different balloons.

What are some ways you can sort these balloons?

Name _____

Show What You Know ✓

Read a Picture Graph

Use the picture graph.

Fruit We Like				
orange				
pear				

1. How many children chose pear? _____ children

2. Circle the fruit the most children chose.

Read a Tally Chart

Complete the tally chart.

Color We Like		Total
green	III	
red	HHH I	
blue	HHH III	

3. How many children chose red?

_____ children

4. Which color did the fewest children choose?

_____

Skip Count by Twos

Count by twos. Write how many.

5.

2, _____, _____, _____, _____, _____, _____

Family note: This page checks your child's understanding of important skills needed for success in Chapter 6.

GO Online Assessment Options Soar to Success Math

Review Words
tally marks
more than
fewer than

Vocabulary Builder

Visualize It

Draw **tally marks** to show the number.

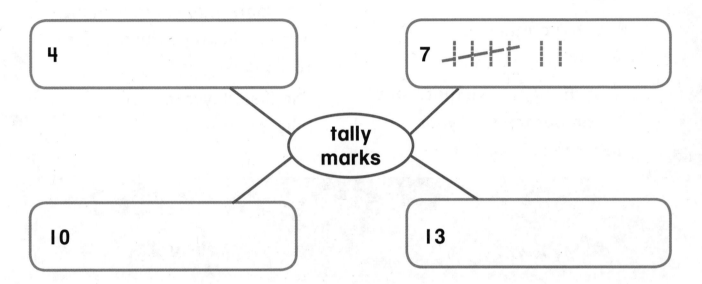

Understand Vocabulary

Write a number to complete the sentence.

1. 10 apples is **more than** _____ apples.

2. 6 bananas is **fewer than** _____ bananas.

3. _____ grapes is **more than** 6 grapes.

4. _____ oranges is **fewer than** 5 oranges.

Game

Making Tens

Materials • • 25 🟦

• small bag

Play with a partner.

1. Put 25 🟦 in a bag.
2. Toss the 🎲. Take that many 🟦 and put them on your ten frame. Take turns.

3. When you collect 10 🟦 on your ten frame, make a tally mark on the tally chart. Then put the 10 🟦 back in the bag.
4. The first player to make ten tally marks wins.

Player 1				

Player 2				

Making Tens

Player	Tally
Player 1	
Player 2	

Name _____

Take a Survey

Essential Question How can you record data when you take a survey?

Listen and Draw

Take turns pulling a cube from the bag.
Draw a tally mark in the chart for each cube.

Cube Colors	
Color	**Tally**
blue	
red	
green	

HOME CONNECTION • Your child made tally marks to record the color of cubes pulled from a bag. This activity prepares children for collecting and recording data in the next several lessons.

Math Talk

Explain how tally marks help you keep track of your count.

Chapter 6

Model and Draw

You can take a **survey** to collect **data**, or information.
You can record the data with tally marks or with numbers.

Greg asked his friends which lunch is their favorite.

This tally chart shows tally marks.

Favorite Lunch

Lunch	Tally
pizza	IIII
sandwich	HHH I
salad	III

This chart shows numbers.

Favorite Lunch

Lunch	Number
pizza	4
sandwich	
salad	

Share and Show

1. Take a survey. Ask 10 classmates which pet is their favorite. Use tally marks to show their answers.

2. How many classmates chose dog as their favorite pet?

   _____ classmates

3. Which pet did the fewest classmates choose?

   _____

Favorite Pet

Pet	Tally
cat	
dog	
fish	
bird	

4. Did more classmates choose cat or dog? _____

   How many more? _____ more classmates

On Your Own

5. Take a survey. Ask 10 classmates which indoor game is their favorite. Use tally marks to show their answers.

Favorite Indoor Game	
Game	**Tally**
board	
card	
computer	
puzzle	

6. Use the tally chart. Record the data in the chart below.

7. How many classmates chose a board game as their favorite game?

_____ classmates

8. Which game did the most classmates choose?

_____

Favorite Indoor Game	
Game	**Number**
board	
card	
computer	
puzzle	

9. Did more classmates choose a card game or a computer game? _____

How many more? _____ more

10. **H.O.T.** How many classmates did not choose a board game or a puzzle? Explain how you know.

_____

_____

Claire asked her classmates to choose their favorite subject. She made a chart with tally marks and numbers.

Favorite Subject		
Subject	**Tally**	**Total**
reading	‖‖ |	6
math	‖‖ ‖‖	
science	‖‖ ‖‖	

11. Complete the chart.

12. How many classmates chose science?

_____ classmates

13. How many more classmates chose math than reading?

_____ more classmates

14. How many classmates in all did Claire ask?   _____ classmates

15. **H.O.T.** Write a question about the data in the chart.

_____

_____

16. ⭐ **Test Prep**   Use the tally chart. Which statement is true?

Favorite Meal	
Meal	**Tally**
breakfast	‖‖ ‖‖
lunch	‖‖ ‖‖
dinner	‖‖ ‖‖ ‖

○ 13 children voted for breakfast.

○ 35 children voted in all.

○ Fewer children voted for lunch than for breakfast.

○ 12 children voted for dinner.

 TAKE HOME ACTIVITY • Make a chart like the one at the bottom of the page with your child. Ask your child to survey family members or friends about their favorite meal.

FOR MORE PRACTICE:
Standards Practice Book, pp. P123 P124

Name _____

Make a List • Surveys

Essential Question How can making a list help you solve a problem?

Madison took a survey of her class. She asked this question.

Which balloon color do you like best, blue, red, or green?

Which color did the most classmates choose?

blue	red	blue
red	green	green
red	red	red
red	green	green
green	red	blue

❓ Unlock the Problem REAL WORLD

What do I need to find?

which _balloon color_ the most classmates chose

What information do I need to use?

number of votes there are for each balloon color

Show how to solve the problem.

Make a list of the choices in a tally chart.
Write tally marks for the votes.
Then write numbers.

Favorite Balloon Color		
Color	**Tally**	**Total**
blue	III	3
red	IIII II	
green		

The most classmates chose _____.

HOME CONNECTION • Your child made a list of answer choices and responses to a survey. Making a list helps your child organize the data in a tally chart.

Try Another Problem

1. Make a tally chart to list the data for the problem.

- What do I need to find?
- What information do I need to use?

Alex took a survey of his class. He asked this question.

Which is your favorite snack, popcorn, apple, or muffin?

He wrote the votes on the board. Which snack did the most classmates choose?

popcorn	muffin	apple
apple	muffin	apple
apple	apple	muffin
muffin	apple	popcorn
popcorn	popcorn	apple

Favorite Snack

Snack	Tally	Total

The most classmates chose _____.

Math Talk
Explain why it is helpful to make a tally chart of the votes.

Name _____

Share and Show

Make a tally chart to solve.

2. Choose a topic from the list for a survey.
   Complete this survey question.

   Which is your favorite _____,

   _____, _____, **or** _____?

insect
vegetable
book
flower
tree
game

3. Use your topic to write a title in the tally chart.

4. Think of three answer choices. Write them in
   the tally chart.

✓ 5. Take your survey. Complete the tally chart.

_____	Tally	Total
_____		

✓ 6. Which answer did the most classmates choose?

   _____

7. Write a question about your chart. Have a classmate
   use your chart to answer the question.

   _____

   _____

On Your Own

Choose a way to solve.
Write or draw to explain.

---

8. Janna counted 26 birds at the feeders in the morning. She counted 35 birds at the feeders in the afternoon. How many birds did she count in all?

_____ birds

---

9. Emma had 52 nickels. She gave 15 nickels to her sister. How many nickels does Emma have now?

_____ nickels

---

10. **H.O.T.** There were 30 roses and 15 daisies in the flower garden. Hanson picked 5 roses and 5 daisies. How many flowers are left in the garden?

_____ flowers

---

11. ⭐ **Test Prep** Gwen collected 38 oak leaves and 15 maple leaves. How many more oak leaves than maple leaves did she collect?

- ○ 13
- ○ 23
- ○ 53
- ○ 63

TAKE HOME ACTIVITY • Ask your child to explain how he or she solved one of the problems on this page.

FOR MORE PRACTICE:
Standards Practice Book, pp. P125–P126

Name _____

Pictographs

Essential Question How does a key on a pictograph help you read the data?

Listen and Draw

Take turns pulling a cube from the bag.
Draw a smiley face in the graph for each cube.

Cube Colors					
blue					
red					
green					
orange					

Math Talk
Explain how you know that the number of smiley faces for blue matches the number of blue cubes.

HOME CONNECTION • Your child made a graph by recording with smiley faces the color of cubes taken from a bag. This activity prepares children for working with pictographs in this lesson.

Model and Draw

A **pictograph** uses pictures to show data.

A **key** tells how many each picture stands for.

Number of Flowers Picked	
Name	**Tally**
Jessie	||||
Inez	卌 |||
Paulo	卌 |

Number of Flowers Picked					
Jessie	🌼	🌼			
Inez	🌼	🌼	🌼	🌼	
Paulo					

Key: Each  stands for 2 flowers.

How many flowers did Inez pick?   Inez picked _____ flowers.

Share and Show [Math Board]

1. Use the tally chart to complete the pictograph.
   Draw a ☺ for every 5 children.

Favorite Sandwich	
Sandwich	**Tally**
cheese	卌 卌
ham	卌
tuna	卌 卌 卌

Favorite Sandwich					
cheese					
ham					
tuna					

Key: Each ☺ stands for 5 children.

Use the pictograph.

✔ 2. How many children chose tuna?   _____ children

✔ 3. How many more children chose cheese than ham?

                                                _____ more children

© Houghton Mifflin Harcourt Publishing Company

Name _____

On Your Own

4. Use the tally chart to complete the pictograph.
Draw a ☺ for every 2 children.

Favorite Fruit	
Fruit	**Tally**
apple	ⵏⵏ ||||
banana	||||
grapes	ⵏⵏ ⵏⵏ

Favorite Fruit				
apple				
banana				
grapes				

Key: Each ☺ stands for 2 children.

5. How many children chose apple?   _____ children

_____

6. Which fruit did the fewest children choose?   _____

_____

7. Use the pictograph. How many pencils does John have?

_____ pencils

Number of Pencils				
Alana	✏	✏	✏	
Teresa	✏	✏	✏	✏
John	✏	✏		

Key: Each ✏ stands for 5 pencils.

8. How many more pencils does Alana have than John?

_____ more pencils

_____

9. How many pencils in all do the three children have?   _____ pencils

10. 🌞 **H.O.T.** Suppose Teresa gives 5 of her pencils to John.
How many pencils will each child have? Explain.

_____

_____

TAKE HOME ACTIVITY • Ask your child to explain how to read a pictograph on this page.

Name _____

 Mid-Chapter Checkpoint

Concepts and Skills

Hannah asked her classmates which season is their favorite. She made this chart. (pp. 265–268)

1. Write numbers to complete the chart.

- -

2. Which season did the most classmates choose?

_____

Favorite Season		
Season	**Tally**	**Total**
spring	卌	
summer	卌 |||	
fall	卌 卌	
winter	||||	

- -

Use the pictograph. (pp. 269–271)

Favorite Ball Game					
soccer	☺	☺	☺	☺	☺
catch	☺	☺	☺		
baseball	☺	☺			

Key: Each ☺ stands for 2 children.

3. How many children chose baseball?

_____ children

- -

4. How many more children chose soccer than baseball?

_____ more children

- -

 Test Prep (pp. 269–271)

5. James made a pictograph. In his pictograph, each ✿ stands for 5 sunny days. How many sunny days do ✿✿✿ stand for?

- ○ 3
- ○ 6
- ○ 8
- ○ 15

© Houghton Mifflin Harcourt Publishing Company

Name _____

Make Bar Graphs

Essential Question How do you make a bar graph
to show data?

Listen and Draw

Look at the key for the pictograph.
Then draw pictures to complete the pictograph.

Writing Objects in the Bag					
chalk					
crayon					
marker					
pencil					

Key: Each ⬤ **stands for I writing object.**

FOR THE TEACHER • Have children make a
pictograph by drawing a circle in the graph for
each writing object you pull from a bag.

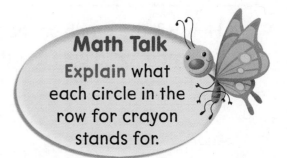

Math Talk
Explain what
each circle in the
row for crayon
stands for.

© Houghton Mifflin Harcourt Publishing Company

Model and Draw

A **bar graph** uses bars to show data.

This bar graph shows that Abel read 2 books, Brad read 1 book, and Cara read 4 books.

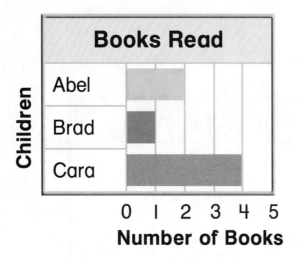

Books Read

Children	
Abel	
Brad	
Cara	

Number of Books
0 1 2 3 4 5

Complete this bar graph to show the same data.

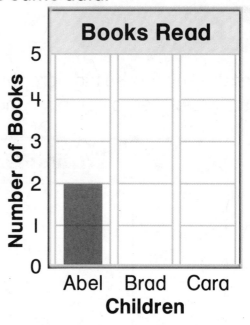

Books Read

Number of Books
5 4 3 2 1 0

Abel   Brad   Cara
Children

Share and Show  Math Board

Ella is making a bar graph to show the kinds of pets her classmates have.

- 5 classmates have a dog.
- 7 classmates have a cat.
- 2 classmates have a bird.
- 3 classmates have fish.

✓ **1.** Write labels and draw bars to complete the graph.

_____

2. How will the graph change if one more child gets a bird?

_____

_____

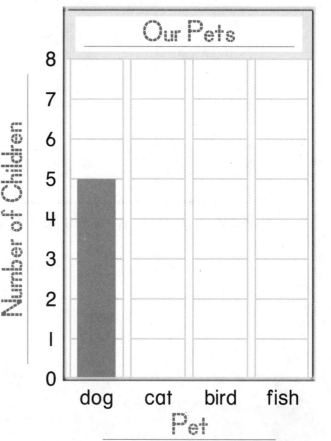

Our Pets

Number of Children
8 7 6 5 4 3 2 1 0

dog   cat   bird   fish
Pet

Name _____

On Your Own

Tomas asked his classmates which pizza topping is their favorite.

- 4 classmates chose peppers.
- 7 classmates chose meat.
- 5 classmates chose mushrooms.
- 2 classmates chose olives.

Complete the bar graph for the data.

3. Write a title and labels.

_____

4. Draw bars in the graph to show the data.

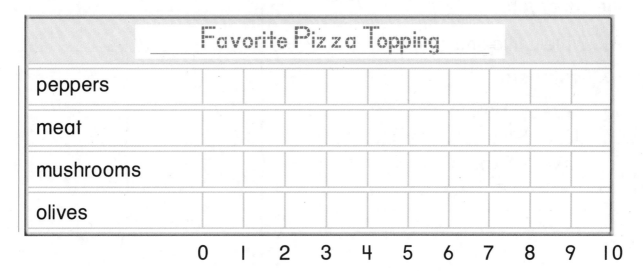

Favorite Pizza Topping

peppers	
meat	
mushrooms	
olives	

0 1 2 3 4 5 6 7 8 9 10

_____

Use the bar graph.

5. Which topping did the most classmates choose? _____

6. 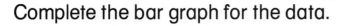 **H.O.T.** Did more classmates choose peppers and olives than meat? Explain. _____

_____

_____

Cody asked his classmates which zoo animal is their favorite. He made this chart.

7. Write numbers to complete the chart.

Favorite Zoo Animal		
Animal	**Tally**	**Total**
bear	‖‖‖ I	6
lion	‖‖‖	
tiger	‖‖‖ ‖	
zebra	‖‖‖	

Use the tally chart to complete the bar graph.

8. Write a title and labels.

9. Draw bars.

10. **H.O.T.** How many classmates did Cody survey? Explain.

_____

_____

_____

_____

8
7
6
5
4
3
2
1
0

bear   lion   tiger   zebra

_____

11. ⭐ **Test Prep** Look at the tally marks. Which animal did the most classmates choose?

○ bear   ○ tiger
○ lion   ○ zebra

TAKE HOME ACTIVITY • Ask your child to explain how the bars in the graph on this page match the data in the tally chart.

FOR MORE PRACTICE:
Standards Practice Book, pp. P129–P130

Name _____

Use Bar Graphs

Essential Question How do you use a bar graph to help you answer questions?

Listen and Draw

Skip count to find the number of . Write the numbers that you say. Draw pictures to show what you did.

FOR THE TEACHER • Have children build eight towers with two cubes in each tower and place them in the top box. Then have them skip count by twos and write the numbers. Repeat for skip counting by fives.

Math Talk
Explain how skip counting helps you count the cubes.

Chapter 6

Model and Draw

Bar graphs can have different **scales**.
The scale shows numbers for the lengths of the bars.

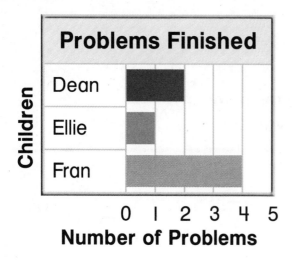

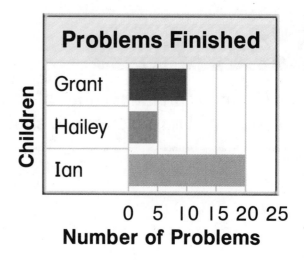

Use the graphs.

Dean finished ___2___ problems. Grant finished _____ problems.

Fran finished _____ problems. Ian finished _____ problems.

Share and Show

Use the bar graph.

1. How many marbles are green?

   _____ marbles

   _____

2. How many more red marbles than purple marbles are there?

   _____ more red marbles

   _____

3. Of which color marble are there the fewest?

   _____

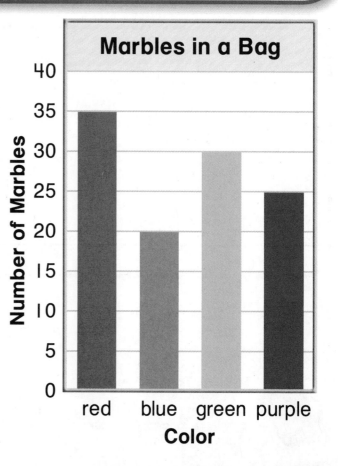

On Your Own

Bradley made a bar graph to show the lunches sold during one week.

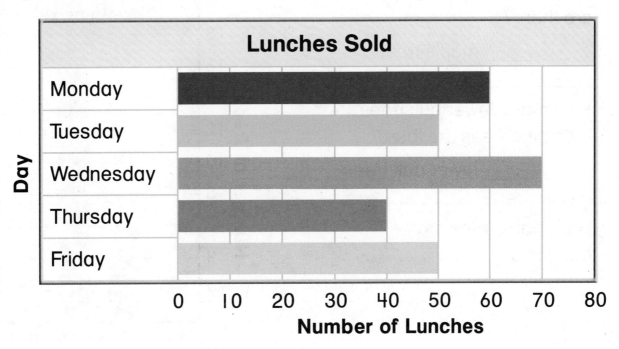

4. How many lunches were sold on Wednesday?

_____ lunches

5. On which day were just 40 lunches sold?

_____

6. On which two days were the same number of lunches sold?

_____

7. How many more lunches were sold on Monday than on Thursday?

_____ more lunches

8. **H.O.T.** On which day were fewer lunches sold than on Friday? Explain how the bars on the graph help you know.

_____

_____

PROBLEM SOLVING

REAL WORLD

Write Math

Use the bar graph.

9. How many maple trees are there?

_____ maple trees

10. How many fewer oak trees than pine trees are there?

_____ fewer oak trees

11. How many trees are there in all?

_____ trees

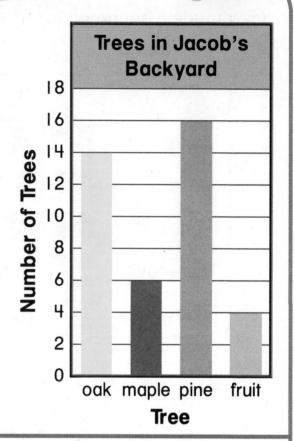

Trees in Jacob's Backyard

Number of Trees / Tree

12. **H.O.T.** Jacob wants to have 12 fruit trees in all. How many more fruit trees are needed? Explain.

_____

_____

_____

13. ⭐ **Test Prep**   Look at the bar graph. How many pine trees are in Jacob's backyard?

○ 6   ○ 9   ○ 16   ○ 18

TAKE HOME ACTIVITY • Ask your child to explain what the scale on the bar graph on this page means.

© Houghton Mifflin Harcourt Publishing Company

FOR MORE PRACTICE:
Standards Practice Book, pp. P131–P132

Name _____

Use Data

Essential Question How do you use a chart or a graph to help you solve problems?

Listen and Draw

Complete the tally chart.

Favorite Color		
Color	**Tally**	**Total**
blue		
red		
green		
purple		

Make a bar graph.

Favorite Color

Color					
blue					
red					
green					
purple					

0   1   2   3   4   5

Number of Children

Math Talk
Explain how the tally chart and the bar graph are alike.

FOR THE TEACHER • Have children take turns naming a favorite color. Have all children record the votes in the tally chart. Then have children shade the cells in the grid to make a bar graph for the data in the tally chart.

Chapter 6

Model and Draw

Sometimes you can compare data in graphs or charts.
Two children made graphs for their classes.

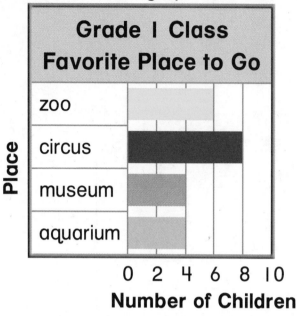

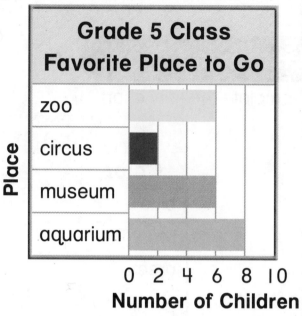

Share and Show

Use the bar graphs.

1. In which class did more children choose the museum?

   _____

☑ 2. In which class did fewer children choose the aquarium?

   _____

☑ 3. How many more children chose the circus in Grade 1 than in Grade 5?

   _____ more children

4. How many children in all are in the Grade 5 class?

   _____ children

5. Was the place chosen by the most children in each class the same? Explain.

   _____

   _____

On Your Own

Two children took surveys in their classes.
They made these charts.

Grade 1 Class Favorite Outdoor Game	
Game	**Tally**
tag	卌 卌 I
soccer	III
jump rope	卌 II
four square	II

Grade 5 Class Favorite Outdoor Game	
Game	**Tally**
tag	
soccer	卌 卌 I
jump rope	II
four square	卌 IIII

Use the tally charts.

6. In which class did more children choose soccer?

_____

7. In which class did fewer children choose four square?

_____

8. How many more children chose tag in Grade 1 than in Grade 5?

_____ more children

9. How many children in all are in Grade 5?

_____ children

10. **H.O.T.** Look at both charts. Write a sentence about what the data in the charts shows.

_____

_____

PROBLEM SOLVING REAL WORLD

Three children collected shells. They made a tally chart to show how many shells they collected.

Shells Collected	
Name	**Tally**
Misha	⊮
Andy	⊮ ⊮ ⊮ ⊮
Pat	⊮ ⊮ ⊮

11. Use the tally chart to complete the pictograph.

Shells Collected					
Misha	●				
Andy					
Pat					

Key: Each ● stands for 5 shells.

12. Use the tally chart to complete the bar graph.

Shells Collected

Children

Misha ▮
Andy
Pat

0 5 10 15 20 25
Number of Shells

13. **H.O.T.** Explain how the chart and the graphs are alike.

_____

14. ⭐ **Test Prep** Look at the tally chart. How many shells did Misha and Pat collect in all?

○ 5   ○ 20

○ 15   ○ 40

TAKE HOME ACTIVITY · Ask your child to explain how the pictograph and the bar graph on this page are alike and how they are different.

FOR MORE PRACTICE:
Standards Practice Book, pp. P133–P134

✓ Chapter 6 Review/Test

Vocabulary

Use a word in the box to complete each sentence.

1. You can take a _____ to collect data.
   (pp. 261–264)

2. A _____ uses pictures to show data in a graph. (pp. 269–271)

bar graph
pictograph
survey

Concepts and Skills

Use the bar graphs. (pp. 281–284)

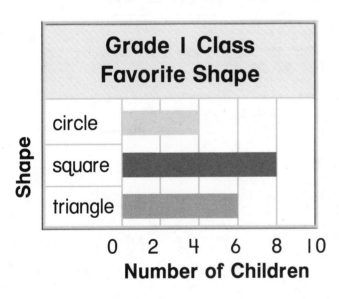

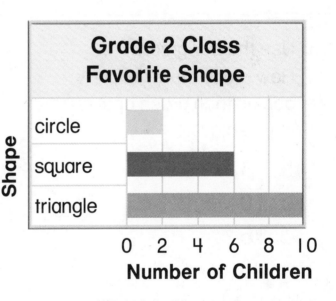

3. In which class did more children choose a square?

   _____

4. In which class did fewer children choose a circle?

   _____

5. How many more children chose triangle in Grade 2 than in Grade 1?

   _____ more children

6. How many children in all are in the Grade 2 class?

   _____ children

Fill in the bubble for the correct answer choice.

7. Use the tally chart.
   Which kind of muffin did the
   most children choose? (pp. 261–264)

   ○ banana

   ○ blueberry

   ○ apple

   ○ lemon

Favorite Muffin	
Muffin	**Tally**
banana	|||
blueberry	ℍℍ ℍℍ	
apple		
lemon	ℍℍ |||

8. Use the bar graph.
   How many more yellow
   apples than green apples
   were sold? (pp. 277–280)

   ○ 3

   ○ 10

   ○ 15

   ○ 20

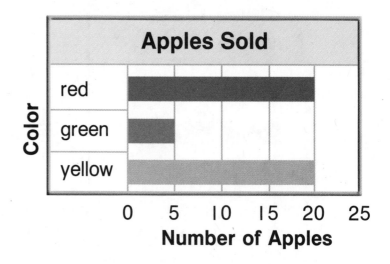

9. Use the pictograph.
   How many stickers do Megan
   and Lin have in all? (pp. 269–271)

   ○ 6

   ○ 12

   ○ 20

   ○ 30

Stickers We Have					
Shane	☺	☺	☺		
Megan	☺	☺			
Lin	☺	☺	☺	☺	

Key: Each ☺ stands for 5 stickers.

Fill in the bubble for the correct answer choice.

10. Use the pictograph.
How many fewer books did
Joy read than Tony? (pp. 269–271)

- ○ 2
- ○ 6
- ○ 8
- ○ 12

Books We Read					
Joy	📖				
Dave	📖	📖	📖	📖	
Sasha	📖	📖	📖		
Tony	📖	📖	📖	📖	

Key: Each 📖 stands for 2 books.

11. Use the tally chart.
What is the missing number
in the chart? (pp. 261–264)

- ○ 9
- ○ 11
- ○ 12
- ○ 15

Favorite Toy		
Toy	**Tally**	**Total**
ball	|||||	5
truck	||||| ||||| ||	
doll	||||| |||	8

12. Use the bar graph.
How many more mums
than roses are in
the garden? (pp. 277–280)

- ○ 2
- ○ 4
- ○ 6
- ○ 10

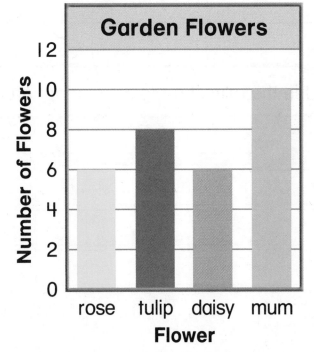

Short Answer

13. Stan made a pictograph with this key.
Each ☺ stands for 2 children.

How many ☺ should he draw to show 8 children? Explain.

_____

_____

Performance Task

14. Jason wants to find out what his classmates like to do after school. What question could he ask them?

_____

Write three answer choices for your question in the chart. Ask 10 classmates your question. Complete the tally chart.

Favorite After-School Activity		
Activity	**Tally**	**Total**

Use the tally chart to make a bar graph.

0   1   2   3   4   5   6   7   8

© Houghton Mifflin Harcourt Publishing Company

Chapter 7

3-Digit Addition and Subtraction

Curious About Math with Curious George

Monarch butterflies roost together during migration.

If you count 83 monarch butterflies on one tree and 72 on another, how many monarch butterflies have you counted altogether?

Name _____

Show What You Know ✓

Model Subtracting Tens

Write the difference.

1.

5 tens − 3 tens = _____ tens

50 − 30 = _____

2.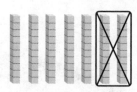

7 tens − 2 tens = _____ tens

70 − 20 = _____

2-Digit Addition

Write the sum.

3.
$$\begin{array}{r} 54 \\ +\ 25 \\ \hline \end{array}$$

4.
$$\begin{array}{r} 35 \\ +\ 18 \\ \hline \end{array}$$

5.
$$\begin{array}{r} 82 \\ +\ 67 \\ \hline \end{array}$$

6.
$$\begin{array}{r} 29 \\ +\ 81 \\ \hline \end{array}$$

Hundreds, Tens, and Ones

Write the hundreds, tens, and ones. Write the number.

7.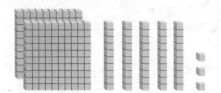

Hundreds	Tens	Ones

_____

8.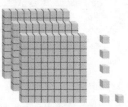

Hundreds	Tens	Ones

_____

 Family note: This page checks your child's understanding of important skills needed for success in Chapter 7.

 Assessment Options
Online Soar to Success Math

© Houghton Mifflin Harcourt Publishing Company

Name _____

Vocabulary Builder

Visualize It

Fill in the graphic organizer by writing examples of ways to **regroup**.

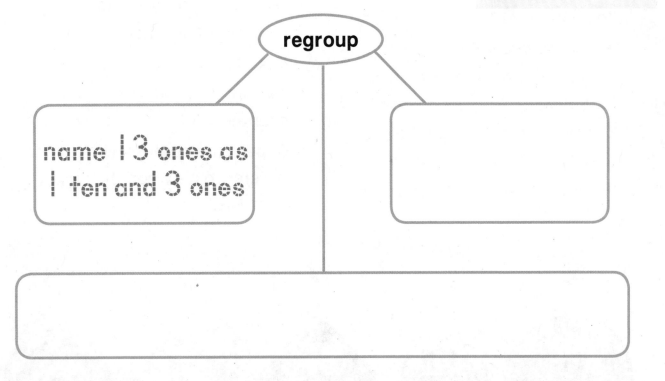

regroup

name 13 ones as 1 ten and 3 ones

Understand Vocabulary

1. Write a number that has 5 **ones**. _____

2. Write a number that has 5 **tens**. _____

3. Write a number that has 5 **hundreds**. _____

4. Write a number that has a **hundreds** digit that is greater than its **tens** digit. _____

GO Online • eStudent Edition • Multimedia eGlossary

 **Game** 2-Digit Shuffle

Materials

- number cards 10–50
- 15   • 15 ●

Play with a partner.

1. Shuffle the number cards. Place them face down in a pile.

2. Take two cards. Say the sum of the two numbers.

3. Your partner checks your sum.

4. If your sum is correct, place a counter on a button. If you regrouped to solve, place a counter on another button.

5. Take turns. Cover all the buttons. The player with more counters on the board wins.

6. Repeat the game, saying the difference between the two numbers.

Name _____

Break Apart 3-Digit Addends

Essential Question How do you break apart addends to add hundreds, tens, and then ones?

Listen and Draw

Write the number. Draw a quick picture for the number. Then write the number in different ways.

_____

____ hundreds ____ tens ____ ones

_____ + _____ + _____

_____

____ hundreds ____ tens ____ ones

_____ + _____ + _____

FOR THE TEACHER • Have children write 258 on the blank in the first box. Ask: How many hundreds, tens, and ones are in 258? Have children draw a quick picture for this number and then complete the other two forms for the number. Repeat the activity for 325.

Math Talk
What number can be written as 400 + 20 + 9?

Chapter 7

two hundred ninety-three **293**

Break apart the addends.
Add the hundreds, the tens, and the ones.
Then find the total sum.

$$538 \longrightarrow 500 + 30 + 8$$
$$+216 \longrightarrow 200 + \underline{\quad} + \underline{\quad}$$
$$700 + \underline{\quad} + \underline{\quad} = \underline{\quad\quad}$$

Share and Show

Break apart the addends. Find the total sum.

1. $321 \longrightarrow \underline{\qquad} + \underline{\qquad} + \underline{\qquad}$

    $+457 \longrightarrow \underline{\qquad} + \underline{\qquad} + \underline{\qquad}$

    $\underline{\qquad} + \underline{\qquad} + \underline{\qquad} = \underline{\qquad}$

2. $744 \longrightarrow \underline{\qquad} + \underline{\qquad} + \underline{\qquad}$

    $+162 \longrightarrow \underline{\qquad} + \underline{\qquad} + \underline{\qquad}$

    $\underline{\qquad} + \underline{\qquad} + \underline{\qquad} = \underline{\qquad}$

3. $254 \longrightarrow \underline{\qquad} + \underline{\qquad} + \underline{\qquad}$

    $+536 \longrightarrow \underline{\qquad} + \underline{\qquad} + \underline{\qquad}$

    $\underline{\qquad} + \underline{\qquad} + \underline{\qquad} = \underline{\qquad}$

On Your Own

Break apart the addends. Find the total sum.

4. 374 ⟶ _____ + _____ + _____

    +518 ⟶ _____ + _____ + _____
    _____

    _____ + _____ + _____ = _____

5. 425 ⟶ _____ + _____ + _____

    +232 ⟶ _____ + _____ + _____
    _____

    _____ + _____ + _____ = _____

6. 849 ⟶ _____ + _____ + _____

    +123 ⟶ _____ + _____ + _____
    _____

    _____ + _____ + _____ = _____

7. **H.O.T.** Write the missing numbers in the problem.

    412 ⟶ _____ + _____ + _____

    + _____ ⟶ 500 + 60 + _____
    _____

    _____ + _____ + 10 = _____

PROBLEM SOLVING REAL WORLD

Write Math

Solve. Write or draw to explain.

8. Mr. Jones has 158 sheets of art paper and 231 sheets of plain paper. How many sheets of paper does he have in all?

_____ sheets of paper

9. **H.O.T.** Wesley added in a different way.

$$
\begin{array}{r}
327 \\
+\ 468 \\
\hline
700 \\
80 \\
+\ \ \ 15 \\
\hline
795
\end{array}
$$

7 hundreds
8 tens
15 ones

Use Wesley's way to find the sum.

$$
\begin{array}{r}
539 \\
+\ 247 \\
\hline
\end{array}
$$

10. ⭐ **Test Prep** There are 324 children at Theo's school. There are 419 children at Latasha's school. How many children are at the two schools?

○ 733
○ 743
○ 745
○ 825

TAKE HOME ACTIVITY • Write 382 + 215. Have your child break apart the numbers and then find the sum.

FOR MORE PRACTICE:
Standards Practice Book, pp. P139–P140

Record 3-Digit Addition: Regroup Ones

Essential Question When do you regroup ones in addition?

Listen and Draw REAL WORLD

Use ▦ ▭ ▪ to model the problem.
Draw quick pictures to show what you did.

Hundreds	Tens	Ones

FOR THE TEACHER • Read the following problem and have children model it with blocks. There were 213 people at the show on Friday and 156 people on Saturday. How many people in all were at the show? Have children draw quick pictures to show how they solved the problem.

Math Talk

Describe how you modeled the problem.

Model and Draw

Add the ones.
$6 + 7 = 13$

Regroup 13 ones as 1 ten 3 ones.

Hundreds	Tens	Ones
	[1]	
2	4	6
+ 1	1	7
		3

Hundreds	Tens	Ones

Add the tens.
$1 + 4 + 1 = 6$

Hundreds	Tens	Ones
	1	
2	4	6
+ 1	1	7
	6	3

Hundreds	Tens	Ones

Add the hundreds.
$2 + 1 = 3$

Hundreds	Tens	Ones
	1	
2	4	6
+ 1	1	7
3	6	3

Hundreds	Tens	Ones

Share and Show

Write the sum.

✓1.

Hundreds	Tens	Ones
	☐	
3	2	8
+ 1	3	4

✓2.

Hundreds	Tens	Ones
	☐	
4	4	5
+	2	3

© Houghton Mifflin Harcourt Publishing Company

Name _____

On Your Own

Write the sum.

3.

Hundreds	Tens	Ones
	☐	
5	2	6
+ 1	0	3

4.

Hundreds	Tens	Ones
	☐	
3	4	8
+	1	9

5.

Hundreds	Tens	Ones
	☐	
6	2	8
+ 3	4	7

6.

Hundreds	Tens	Ones
	☐	
2	3	5
+ 2	5	7

7.

Hundreds	Tens	Ones
	☐	
5	6	2
+ 3	2	9

8.

Hundreds	Tens	Ones
	☐	
1	4	7
+ 1	2	5

9.

Hundreds	Tens	Ones
	☐	
4	3	5
+ 2	1	4

10.

Hundreds	Tens	Ones
	☐	
3	2	9
+ 2	4	8

Solve. Write or draw to explain.

11. The gift shop is 140 steps away from the zoo entrance. The train stop is 235 steps away from the gift shop. How many total steps is this?

_____ steps

12. H.O.T. On Thursday, there were 326 visitors at the zoo. There were 200 more visitors at the zoo on Friday than on Thursday. How many visitors in all were at the zoo on both days?

_____ visitors

13. ⭐ **Test Prep** On Thursday, 175 drinks were sold at the zoo. On Friday, 219 drinks were sold. How many drinks were sold on both days?

○ 484
○ 464
○ 404
○ 394

TAKE HOME ACTIVITY · Ask your child to explain why he or she regrouped in only some of the problems in this lesson.

FOR MORE PRACTICE:
Standards Practice Book, pp. P141–P142

Record 3-Digit Addition: Regroup Tens

Essential Question When do you regroup tens in addition?

Listen and Draw REAL WORLD

Use [grid] _____ to model the problem.
Draw quick pictures to show what you did.

Hundreds	Tens	Ones

FOR THE TEACHER • Read the following problem and have children model it with blocks. On Monday, 253 children visited the aquarium. On Tuesday, 324 children visited the aquarium. How many children visited the aquarium those two days? Have children draw quick pictures to show how they solved the problem.

Math Talk
Explain how your quick pictures show what happened in the problem.

Model and Draw

Add the ones.
$2 + 5 = 7$

Hundreds	Tens	Ones
☐	☐	
1	4	2
+ 2	8	5
		7

Hundreds	Tens	Ones

Add the tens.
$4 + 8 = 12$

Regroup 12 tens as
1 hundred 2 tens.

Hundreds	Tens	Ones
☐	☐	
1	4	2
+ 2	8	5
	2	7

Hundreds	Tens	Ones

Add the hundreds.
$1 + 1 + 2 = 4$

Hundreds	Tens	Ones
1	☐	
1	4	2
+ 2	8	5
4	2	7

Hundreds	Tens	Ones

Share and Show

Math Board

Write the sum.

1.
Hundreds	Tens	Ones
☐	☐	
3	4	7
+ 2	9	1

2.
Hundreds	Tens	Ones
☐	☐	
1	6	5
+ 3	5	4

3.
Hundreds	Tens	Ones
☐	☐	
5	3	8
+ 1	7	0

Name _____

On Your Own

Write the sum.

4.

Hundreds	Tens	Ones
☐	☐	
1	5	6
+	4	2

5.

Hundreds	Tens	Ones
☐	☐	
7	6	4
+ 1	5	3

6.

Hundreds	Tens	Ones
☐	☐	
3	7	2
+ 1	8	5

7.

2	2	4
+ 1	5	7

8.

2	5	4
+		5

9.

6	4	4
+	9	2

10.

1	3	2
+ 2	5	8

11.

3	1	4
+ 4	3	5

12.

7	5	3
+ 1	5	2

Rewrite the numbers. Then add.

13. 760 + 178

14. 216 + 346

15. 423 + 285

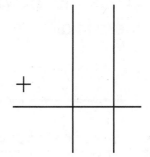

PROBLEM SOLVING REAL WORLD

These are the pieces of fruit that
Mr. Olson and Mr. Lee sold at the market.

Mr. Olson	**Mr. Lee**
257 apples	314 pears
281 plums	229 peaches

Write or draw to explain.

16. How many pieces of fruit
    did Mr. Olson sell?

    _____ pieces of fruit

17. **H.O.T.** Who sold more pieces
    of fruit? How many more?

    _____

    _____ more pieces of fruit

18. ⭐ **Test Prep** There are 465 oranges
    packed in boxes. There are 253 oranges
    in baskets. How many oranges are
    there in all?

    ○ 718
    ○ 708
    ○ 698
    ○ 612

TAKE HOME ACTIVITY · Have your child choose a new combination
of two fruits on this page and find the total number of pieces of
the two types of fruit.

FOR MORE PRACTICE:
Standards Practice Book, pp. P143–P144

Name _____

3-Digit Addition

Essential Question How do you know when to regroup in addition?

Listen and Draw REAL WORLD

Write an addition problem to find each answer. Draw a quick picture to prove that the sum is correct.

FOR THE TEACHER • Read the following problem and have children solve it. There are 259 girls and 304 boys at Elm Street School. How many children are at Elm Street School? Repeat the activity for 462 + 374.

Math Talk
Did you regroup in the same way for both problems? **Explain.**

Model and Draw

Sometimes you will regroup more than once in addition problems.

$$\begin{array}{r} 2\,5\,9 \\ +\ 4\,7\,6 \\ \hline 7\,3\,5 \end{array}$$

9 ones + 6 ones = 15 ones, or 1 ten 5 ones

1 ten + 5 tens + 7 tens = 13 tens, or 1 hundred 3 tens

1 hundred + 2 hundreds + 4 hundreds = 7 hundreds

THINK:
Are there 10 or more ones?
Are there 10 or more tens?

Share and Show

Write the sum.

1.
$$\begin{array}{r} 1\,8\,4 \\ +\ 3\,2\,9 \\ \hline \end{array}$$

2.
$$\begin{array}{r} 5\,4\,6 \\ +\ 2\,7\,8 \\ \hline \end{array}$$

3.
$$\begin{array}{r} 3\,2\,7 \\ +\ 3\,5\,3 \\ \hline \end{array}$$

4.
$$\begin{array}{r} 2\,9\,4 \\ +\ 1\,5\,8 \\ \hline \end{array}$$

✅ 5.
$$\begin{array}{r} 3\,7\,5 \\ +\ 2\,7\,2 \\ \hline \end{array}$$

✅ 6.
$$\begin{array}{r} 1\,8\,9 \\ +\ 6\,2\,3 \\ \hline \end{array}$$

On Your Own

Write the sum.

7.
$$\begin{array}{c c c} 5 & 7 & 4 \\ + \; 2 & 8 & 1 \\ \hline \end{array}$$

8.
$$\begin{array}{c c c} 4 & 1 & 6 \\ + \; 4 & 8 & 3 \\ \hline \end{array}$$

9.
$$\begin{array}{c c c} 3 & 4 & 6 \\ + \; 5 & 9 & 7 \\ \hline \end{array}$$

10.
$$\begin{array}{c c c} 3 & 6 & 5 \\ + \; 2 & 8 & 3 \\ \hline \end{array}$$

11.
$$\begin{array}{c c c} 6 & 4 & 7 \\ + \; 1 & 0 & 9 \\ \hline \end{array}$$

12.
$$\begin{array}{c c c} 5 & 4 & 6 \\ + \; 3 & 5 & 6 \\ \hline \end{array}$$

Rewrite the numbers. Then find the sum.

13. $348 + 631$

$+$ _____

14. $455 + 139$

$+$ _____

15. $563 + 245$

$+$ _____

 Write the missing digits.

16.
$$\begin{array}{c c c} \blacksquare & \blacksquare & 6 \\ + \; 4 & 5 & \blacksquare \\ \hline 6 & 9 & 0 \end{array}$$

17.
$$\begin{array}{c c c} 6 & & 7 \\ + \; 2 & 3 & \blacksquare \\ \hline \blacksquare & 6 & 2 \end{array}$$

18.
$$\begin{array}{c c c} 1 & 3 & 4 \\ + \; \blacksquare & 7 & \blacksquare \\ \hline 5 & \blacksquare & 3 \end{array}$$

PROBLEM SOLVING

REAL WORLD

Write Math

Solve. Write or draw to explain.

19. Diane and Matthew each have 46 sheets of paper. Together they use a total of 17 sheets of paper for a project. How many sheets of paper do they have left?

_____ sheets of paper

20. **H.O.T.** Thomas has 173 stickers. Lisa has 10 fewer stickers than Thomas has. How many stickers do they have in all?

_____ stickers

21. ⭐ **Test Prep** Mr. Jennings has 145 yellow cards and 263 blue cards. How many cards does he have altogether?

- ○ 118
- ○ 322
- ○ 408
- ○ 418

TAKE HOME ACTIVITY · Ask your child to write an addition problem with a pair of 3-digit numbers for which there will be no regrouping.

FOR MORE PRACTICE:
Standards Practice Book, pp. P145–P146

Name _____

Practice 3-Digit Addition

Essential Question How do you record the steps when adding 3-digit numbers?

Listen and Draw REAL WORLD

Choose one way to solve the problem.
Draw or write to show what you did.

FOR THE TEACHER • Read the following problem and have children solve it. Last week 735 adults and 623 children went to the science museum. How many people went to the museum last week?

Math Talk
Explain why you chose your way to solve the problem.

Chapter 7

three hundred nine **309**

Mr. Smith sells balloons at the zoo.
He sold 728 balloons on Saturday.
He sold 535 balloons on Sunday.
How many balloons did he sell on
those two days in all?

Step 1 Add the
ones.

$8 + 5 = 13$

Regroup
13 ones as
1 ten 3 ones.

$$
\begin{array}{r}
\overset{\text{1}}{7}28 \\
+\ 535 \\
\hline
3
\end{array}
$$

Step 2 Add the
tens.

$1 + 2 + 3 = 6$

$$
\begin{array}{r}
\overset{\text{1}}{7}28 \\
+\ 535 \\
\hline
63
\end{array}
$$

Step 3 Add the
hundreds.

$7 + 5 = 12$

12 hundreds
is the same as
1 thousand
2 hundreds.

$$
\begin{array}{r}
\overset{\text{1}}{7}28 \\
+\ 535 \\
\hline
63
\end{array}
$$

Step 4 Write
the thousands
digit and the
hundreds digit
in the sum.

$$
\begin{array}{r}
\overset{\text{1}}{7}28 \\
+\ 535 \\
\hline
1,263
\end{array}
$$

Share and Show

Write the sum.

1.
$$
\begin{array}{r}
623 \\
+\ 491 \\
\hline
\end{array}
$$

☑ 2.
$$
\begin{array}{r}
327 \\
+\ 563 \\
\hline
\end{array}
$$

☑ 3.
$$
\begin{array}{r}
956 \\
+\ 823 \\
\hline
\end{array}
$$

Name _____

On Your Own

Write the sum.

4.	5.	6.
586 + 237	629 + 856	392 + 58

7.	8.	9.
734 + 625	443 + 261	226 + 135

10.	11.	12.
580 + 793	312 + 398	715 + 247

H.O.T. Find the error. Then rewrite the problem and solve it correctly.

13.

537
+ 65
1,187

14.

784
+ 155
839

TAKE HOME ACTIVITY · Ask your child to choose two numbers from 529, 642, 387, and 851, and find the sum of those numbers.

Chapter 7 · Lesson 5

FOR MORE PRACTICE:
Standards Practice Book, pp. P147–P148   three hundred eleven **311**

© Houghton Mifflin Harcourt Publishing Company

Name _____

✓ Mid-Chapter Checkpoint

Concepts and Skills

Break apart the addends. Find the total sum. (pp. 293–296)

1. 567 ⟶ _____ + _____ + _____

    +324 ⟶ _____ + _____ + _____
    _____

    _____ + _____ + _____ = _____

2. 635 ⟶ _____ + _____ + _____

    +148 ⟶ _____ + _____ + _____
    _____

    _____ + _____ + _____ = _____

Write the sum. (pp. 297–304)

3.
```
    2 | 4 | 8
 +  3 | 4 | 6
```

4.
```
    6 | 1 | 0
 +  2 | 6 | 4
```

5.
```
    3 | 9 | 1
 +  5 | 3 | 7
```

 Test Prep

6. There are 148 small sand dollars and 119 large sand dollars at the store. How many sand dollars in all are at the store? (pp. 297–300)

    ○ 257
    ○ 267
    ○ 357
    ○ 367

Name _____

Make a Model • 3-Digit Subtraction

Essential Question How can you make a model to solve a problem?

There were 436 people at the art show. 219 people left the art show early. How many people stayed at the art show?

🔑 Unlock the Problem

What do I need to find?

how many people
_____

stayed at the art show

What information do I need to use?

_____ people were there.

_____ people left the show.

Show how to solve the problem.

Make a model.

HOME CONNECTION • Your child made a model to represent the problem and solve the subtraction problem.

Try Another Problem

Make a model. Show how you solved the problem.

- What do I need to find?
- What information do I need to use?

1. There are 532 pieces of art at the show. 319 pieces of art are paintings. How many pieces of art are not paintings?

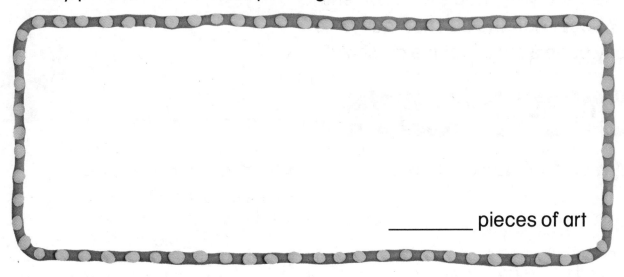

_____ pieces of art

2. 245 children go to the face-painting event. 114 of the children are boys. How many of the children are girls?

_____ girls

Math Talk
Explain how you solved the first problem on this page.

Share and Show

Make a model. Show how you
solved the problem.

☑ **3.** There were 237 books on the
shelves. Mr. Davies took
126 books off the shelves.
How many books were still on
the shelves?

_____ books

☑ **4.** 164 children and 31 adults
saw the movie in the morning.
125 children saw the movie in
the afternoon. How many more
children saw the movie in the
morning than in the afternoon?

_____ more children

---

5. There are 232 postcards
on the table. Janet uses
118 postcards to cover the
bulletin board. How many
postcards did not get used?

_____ postcards

On Your Own

Choose a way to solve. Write or draw to explain.

6. Ted has some grapes. He gives 5 grapes to each of 4 friends. How many grapes does he give to his friends?

_____ grapes

7.  **H.O.T.** Maria has 127 animal cards. Ellen has twice that number of cards. How many animal cards do the girls have in all?

_____ animal cards

8. ⭐ **Test Prep** Mr. Gilmore has 350 balloons. He sells 133 balloons at the park. How many balloons does he have left?

- ○ 217
- ○ 223
- ○ 423
- ○ 483

 TAKE HOME ACTIVITY · Ask your child to choose one of the problems in this lesson and solve it in a different way.

FOR MORE PRACTICE:
Standards Practice Book, pp. P149–P150

Name _____

Record 3-Digit Subtraction: Regroup Tens

Essential Question When do you regroup tens in subtraction?

Listen and Draw REAL WORLD

Make a model. Show how you solved the problem.

Hundreds	Tens	Ones

FOR THE TEACHER • Read the following problem and have children model it with blocks. 473 people went to the football game on Saturday. 146 people were still there at the end of the game. How many people left before the end of the game? Have children draw quick pictures of their models.

Math Talk

Describe what to do when there are not enough ones to subtract from.

Chapter 7

$354 - 137 = ?$

Are there enough ones to subtract 7?

yes   (no)

Regroup 1 ten as 10 ones.

Hundreds	Tens	Ones
	4	14
3	5̶	4̶
− 1	3	7

Hundreds	Tens	Ones

Now there are enough ones.

Subtract the ones.

$14 - 7 = 7$

Hundreds	Tens	Ones
	4	14
3	5̶	4̶
− 1	3	7
		7

Hundreds	Tens	Ones

Subtract the tens.

$4 - 3 = 1$

Subtract the hundreds.

$3 - 1 = 2$

Hundreds	Tens	Ones
	4	14
3	5̶	4̶
− 1	3	7
2	1	7

Hundreds	Tens	Ones

Share and Show

Solve. Write the difference.

✓ 1.

Hundreds	Tens	Ones
	☐	☐
4	3	1
− 3	2	6

✓ 2.

Hundreds	Tens	Ones
	☐	☐
6	5	8
− 2	3	7

Name _____

On Your Own

Solve. Write the difference.

3.

Hundreds	Tens	Ones
	☐	☐
7	2	8
− 1	0	7

4.

Hundreds	Tens	Ones
	☐	☐
4	5	2
− 2	1	6

5.

Hundreds	Tens	Ones
	☐	☐
9	6	5
− 2	3	8

6.

Hundreds	Tens	Ones
	☐	☐
4	8	9
− 1	4	9

7.

Hundreds	Tens	Ones
	☐	☐
6	4	5
− 2	2	7

8.

Hundreds	Tens	Ones
	☐	☐
6	7	0
− 1	3	8

9.

Hundreds	Tens	Ones
	☐	☐
8	7	4
− 4	3	8

10.

Hundreds	Tens	Ones
	☐	☐
9	8	4
− 7	1	5

Solve. Write or draw to explain.

11. There are 42 bells and 235 whistles in the store. Ryan counts 128 whistles on the shelf. How many whistles are not on the shelf?

_____ whistles

12.  **H.O.T.** There were 287 music books in the store. After some of the music books were sold, there are 159 music books left. How many music books were sold?

_____ music books

13. **Test Prep** Ms. Watson has 254 stickers. She gives 123 stickers to her students. How many stickers does she have left?

○ 121
○ 127
○ 131
○ 137

© Houghton Mifflin Harcourt Publishing Company

TAKE HOME ACTIVITY · Ask your child to explain why he or she regrouped in only some of the problems in this lesson.

FOR MORE PRACTICE:
Standards Practice Book, pp. P151–P152

Name _____

Record 3-Digit Subtraction: Regroup Hundreds

Essential Question When do you regroup hundreds in subtraction?

Listen and Draw REAL WORLD

Draw quick pictures to show the problem.

Hundreds	Tens	Ones

FOR THE TEACHER • Read the following problem and have children model it with quick pictures. The Reading Club collected 349 books. 173 books were fiction books. The other books were nonfiction books. How many nonfiction books were there?

Math Talk

Describe what to do when there are not enough tens to subtract from.

three hundred twenty-one **321**

Model and Draw

428 − 153 = ?

Subtract the ones.
8 − 3 = 5

Hundreds	Tens	Ones
☐	☐	☐
4	2	8
− 1	5	3
		5

Hundreds	Tens	Ones

There are not enough tens to subtract from.

Regroup 1 hundred. 4 hundreds 2 tens is now 3 hundreds 12 tens.

Hundreds	Tens	Ones
3	12	☐
4	2	8
− 1	5	3
		5

Hundreds	Tens	Ones

Subtract the tens.
12 − 5 = 7

Subtract the hundreds.
3 − 1 = 2

Hundreds	Tens	Ones
3	12	☐
4	2	8
− 1	5	3
2	7	5

Hundreds	Tens	Ones

Share and Show

Solve. Write the difference.

1.

Hundreds	Tens	Ones
☐	☐	☐
4	7	8
− 3	5	6

2.

Hundreds	Tens	Ones
☐	☐	☐
8	1	4
− 2	6	3

On Your Own

Solve. Write the difference.

3.

Hundreds	Tens	Ones
☐	☐	☐
6	2	9
− 4	8	2

4.

Hundreds	Tens	Ones
☐	☐	☐
9	3	6
− 1	7	3

5.

4	3	5
− 1	9	2

6.

3	8	7
−	4	7

7.

5	8	8
− 4	5	0

8.

3	4	5
− 2	6	3

Rewrite the numbers. Then subtract.

9. 567 − 183

10. 718 − 467

Solve.

11. **H.O.T.** Michael built two towers.
He used 139 blocks for the first tower.
He used 276 blocks in all. For which tower
did he use more blocks?

_____

12. Explain how you solved the problem above.

_____

_____

_____

_____

13. ⭐ **Test Prep** Mr. Simms has a box with
315 paper hats in it. He gives 140 paper
hats to students in the parade. How many
paper hats does he have now?

○ 255
○ 235
○ 215
○ 175

TAKE HOME ACTIVITY • Have your child explain how to
find the difference for 745 − 381.

FOR MORE PRACTICE:
Standards Practice Book, pp. P153–P154

✓ Chapter 7 Review/Test

Vocabulary

Use a word in the box to complete each sentence.

| sum |
| regroup |
| difference |

1. You can _____ 7 hundreds 1 ten as 6 hundreds 11 tens. (pp. 297–300)

2. In 235 − 108 = 127, 127 is the _____. (pp. 313–316)

Concepts and Skills

Break apart the addends. Find the total sum. (pp. 293–296)

3.   413 ⟶ _____ + _____ + _____

  +278 ⟶ _____ + _____ + _____
  _____

  _____ + _____ + _____ = _____

Write the sum. (pp. 297–300)

4.

Hundreds	Tens	Ones
	☐	
1	7	4
+ 4	1	9

Write the difference. (pp. 317–320)

5.

Hundreds	Tens	Ones
	☐	☐
5	9	3
− 4	2	6

Fill in the bubble for the correct answer choice.

6. Mr. Kent's art class used 234 craft sticks.
Ms. Reed's art class used 358 craft sticks.
How many craft sticks were used by the
two classes? (pp. 297–300)

   ○ 524

   ○ 582

   ○ 592

   ○ 692

7. At the marine park, 563 people were at
the dolphin show. 318 people were at
the otter show.

   How many people in all were at the two shows? (pp. 297–300)

   ○ 881

   ○ 891

   ○ 981

   ○ 991

8. 116 girls and 122 boys saw the school play.
How many children in all saw the school play? (pp. 293–296)

   ○ 338

   ○ 238

   ○ 234

   ○ 226

Fill in the bubble for the correct answer choice.

9. Mr. Briner had 542 baseball cards in his collection. He sold 128 of the cards. How many cards does he have now? (pp. 317–320)

- ○ 676
- ○ 670
- ○ 426
- ○ 414

10. The library has 668 books and magazines. There are 565 books at the library. How many magazines are there? (pp. 313–316)

- ○ 13
- ○ 103
- ○ 403
- ○ 1,233

11. Mrs. Pilar had 459 leaves. She gave 274 leaves to her students.

How many leaves does she still have? (pp. 321–324)

- ○ 125
- ○ 185
- ○ 225
- ○ 733

Short Answer

12. Find the sum for each problem.

```
   1 5 6            5 7 2
 + 4 0 8          + 1 3 5
 ─────────        ─────────
```

Explain how these problems are different.

_____

_____

Performance Task

13. This is how many blocks each child used.

Anna
118 blocks

Rafael
152 blocks

Terry
346 blocks

How many blocks did Anna and Terry use in all?
Draw or write to show how you found your answer.

```
┌─────────────────────────────────────────────┐
│                                             │
│                                             │
│                                             │
│                                             │
└─────────────────────────────────────────────┘
```

How many more blocks did Terry use than Rafael?
Draw or write to show how you found your answer.

```
┌─────────────────────────────────────────────┐
│                                             │
│                                             │
│                                             │
│                                             │
└─────────────────────────────────────────────┘
```

Multiplication Concepts

Curious About Math with *Curious George*

Hot air rises. A balloon filled with hot air will float up high into the sky.

Suppose the basket on a hot-air balloon can hold 5 people. How many people can ride in 2 balloons? 3 balloons?

Name _____

Show What You Know ✓

Add Doubles

Write the doubles fact.

1.

2.

_____ + _____ = _____   _____ + _____ = _____

Skip Count by Twos and Fives

Skip count. Write how many in all.

3.

2, _____, _____, _____, _____, _____, _____
shoes

4.

5, _____, _____, _____, _____, _____, _____
paints

Draw to Show Addition

Draw a picture. Complete the addition sentence.

5. There are 3 apples in a bowl. Then Ed
puts in 2 more apples. How many apples
are in the bowl now?

_____ + _____ = _____

 Family note: This page checks your child's understanding of important skills needed for success in Chapter 8.

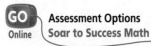 **GO** Online Assessment Options Soar to Success Math

© Houghton Mifflin Harcourt Publishing Company

Name _____

Vocabulary Builder

Visualize It

Write numbers in the graphic organizer to show **even** and **odd** numbers.

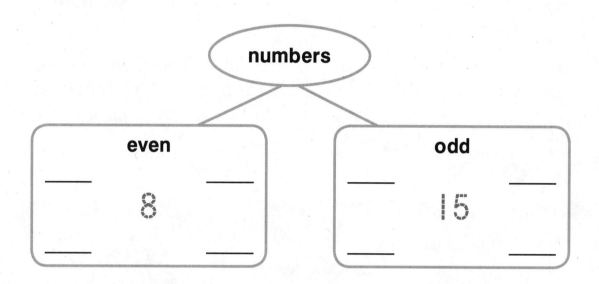

numbers

even
___ ___
8
___ ___

odd
___ ___
15
___ ___

Understand Vocabulary

Look at the **hundred chart**.

1. Start on 10. Use yellow to shade the numbers as you count by tens to 50.

2. Start on 2. Use blue to shade the numbers as you count by twos to 8.

3. Circle numbers to show a **pattern** of counting by fives.

1	2	3	4	5	6	7	8	9	10
11	12	13	14	15	16	17	18	19	20
21	22	23	24	25	26	27	28	29	30
31	32	33	34	35	36	37	38	39	40
41	42	43	44	45	46	47	48	49	50
51	52	53	54	55	56	57	58	59	60
61	62	63	64	65	66	67	68	69	70
71	72	73	74	75	76	77	78	79	80
81	82	83	84	85	86	87	88	89	90
91	92	93	94	95	96	97	98	99	100

Game
Triple Play

Materials

- 3 🎲
- 6 🔴
- 6 🟡

Play with a partner.

1. Toss the 3 🎲. Choose red or yellow 🟡

2. Add the 3 numbers. Your partner checks the sum.

3. If the sum is correct, find the sum on a baseball. Put one of your 🔴 on the baseball.

4. If all three numbers you tossed match, take another turn!

5. Take turns until one player has placed all 6 counters on the board. That player is the winner.

3   4   5   6

7   8   9   10

11   12   13   14

15   16   17   18

Skip Count on a Hundred Chart

Essential Question How do you extend a skip counting pattern?

Listen and Draw REAL WORLD

Shade the numbers in the skip counting pattern.

1	2	3	4	5	6	7	8	9	10
11	12	13	14	15	16	17	18	19	20
21	22	23	24	25	26	27	28	29	30
31	32	33	34	35	36	37	38	39	40
41	42	43	44	45	46	47	48	49	50
51	52	53	54	55	56	57	58	59	60
61	62	63	64	65	66	67	68	69	70
71	72	73	74	75	76	77	78	79	80
81	82	83	84	85	86	87	88	89	90
91	92	93	94	95	96	97	98	99	100

Math Talk

Describe how the digits change when you skip count by tens.

FOR THE TEACHER • Read the following problem. Have children skip count on the hundred chart to solve. Paulo has 100 pennies. How many stacks of ten pennies can he make?

The shaded numbers show a pattern.
Skip count by twos.

The numbers in the ones places
of the shaded numbers are

_2_, ____, ____, ____, or ____.

1	2	3	4	5	6	7	8	9	10
11	12	13	14	15	16	17	18	19	20
21	22	23	24	25	26	27	28	29	30
31	32	33	34	35	36	37	38	39	40
41	42	43	44	45	46	47	48	49	50
51	52	53	54	55	56	57	58	59	60
61	62	63	64	65	66	67	68	69	70
71	72	73	74	75	76	77	78	79	80
81	82	83	84	85	86	87	88	89	90
91	92	93	94	95	96	97	98	99	100

Continue skip counting. Shade the squares.

Share and Show

Skip count. Show the pattern
on the hundred chart.

✓ 1. Count by tens.
   Circle the numbers.

_____

✓ 2. Count by fives.
   Color the squares blue.

1	2	3	4	5	6	7	8	9	10
11	12	13	14	15	16	17	18	19	20
21	22	23	24	25	26	27	28	29	30
31	32	33	34	35	36	37	38	39	40
41	42	43	44	45	46	47	48	49	50
51	52	53	54	55	56	57	58	59	60
61	62	63	64	65	66	67	68	69	70
71	72	73	74	75	76	77	78	79	80
81	82	83	84	85	86	87	88	89	90
91	92	93	94	95	96	97	98	99	100

_____

3. Write the pattern made with
   the circled numbers.

10, 20, ____, ____, ____, ____, ____, ____, ____, ____

On Your Own

Skip count. Show the pattern
on the hundred chart.

1	2	3	4	5	6	7	8	9	10
11	12	13	14	15	16	17	18	19	20
21	22	23	24	25	26	27	28	29	30
31	32	33	34	35	36	37	38	39	40
41	42	43	44	45	46	47	48	49	50
51	52	53	54	55	56	57	58	59	60
61	62	63	64	65	66	67	68	69	70
71	72	73	74	75	76	77	78	79	80
81	82	83	84	85	86	87	88	89	90
91	92	93	94	95	96	97	98	99	100

4. Count by fours.
   Circle the numbers.

_____

5. Count by threes.
   Color the squares blue.

_____

6. Write the numbers to show the pattern.
   Start at 12. Count by twos.

12, _____, _____, _____, _____, _____, _____

 Use the hundred chart.

7. Start at 30. Skip count backward by threes.
   Write **even** or **odd** under each number to describe it.

   30 , _____, _____, _____, _____

   even   _____   _____   _____   _____

8. Write your own number pattern in which
   you skip count backward by twos.

   _____, _____, _____, _____, _____, _____

1	2	3	4	5	6	7	8	9	10
11	12	13	14	15	16	17	18	19	20
21	22	23	24	25	26	27	28	29	30
31	32	33	34	35	36	37	38	39	40
41	42	43	44	45	46	47	48	49	50

Choose a way to solve.

9. Joel skip counts by fives. He starts on 5. Which of the following numbers will he say? Circle them.

   35   53   40

   65   89

10. Cindy skip counts by twos. She starts on 2 and stops on 72. Which of the following numbers will she say? Circle them.

   24   38   67

   55   70

11. **H.O.T.** Brett wanted to show a pattern of skip counting by fours on the chart.

1	2	3	4	5	6	7	8	9	10
11	12	13	14	15	16	17	18	19	20
21	22	23	24	25	26	27	28	29	30

   Describe his mistake. List the numbers that should be shaded.

   _____

   _____

12. ⭐ **Test Prep**   Pat skip counts by tens. Which numbers show skip counting by tens?

   ○ 20, 25, 30, 35   ○ 10, 12, 14, 16

   ○ 20, 30, 40, 50   ○ 10, 15, 20, 25

TAKE HOME ACTIVITY · Practice skip counting by twos, fives, and tens with your child.

FOR MORE PRACTICE:
Standards Practice Book, pp. P159–P160

Name _____

Act It Out • Patterns

Essential Question How can acting out a problem
help show a pattern?

Theo wants to put 3 stickers on each card.
How many stickers will he put on 5 cards?

🔑 Unlock the Problem

What do I need to find?

how many stickers Theo will put on

5 cards

**What information do
I need to use?**

3 stickers on each card

5 cards

Show how to solve the problem.

HOME CONNECTION • Your child used counters to act out
the problem. Counters are a concrete tool to show how a skip
counting pattern can be used to solve the problem.

Try Another Problem

Act out the problem.
Draw to show what you did.

• What do I need to find?
• What information do I need to use?

1. Jenna and her dad are building toy cars. They put 4 wheels on each car. How many wheels do they need to build 3 cars?

_____ wheels

2. Jamal puts 6 toys in each box. How many toys will he put in 3 boxes?

_____ toys

Math Talk
Explain how acting it out and skip counting helped you solve the second problem.

Name _____

Share and Show

Act out the problem.
Draw to show what you did.

☑ **3.** Mr. Fulton puts 3 bananas on each tray. How many bananas does he put on 4 trays?

_____ bananas

☑ **4.** Ms. Davis needs to have 3 apples in each bowl. There are 5 bowls. How many apples in all does she need in these bowls?

_____ apples

5. Dexter puts 5 grapes on each plate. How many grapes in all does he put on 4 plates?

_____ grapes

On Your Own

Choose a way to solve.
Write or draw to explain.

6. Jon has 6 marbles. Amy gives him some more. Now he has 13 marbles. How many marbles did Amy give to him?

_____ marbles

7. **H.O.T.** Angela used these counters to act out a problem.

Write a problem that Angela could have solved with these counters.

_____

_____

_____

8. ⭐ **Test Prep** Brett has 3 bags of shells. He has 4 shells in each bag. How many shells does he have in all?

○ 6
○ 7
○ 12
○ 15

 TAKE HOME ACTIVITY • Ask your child to explain how he or she solved the problem in Exercise 8.

FOR MORE PRACTICE:
Standards Practice Book, pp. P161–P162

Name _____

Algebra: Extend Patterns

Essential Question How do you extend a number pattern?

Listen and Draw REAL WORLD

Draw pictures to show the pattern in the story.

———— , ———— , ———— , ————

Math Talk

Describe how your pictures would be different if the story was about tricycles.

FOR THE TEACHER • Read the following problem. Have children draw pictures to represent the problem and then write the counting pattern. There are 4 bicycles in Tim's garage. Each bicycle has 2 wheels. How many wheels do the bicycles have in all?

Chapter 8

A table can be used to show a pattern. There are 4 wheels on each wagon. Use the table to find the number of wheels on 4 wagons.

number of wagons	1	2	3	4
number of wheels	4			

There are _____ wheels on 4 wagons.

Share and Show

1. There are 3 stickers in each pack. How many stickers are in 5 packs?

number of packs	1	2	3	4	5
number of stickers					

There are _____ stickers in 5 packs.

2. There are 2 wheels on each scooter. How many wheels are on 6 scooters?

number of scooters	1	2	3	4		
number of wheels						

There are _____ wheels on 6 scooters.

© Houghton Mifflin Harcourt Publishing Company

On Your Own

3. There are 5 apples in each bag.
How many apples are in 5 bags?

number of bags	1	2	3		
number of apples					

There are _____ apples in 5 bags.

---

4. There are 10 crayons in each box.
How many crayons are in 6 boxes?

number of boxes	1	2				
number of crayons						

There are _____ crayons in 6 boxes.

5. **H.O.T.** The chart below shows the numbers of wheels on carts. Write the missing information in the table.

number of _____		2			
number of _____		8			20

TAKE HOME ACTIVITY · Work with your child to show a pattern in a table to find the number of wings on 6 birds.

Name _____

Concept and Skills

Skip count. (pp. 333–336)

1. Count by threes.

3, _____, _____, _____, _____, _____, _____

2. Start at 30. Count by fives.

30, _____, _____, _____, _____, _____, _____

Choose a way to solve.
Draw or write to explain. (pp. 337–340)

3. Matt has 2 baskets. He has
5 apples in each basket. How
many apples does he have?

_____ apples

Complete the table to solve. (pp. 341–343)

4. There are 10 pens in each box.
How many pens are in 5 boxes?

number of boxes	1	2			
number of pens					

There are _____ pens in 5 boxes.

5. ⭐ **Test Prep** Lee has 3 flower pots.
She plants 6 seeds in each pot. How
many seeds does she plant? (pp. 337–343)

○ 18
○ 15
○ 9
○ 3

Name _____

Connect Addition and Multiplication

Essential Question When and how can you use multiplication to show addition?

Listen and Draw REAL WORLD

Use ⬤. Model the problems. Then draw what you modeled.

FOR THE TEACHER • Read the following two problems. For each problem, have students model with counters and then draw a picture and show the addition. Carlos has 3 red marbles, 2 blue marbles, and 5 black marbles. How many marbles does Carlos have in all? Sam has 5 red marbles, 5 blue marbles, and 5 black marbles. How many marbles does Sam have in all?

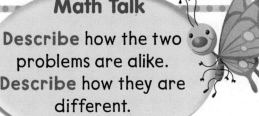

Math Talk

Describe how the two problems are alike. **Describe** how they are different.

Chapter 8

Model and Draw

When you **multiply**, you add **equal groups**.

3 groups of 4

Add to find how many in all.

$$\begin{array}{r} 4 \\ 4 \\ +\ 4 \\ \hline \end{array}$$

Multiply to find how many in all.

3 groups   4 in each group   12 in all

$$3 \times 4 = \underline{}$$

Read the **multiplication sentence**.
Three times four equals twelve.

Share and Show

Show the addition. Then write the multiplication sentence.

☑ I. 3 groups of 2

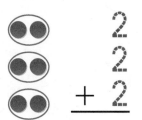

$$\begin{array}{r} 2 \\ 2 \\ +\ 2 \\ \hline \end{array}$$

$$2 \times 3 = \underline{}$$

☑ 2. 4 groups of 3

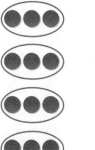

$$+ \underline{}$$

$$\underline{}$$

On Your Own

Show the addition. Then write the multiplication sentence.

3. 2 groups of 3

$+$ ___

_____

4. 2 groups of 4

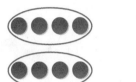

$+$ ___

_____

5. 4 groups of 4

$+$ ___

_____

6. 4 groups of 2

$+$ ___

_____

 Complete the addition sentence.
Then show the addition using multiplication.

7. $5 + 5 + 5 + 5 + 5 + 5 =$ ___   _____

PROBLEM SOLVING

 **REAL WORLD**

Choose a way to solve.
Draw or write to explain.

8. Glen has 3 fish bowls. There are 5 fish in each. How many fish are there in all?

_____ fish

9. Brianna has 48 yellow beads, 36 red beads, and 24 blue beads. How many more red beads than blue beads does she have?

_____ more red beads

10. **H.O.T.** Four girls share 12 buttons. Each girl gets the same number of buttons. How many does each girl get?

_____ buttons

11. ★ **Test Prep** Samantha buys 4 packs of cups. Each pack has 6 cups. How many cups does she buy?

- ○ 2
- ○ 10
- ○ 20
- ○ 24

 TAKE HOME ACTIVITY · Have your child explain how he or she solved one of the problems on this page.

© Houghton Mifflin Harcourt Publishing Company

FOR MORE PRACTICE:
Standards Practice Book, pp. P165–P166

Name _____

Model Multiplication

Essential Question How can you make a model to show multiplication?

Listen and Draw REAL WORLD

Use ●.

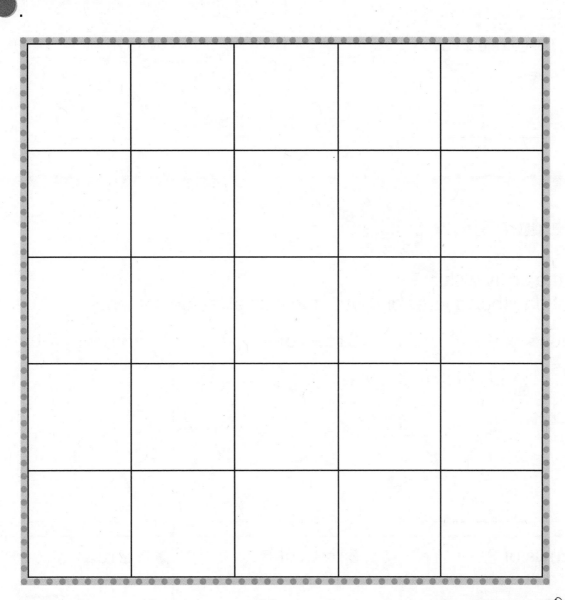

FOR THE TEACHER • Read the following problem. Have children place counters in the squares to solve. Then have them shade the squares where they placed the counters. Mrs. Hunter makes 3 rows of chairs. She puts 4 chairs in each row. How many chairs does she use?

Math Talk
Would the number of chairs be the same if she made 4 rows of 3? **Explain.**

Chapter 8

three hundred forty-nine **349**

You can use a model to multiply.

You can show an **array** with .

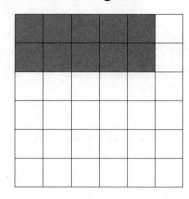

You can shade a grid.

There are 2 rows of 5.

$2 \times 5 =$ _____

$2 \times 5 =$ _____

Share and Show

Make the array with ⬤.

Then shade the squares and write the multiplication sentence.

1. 2 rows of 4

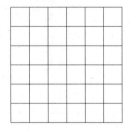

_____

2. 3 rows of 4

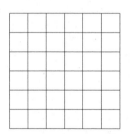

_____

3. 4 rows of 1

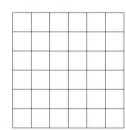

_____

4. 3 rows of 3

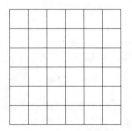

_____

✓ 5. 5 rows of 3

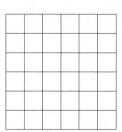

_____

✓ 6. 2 rows of 6

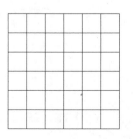

_____

Name _____

On Your Own

Make an array with 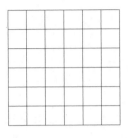.
Then shade the squares and write the multiplication sentence.

7. 2 rows of 3

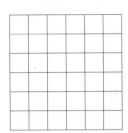

_____

8. 4 rows of 3

_____

9. 5 rows of 2

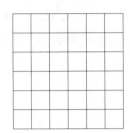

_____

10. 3 rows of 6

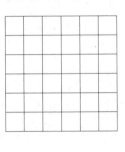

_____

11. 5 rows of 4

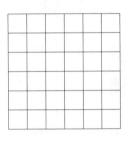

_____

12. I row of 5

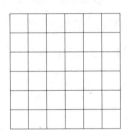

_____

H.O.T. Shade the squares.
Then write the multiplication sentence.

13. Make a model that is a square.

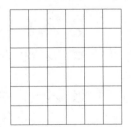

_____

14. Make a model that is not a square.

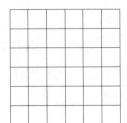

_____

Choose a way to solve.
Write or draw to explain.

15. Manny has 3 rows of stickers with 4 stickers in each row. How many stickers does he have?

_____ stickers

16. Brett collected 12 bottles and 54 cans to recycle. How many more cans than bottles did he collect?

_____ more cans

17. **H.O.T.** Jimmy hangs 6 photos on a wall. He puts them in an array with 3 rows. How many photos are in each row?

_____ photos

18. ⭐ **Test Prep** Which multiplication sentence does the model show?

○ $2 \times 6 = 12$
○ $3 \times 4 = 12$
○ $3 \times 6 = 18$
○ $4 \times 2 = 8$

TAKE HOME ACTIVITY • Have your child use pennies or other small objects to make an array. Have him or her write a multiplication sentence for the array.

© Houghton Mifflin Harcourt Publishing Company

FOR MORE PRACTICE:
Standards Practice Book, pp. P167–P168

Name _____

Multiply with 2

Essential Question How can skip counting help you multiply with 2?

Listen and Draw REAL WORLD

Draw pictures to solve. Then skip count to find the answer.

FOR THE TEACHER • Read the following problem. Have children draw pictures and then skip count to solve the problem. Lucy makes smiley-face pillows. She uses buttons for the eyes. How many buttons does she need to make 8 pillows?

Math Talk
Describe another way to solve the problem.

Chapter 8

Model and Draw

You can skip count by twos to multiply with 2.

__2__, __4__, __6__, ____, ____, ____

balloons

$$6 \times 2 = 12$$

Share and Show

Skip count by twos. Write the multiplication sentence.

1.

$$1 \times 2 =$$

_____

2.

_____

3.

_____

☑ 4.

_____

☑ 5.

_____

Name _____

On Your Own

Skip count by twos. Write the multiplication sentence.

6.

_____

7.

_____

8.

_____

9.

_____

H.O.T. Multiply.

10. $4 \times 2 = $ ____

11. $5 \times 2 = $ ____

12. $3 \times 2 = $ ____

13. $1 \times 2 = $ ____

14. $7 \times 2 = $ ____

15. $9 \times 2 = $ ____

Chapter 8 • Lesson 6

three hundred fifty-five **355**

PROBLEM SOLVING

Choose a way to solve.
Write or draw to explain.

16. Dylan has 4 dogs at his house.
He buys each dog 2 new bones.
How many bones does he buy?

_____ bones

17. **H.O.T.** Explain how you could find 10 × 2.

_____

_____

_____

18. ⭐ **Test Prep** Maria has 7 plates.
She puts 2 apples on each plate.
How many apples does she use?

○ 14
○ 12
○ 9
○ 5

TAKE HOME ACTIVITY · Ask your child to show you how to use skip counting
to find 9 × 2.

356 three hundred fifty-six

FOR MORE PRACTICE:
Standards Practice Book, pp. P169–P170

© Houghton Mifflin Harcourt Publishing Company

Name _____

Multiply with 5

Essential Question How can you use skip counting to multiply with 5?

Listen and Draw REAL WORLD

Use the hundred chart to skip count and solve the problem.

1	2	3	4	5	6	7	8	9	10
11	12	13	14	15	16	17	18	19	20
21	22	23	24	25	26	27	28	29	30
31	32	33	34	35	36	37	38	39	40
41	42	43	44	45	46	47	48	49	50
51	52	53	54	55	56	57	58	59	60
61	62	63	64	65	66	67	68	69	70
71	72	73	74	75	76	77	78	79	80
81	82	83	84	85	86	87	88	89	90
91	92	93	94	95	96	97	98	99	100

Math Talk

Explain how you knew when to stop skip counting.

FOR THE TEACHER • Read the following problem. Have children skip count and shade boxes on the hundred chart to solve the problem. Madison bought 9 packs of stickers. Each pack had 5 stickers. How many stickers did she buy?

© Houghton Mifflin Harcourt Publishing Company

Chapter 8

three hundred fifty-seven **357**

You can skip count by fives to multiply with 5.

5 , 10 , 15 , _____ , _____ , _____
fingers

6 × 5 = 30

Share and Show

Skip count by fives. Write the multiplication sentence.

1.

   1 × 5 =
   _____

2.

   _____

 3.

   _____

 4.

   _____

On Your Own

Skip count by fives. Write the multiplication sentence.

5.

_____

6.

_____

7.

_____

8.

_____

9.

_____

 **Multiply.**

10. $7 \times 5 =$ _____	11. $4 \times 5 =$ _____	12. $8 \times 5 =$ _____
13. $5 \times 5 =$ _____	14. $3 \times 5 =$ _____	15. $6 \times 5 =$ _____

Choose a way to solve.
Write or draw to explain.

16. Mr. Smith has 10 bunches of bananas for sale. Each bunch has 5 bananas. He sells 6 bunches. How many bananas does he sell?

_____ bananas

17. **H.O.T.** Carey has 3 bags with 5 marbles in each. Helen has 5 bags with 4 marbles in each. Who has more marbles, Carey or Helen?

_____

18. Mrs. Ray had some books. She gave 15 books to John. Now she has 23 books. How many books did she have to start with?

_____ books

19. ⭐ **Test Prep** Maria buys 8 packs of pencils. Each pack has 5 pencils. How many pencils does she buy?

○ 3
○ 13
○ 40
○ 45

TAKE HOME ACTIVITY • Ask your child to show you how he or she solved one of the problems on this page.

© Houghton Mifflin Harcourt Publishing Company

FOR MORE PRACTICE:
Standards Practice Book, pp. P171–P172

Name _____

✓ Chapter 8 Review/Test

Vocabulary

Use a word in the box to complete each sentence.

1. To find 3×5, you can _____ by fives. (pp. 333–337)

2. To show addition using multiplication, you must have _____. (pp. 345–348)

3. When you put counters in equal rows, you make an _____. (pp. 349–352)

Concepts and Skills

Show the addition.
Then write the multiplication sentence. (pp. 345–348)

4. 3 groups of 5

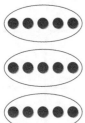

____ + ____

_____

Shade the squares.
Then write the multiplication sentence. (pp. 349–352)

5. 2 rows of 3

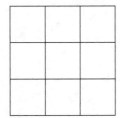

_____

Fill in the bubble for the correct answer choice.

6. Anna starts at 4 and skip counts by fours. What numbers does she say? (pp. 333–336)

- ○ 4, 6, 8, 10, 12
- ○ 4, 8, 12, 16, 20
- ○ 4, 5, 6, 7, 8
- ○ 4, 14, 24, 34, 44

1	2	3	4	5	6	7	8	9	10
11	12	13	14	15	16	17	18	19	20
21	22	23	24	25	26	27	28	29	30
31	32	33	34	35	36	37	38	39	40
41	42	43	44	45	46	47	48	49	50

7. Shelby wants to put 3 flowers in each vase. There are 4 vases. How many flowers will she need in all? (345–348)

- ○ 3
- ○ 7
- ○ 12
- ○ 34

8. There are 5 oranges in each basket.

number of baskets	1	2	3			
number of oranges	5					

How many oranges are in 6 baskets? (pp. 341–343)

- ○ 30
- ○ 15
- ○ 11
- ○ 6

Name _____

Fill in the bubble for the correct answer choice.

9. A room has 5 tables in it. Each table has 4 chairs. How many chairs are there? (pp. 345–348)

   ○ 9
   ○ 10
   ○ 15
   ○ 20

10. A parking lot has 2 rows of cars. There are 7 cars in each row. How many cars are in the parking lot? (pp. 349–352)

   ○ 16
   ○ 14
   ○ 9
   ○ 5

11. Which multiplication sentence does this array show? (pp. 349–352)

   ○ 2 × 6 = 12
   ○ 2 × 9 = 18
   ○ 3 × 6 = 18
   ○ 3 × 9 = 24

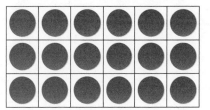

Short Answer

12. Maria makes sock puppets. She uses 2 buttons on each puppet. How many buttons does she need to make 4 puppets?

Write the multiplication sentence to show this problem. Explain how the sentence shows the problem.

_____

_____

_____

_____

Performance Task

13. Jorge makes 7 fruit baskets. He puts 5 bananas in each basket. How many bananas does he use?

Show two different ways to solve this problem.

One way:

Another way:

Jorge uses _____ bananas.

Making a Kite

by Kathryn Krieger and Christine Ruiz

Developing an understanding of linear measurement and facility in measuring lengths

365

Ellie and Mike get the materials to make a kite. Then they make the body of the kite.

Materials

paper kite pattern
tape
straw
10 small paper clips
scissors
hole punch
string
3 sheets of paper
streamer paper

1 Fold the pattern in half.

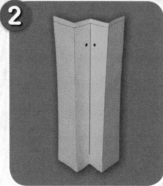

2 Fold along both dashed lines.

3 Tape on each end.

What are the parts of a kite?

Mike does not want the front of the kite to bend too much. He uses a straw to make the kite stronger.

4 Measure 3 paper clips long. Cut.

5 Tape straw on the line.

Science

Why is a straw used as part of the kite?

The kite must have a string for Ellie or Mike to hold. If the kite does not have a string, it will blow away. Ellie will tie the string onto the kite.

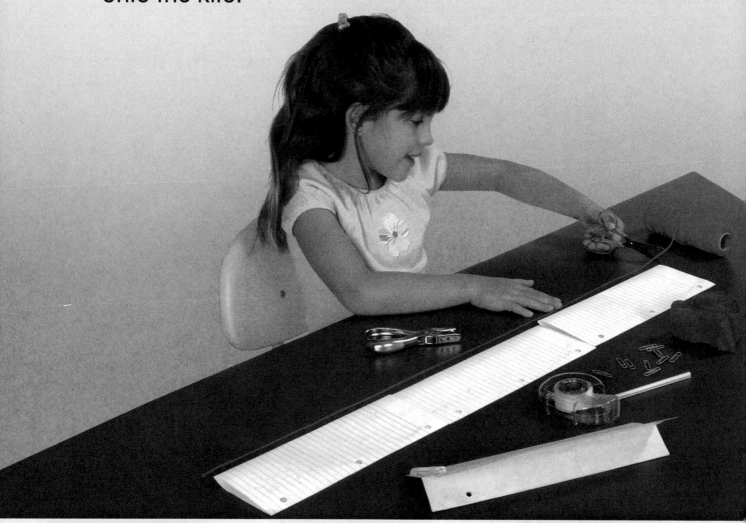

6

Punch one hole.

7

Measure 3 paper-lengths of string. Cut.

8

Put the string through the hole and tie it.

© Houghton Mifflin Harcourt Publishing Company

Science

Why is a string needed on a kite?

A tail will help the kite fly straight. Mike measures streamer paper and will tape it to the kite. Then the kite will be finished!

Measure 10 paper-clip-lengths of streamer paper. Cut.

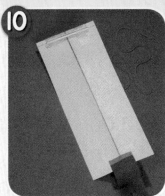

Tape the streamer to the kite as a tail.

Why is a tail needed on a kite?

You can make a kite too.
Start at the beginning of
this story. Follow the steps.

How do all of the parts help the kite fly?

Write About the Story

Draw and write a story about making a kite. Explain how to measure the parts of the kite in your story.

Vocabulary Review

measure

length

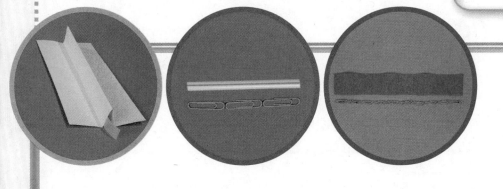

_____

_____

_____

_____

_____

What is the length?

Estimate the length of each straw.
Then measure the length of each
straw using paper clips.

1. Estimate: about _____ paper clips long

Measure: about _____ paper clips long

2. Estimate: about _____ paper clips long

Measure: about _____ paper clips long

3. Estimate: about _____ paper clips long

Measure: about _____ paper clips long

Look around the classroom. Find other
objects to measure. Measure the length
of each object using paper clips.

372

Curious About Math with Curious George

The Missouri River is the longest river in the United States.

What is the longest piece of furniture in your classroom? How would you find out?

Show What You Know ✓

Compare Lengths

1. Order the pencils from shortest to longest.
   Write 1, 2, 3.

_____

_____

_____

Use Nonstandard Units to Measure Length

Use real objects and ▪ to measure.

2. about _____ ▪

3. Crayon about _____ ▪

Measure Length Twice: Nonstandard Units

Use ▭ and ▪.
Measure the length of the pencil.

4. about _____ ▭   5. about _____ ▪

Family note: This page checks your child's understanding of important skills needed for success in Chapter 9.

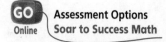

GO Online   Assessment Options
Soar to Success Math

© Houghton Mifflin Harcourt Publishing Company

Name _____

Vocabulary Builder

Visualize It

Fill in the graphic organizer to describe the lengths of two different objects.

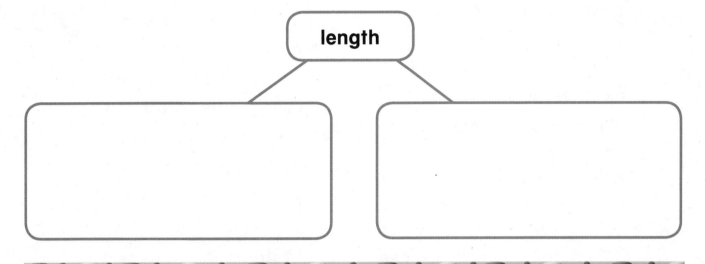

length

Understand Vocabulary

Use review words. Complete the sentences.

1. The red pencil is _____ than the yellow pencil.

2. The blue pencil is _____ than the yellow pencil.

3. The blue pencil is the _____ pencil.

4. The red pencil is the _____ pencil.

GO
Online
• eStudent Edition
• Multimedia eGlossary

Game — Longer or Shorter?

Materials

- 9 ▣
- 9 ▣
- 🔵 Longer Shorter

Play with a partner.

1. Choose a picture on the board. You and your partner each find a real object that matches the picture.

2. Place the objects next to each other to find out which is longer and which is shorter. If the objects are the same length, choose another object.

3. Spin the pointer on the spinner. The player with the object that matches the spinner puts a cube on that picture on the board.

4. Take turns until all the pictures have a cube. The player with more cubes on the board wins.

Longer | Shorter

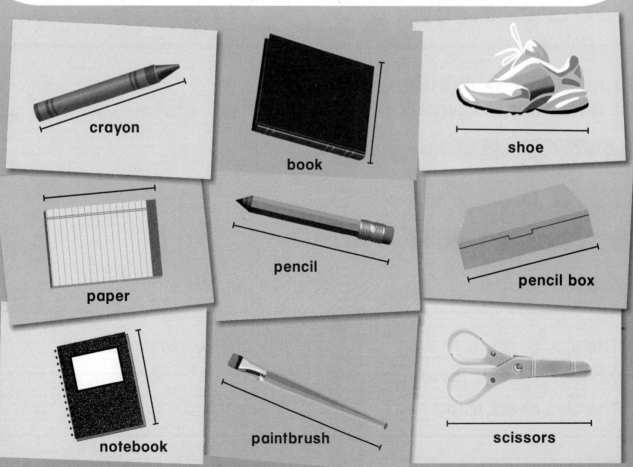

crayon

book

shoe

paper

pencil

pencil box

notebook

paintbrush

scissors

Name _____

Indirect Measurement

Essential Question How can you compare the lengths of two objects that you cannot place side by side?

Listen REAL WORLD

Cut a paper strip to match the length of each string.

Math Talk
For each string, **explain** how you know that your paper strip is the same length.

HOME CONNECTION · In this activity, your child learned to make measurement models to compare lengths.

© Houghton Mifflin Harcourt Publishing Company

How can you compare the lengths or widths of objects that are not near each other?

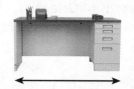

Cut a piece of string to match the length of one of the objects.

Compare the length of the string to the length of the other object.

The desk is longer than the string. So, the desk is longer than the bookcase.

Share and Show

Find the real objects. Use string and scissors.
Circle the picture that answers the question.

I. **Which is longer?**

chalkboard   teacher's desk

2. **Which is wider?**

door   your desk

MR. MARTIN'S CLASS

✓ 3. **Which is longer?**

map   chalkboard

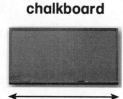

✓ 4. **Which is wider?**

your desk   computer

Name _____

On Your Own

Find the real objects. Use string and scissors.
Circle the picture that answers the question

5. Which is wider?

bookcase	bulletin board
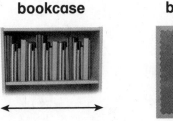 

6. Which is shorter?

your desk	teacher's desk
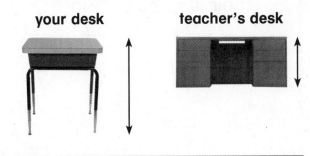

7. Which is taller?

easel	your desk

8. Which is wider?

map	door

9. Cut string to match the width of
one of the objects.
Compare it to the other two objects.
Which is the widest? Circle it.

computer	chair	door

10. **H.O.T.** A pencil and a marker are the same length. A pen is shorter than the pencil. Draw pictures of the objects to show how their lengths compare.

How do the pen and the marker compare?

_____

11. ⭐ **Test Prep**   Compare the lengths of the blue ribbon, the chain, and the paper clip.

Which statement is true?

○ The ribbon is shorter than the chain.

○ The paper clip is shorter than the ribbon.

○ The three objects are the same length.

○ The chain is longer than the ribbon.

TAKE HOME ACTIVITY • Ask your child to compare the lengths of three different objects.

FOR MORE PRACTICE:
Standards Practice Book, pp. P177–P178

Name _____

Compare Lengths

Essential Question How do you compare lengths
of three objects?

Listen and Draw

Use 🖍 🖍. Draw pairs of crayons that your
teacher describes.

Math Talk
Explain how you
know that the
crayons are drawn
correctly.

FOR THE TEACHER • Give the following instructions
for the first box: Draw a red crayon and a blue crayon.
The red crayon should be longer than the blue crayon.
Repeat for the second box, except that the red
crayon should be shorter than the blue crayon.

Chapter 9

If a new string is shorter than the green string,
how does the blue string compare to the new string?

You can draw a string to check your answer.

The blue string is  _____ the new string.

Share and Show

Write **shorter than** or **longer than**.

✓ 1. If a new string is longer than the red string,
how does the green string compare to the new string?

The green string is _____ the new string.

✓ 2. If a new string is shorter than the red string,
how does the blue string compare to the new string?

The blue string is _____ the new string.

On Your Own

Write **shorter than** or **longer than**.

3. Jill's street is longer than
Greg's street. Greg's street
is longer than Paul's street.

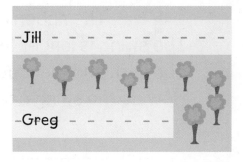

Jill's street is _____ Paul's street.

4. Sasha's book is shorter than Tom's
book. Tom's book is shorter than
Rita's book.

Sasha   Tom

Sasha's book is _____ Rita's book.

5. Jake's wagon is longer than Mary's
wagon. Mary's wagon is longer than
Steve's wagon.

Jake's wagon is _____ Steve's wagon.

6. Dave's poster is shorter than Jan's
poster. Jan's poster is shorter than
Katie's poster.

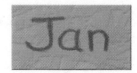

Dave's poster is _____ Katie's poster.

7. **H.O.T.** The ribbon is longer than the yarn.
The string is longer than the ribbon.
The yarn and the tape are the same length.
How do the string and the tape compare?

_____

Draw a picture to prove your answer.

8. ⭐ **Test Prep** Which red string is longer than this string?

○

○

○

○

TAKE HOME ACTIVITY · With your child, predict how an object that you see in a room will compare in length to an object in another room. Check the prediction.

FOR MORE PRACTICE:
Standards Practice Book, pp. P179–P180

Name _____

Measure with Inch Models

Essential Question How can you use inch models to measure length?

Listen and Draw

Use color tiles to measure the length.

_____ color tiles

_____ color tiles

_____ color tiles

HOME CONNECTION • Your child used color tiles as an introduction to measurement of length before using standard measurement tools.

Math Talk
Describe how to use color tiles to measure length.

A color tile is about 1 **inch** long.

How many inches long is this string?

Count the color tiles to find how many inches long the string is.

The string is 4 color tiles long.

So, it is  _____ inches long.

Share and Show

Math Board

Use color tiles. Measure the length of the object in inches.

1.

_____ inches

2.

_____ inches

✔ 3.

_____ inches

✔ 4.

_____ inches

On Your Own

Use color tiles. Measure the length of the object in inches.

5.

_____ inches

6.

_____ inches

7.

_____ inches

8.

_____ inches

9.

_____ inches

10.

_____ inches

PROBLEM SOLVING REAL WORLD

Look around your classroom. Find objects that are about 2 inches long. Draw and label the objects.

11.

_____

12.

_____

13. Andy has a piece of ribbon that is 6 inches long. He needs to cut it into pieces that are each 2 inches long.
How many pieces can he make?

_____ pieces

14. ⭐ **Test Prep** Jeremy used color tiles to measure a string.

Which is the best choice for the length of the string?

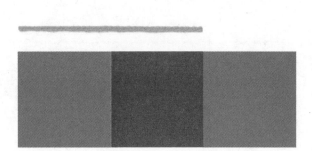

○ 1 inch

○ 2 inches

○ 3 inches

○ 4 inches

 TAKE HOME ACTIVITY • Have your child use small paper clips to measure the lengths of some small objects around your home.

FOR MORE PRACTICE:
Standards Practice Book, pp. P181–P182

Name _____

Make and Use a Ruler

Essential Question Why is using a ruler similar to using a row of color tiles to measure length?

Listen and Draw REAL WORLD

Make a row of color tiles. Trace along the edge to show these lengths.

4 inches

2 inches

3 inches

Math Talk
Describe how you knew how many color tiles to use for each length.

HOME CONNECTION • Your child used color tiles as 1-inch models to show different lengths. This activity helps to make inch units a more familiar concept.

Use a color tile to make a ruler on a paper strip.
Color 6 parts that are each about 1 inch long.

How to use your ruler:
Line up the left edge of an object with the first mark.

Share and Show

Measure the length with your ruler.
Count the inches.

1.

_____ inches

2.

_____ inches

3.

_____ inches

Name _____

On Your Own

Measure the length with your ruler.
Count the inches.

4.

_____ inches

5.

_____ inches

6.

_____ inches

7.

_____ inches

8.

_____ inches

Write Math

Work with a classmate.

9. **H.O.T.** Together, use both of your
   rulers to measure the length of
   a bulletin board or a window.
   What is the length?

   about _____ inches

10. Describe what you did in Exercise 9.
    How did you measure a length that is
    longer than your rulers?

    _____

    _____

    _____

    _____

11. ⭐ **Test Prep**   Use your ruler.
    What is the best choice for the length
    of this piece of yarn?

    ○ 6 inches

    ○ 5 inches

    ○ 4 inches

    ○ 3 inches

TAKE HOME ACTIVITY · Choose one of the objects in this lesson.
Have your child look for objects that are longer, about the same length,
and shorter.

FOR MORE PRACTICE:
Standards Practice Book, pp. P183–P184

Name _____

Estimate Lengths

Essential Question How can you estimate the lengths of objects in inches?

Listen and Draw REAL WORLD

Choose three small objects. Use your ruler to measure their lengths. Draw the objects and write their lengths.

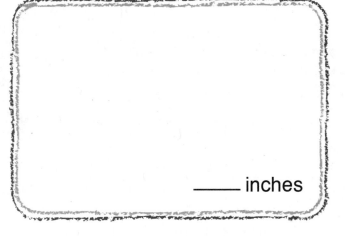

_____ inches

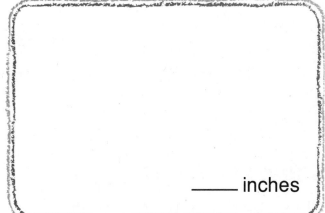

_____ inches

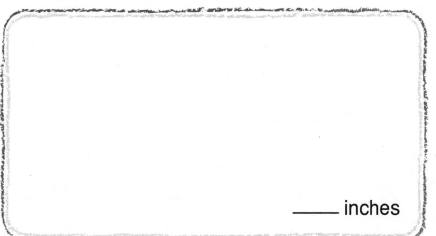

_____ inches

FOR THE TEACHER • Provide a collection of small objects, 2 to 6 inches in length, for the children to measure. Have them select one object, measure it, and return it before selecting another.

Math Talk
Describe how the three lengths compare. Which object is longest?

Chapter 9

The bead is 1 inch long. Use this bead to help find how many beads will fit on the string. Which is the best estimate for the length of the string?

2 inches

(5 inches)

8 inches

2 inches is too short.

5 inches is about right.

8 inches is too long.

Share and Show

Circle the best estimate for the length of the string.

1.

1 inch   3 inches   5 inches

✓ 2.

2 inches   4 inches   6 inches

✓ 3.

4 inches   6 inches   8 inches

On Your Own

Circle the best estimate for the length of the string.

4.

| 4 inches | 7 inches | 10 inches |

5.

| 3 inches | 6 inches | 9 inches |

6.

| 1 inch | 3 inches | 5 inches |

7. Use the 1-inch mark. Estimate the length of each ribbon.

1 inch

Estimates:

red ribbon: about ____ inches

blue ribbon: about ____ inches

PROBLEM SOLVING

Solve. Write or draw to explain.

8.  **H.O.T.** Sasha has a string that is the length of 5 beads. Each bead is 2 inches long. What is the length of the string?

_____ inches

9. **H.O.T.** Maurice has a string that is the length of 6 beads. Each bead is 3 inches long. What is the length of the string?

_____ inches

10. ⭐ **Test Prep** Tameka has this string. She has many beads that are 1 inch long, like this blue bead.

Which is the best estimate for the length of the string?

○ 10 inches

○ 5 inches

○ 2 inches

○ 1 inch

TAKE HOME ACTIVITY • With your child, estimate the lengths of some small objects, such as books.

FOR MORE PRACTICE:
Standards Practice Book, pp. P185–P186

Name _____

Measure with an Inch Ruler

Essential Question How do you use an inch ruler to measure lengths?

Listen and Draw REAL WORLD

Draw each caterpillar to match the given length.

FOR THE TEACHER • Have children use the rulers they made in Lesson 9.4 to draw a caterpillar that is 1 inch long. Using this as a guide, have children draw a caterpillar that is 2 inches long and a caterpillar that is 3 inches long without using their rulers.

Math Talk
Describe how you decided how long to draw the 2-inch and 3-inch caterpillars.

Chapter 9

three hundred ninety-seven **397**

Model and Draw

What is the length of the string to the nearest inch?

Step 1

Line up the end of the string with the zero mark on the ruler.

Step 2

Find the inch mark that is closest to the other end of the string.

_2_ inches

Share and Show [Math Board]

Measure the length to the nearest inch.

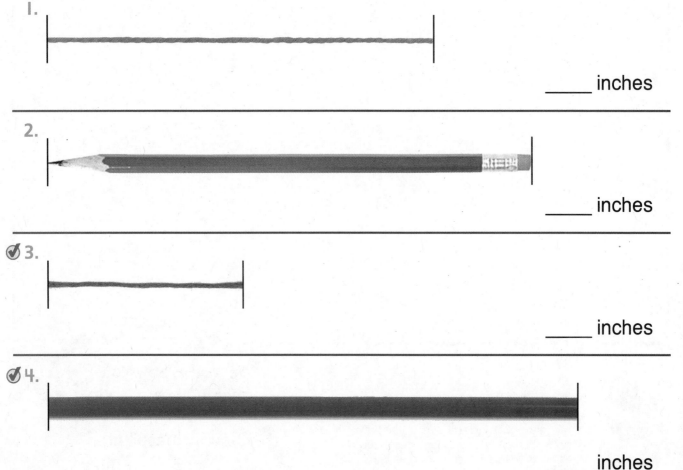

1.

____ inches

2.

____ inches

✓ 3.

____ inches

✓ 4.

____ inches

398 three hundred ninety-eight

On Your Own

Measure the length to the nearest inch.

5.

_____ inches

6.

_____ inches

7.

_____ inches

8.

_____ inches

9.

_____ inches

10.

_____ inches

PROBLEM SOLVING

REAL WORLD

Write Math

Solve.

11. Measure. What is the total length?

_____ inches

12. Measure. What is the total length?

_____ inches

13. **H.O.T.** How much longer is the red string than the blue string?

_____ inches longer

14. **H.O.T.** If the red and blue strings were straight and placed end to end, how long would they be in all?

_____ inches

15. ⭐ **Test Prep** Use an inch ruler. What is the length of the pencil to the nearest inch?

○ 1 inch

○ 2 inches

○ 3 inches

○ 5 inches

TAKE HOME ACTIVITY • Have your child measure the lengths of some objects to the nearest inch.

FOR MORE PRACTICE:
Standards Practice Book, pp. P187–P188

Name _____

Estimate and Measure Length

Essential Question How can you use a 1-inch mark to estimate length?

Listen and Draw REAL WORLD

Choose three small objects.
Measure to the nearest inch.
Draw the objects and write their lengths.

_____ inches

_____ inches

_____ inches

Math Talk

What is the difference in length between the longest and shortest object? **Explain.**

FOR THE TEACHER • Provide a collection of small objects, 2 to 6 inches in length, for the children to measure. Have them select an object, measure it, and return it before selecting another.

Model and Draw

Estimate the length of the object in inches.
Use the 1-inch mark as a guide to help you
estimate. Draw pencil marks showing
1-inch spaces along the top of the object.

| 1 inch

estimated length: _____ inches

Then use your ruler to measure the length of the
object to the nearest inch.

actual length: _____ inches

> How does your estimate compare to the actual measurement?

Share and Show

Estimate the length of each object, using the 1-inch
mark as a guide. Then use your ruler to measure the
length to the nearest inch.

1.

| 1 inch

estimated length: _____ inches

actual length: _____ inches

2.

| 1 inch

estimated length: _____ inches

actual length: _____ inches

Name _____

On Your Own

Estimate the length of each object, using the 1-inch mark as a guide. Then use your ruler to measure the length to the nearest inch.

3.

| 1 inch |

estimated length: _____ inches

actual length: _____ inches

4.

| 1 inch |

estimated length: _____ inches

actual length: _____ inches

5.

| 1 inch |

estimated length: _____ inches

actual length: _____ inches

6.

| 1 inch |

estimated length: _____ inches

actual length: _____ inches

7. On the treasure map, the distance from the tree to the rock is about 2 inches. Estimate and then measure the distance from the rock to the *X*.

> tree   rock   X
> ●   ●   ●

rock to *X* : estimated distance: _____ inches

actual distance: _____ inches

8. **H.O.T.** On the map above, if 1 inch is equal to 100 steps, how many steps are between the tree and the *X*? Explain your answer.

_____

_____

9. ⭐ **Test Prep**   A bracelet has 3 beads for every inch. The bracelet is about 7 inches long. How many beads does it have?

- ○ 3
- ○ 7
- ○ 10
- ○ 21

TAKE HOME ACTIVITY · Ask your child to estimate the length of a small object in inches and then measure the length to the nearest inch using a ruler.

FOR MORE PRACTICE:
Standards Practice Book, pp. P189–P190

Name _____

Measure in Inches and Feet

Essential Question Why is measuring in feet different from measuring in inches?

Listen and Draw REAL WORLD

Draw or write to describe how you measured each distance.

Distance 1

Distance 2

Math Talk
Describe how the length of a sheet of paper is different from the length of an inch.

FOR THE TEACHER • Have pairs of children stand apart and measure the distance between them with sheets of paper folded in half lengthwise. Repeat for a greater distance.

I 2 inches is the same as 1 **foot**.
You can measure lengths in inches
and also in feet.

The real desk is about 24 inches wide.
The real desk is also about 2 feet wide.

Share and Show

Measure to the nearest inch.
Then measure to the nearest foot.

Find the real object.	Measure.
1. **table**	_____ inches _____ feet
☑ 2. **window**	_____ inches _____ feet
☑ 3. **door** MR. MARTIN'S CLASS	_____ inches _____ feet

Name _____

On Your Own

Measure to the nearest inch.
Then measure to the nearest foot.

Find the real object.	Measure.
chalkboard	____ inches ____ feet
poster	____ inches ____ feet
teacher's desk	____ inches ____ feet
easel	____ inches ____ feet
bulletin board	____ inches ____ feet

4.

5.

6.

7.

8.

9. Use a ruler to measure the length of a real shelf in inches and in feet.

Measurements:

_____ inches

_____ feet

10. **H.O.T.** Look at your measurements for the shelf. Why is the number of inches different from the number of feet?

_____

_____

_____

11. ⭐ **Test Prep** Stephen is telling his brother about using a ruler to measure length. Which sentence is true?

○ I inch is the same length as I foot.

○ I foot is a greater length than I inch.

○ I inch is a greater length than I foot.

○ Inches are not used to measure length.

TAKE HOME ACTIVITY · Have your child measure the longer edge of a pillowcase in inches and in feet.

FOR MORE PRACTICE:
Standards Practice Book, pp. P191–P192

Name _____

Measure in Feet and Yards

Essential Question Why is measuring in yards different from measuring in feet?

Listen and Draw REAL WORLD

Draw or write to describe how you measured each distance.

Distance 1

Distance 2

Math Talk

Describe how the length of your piece of yarn is different from the length of a 12-inch ruler.

FOR THE TEACHER • Each small group uses a 1-yard piece of yarn to measure a distance marked on the floor with masking tape. Repeat for a different distance.

3 feet is the same as 1 **yard**.
You can measure length in feet
and also in yards.

The real bat is about 3 feet long.
The real bat is also about 1 yard long.

Share and Show

Measure to the nearest foot.
Then measure to the nearest yard.

Find the real object.	Measure.
wall 1.	_____ feet _____ yards
teacher's desk ✓2.	_____ feet _____ yards
bulletin board ✓3.	_____ feet _____ yards

On Your Own

Measure to the nearest foot.
Then measure to the nearest yard.

Find the real object.	Measure.
map 4.	____ feet ____ yards
table 5.	____ feet ____ yards
chalkboard 6.	____ feet ____ yards
window 7.	____ feet ____ yards

TAKE HOME ACTIVITY · With your child, measure the lengths
of some objects in feet and in yards.

FOR MORE PRACTICE:
Standards Practice Book, pp. P193–P194

Mid-Chapter Checkpoint

Concepts and Skills

Write **shorter than** or **longer than**. (pp. 381–384)

1. If a new string is shorter than the red string, how does the blue string compare to the new string?

The blue string is _____ the new string.

Use color tiles. Measure the length of the object in inches. (pp. 385–388)

2.

_____ inches

The bead is 1 inch long. Circle the best estimate for the length of the string. (pp. 393–396)

3.

    1 inch   2 inches   5 inches

4. ⭐ **Test Prep**   Use an inch ruler. What is the length of the string to the nearest inch? (pp. 397–400)

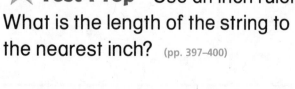

    ○ 1 inch

    ○ 3 inches

    ○ 5 inches

    ○ 7 inches

Name _____

Measure with a Centimeter Model

Essential Question How can you use a
centimeter model to measure length?

Listen and Draw REAL WORLD

Use ▢ to measure the length.

_____

_____ unit cubes

_____

_____ unit cubes

_____

_____ unit cubes

Math Talk
Describe how to
use unit cubes to
measure length.

HOME CONNECTION • Your child used unit
cubes as an introduction to measurement of
length before using metric measurement tools.

© Houghton Mifflin Harcourt Publishing Company

Model and Draw

A unit cube is about 1 **centimeter** long.

How many centimeters long is this string?

> You can make a mark for each centimeter to keep track and to count.

| 1 | 2 | 3 | 4 | 5 | 6 | 7 | 8 | 9 | 10 | 11 |

The string is __11__ centimeters long.

Share and Show

Use a unit cube. Measure the length in centimeters.

1.

_____ centimeters

✔ 2.

_____ centimeters

✔ 3.

_____ centimeters

414 four hundred fourteen

On Your Own

Use a unit cube. Measure the length in centimeters.

4.

_____ centimeters

5.

_____ centimeters

6.

_____ centimeters

7.

_____ centimeters

8.

_____ centimeters

Solve. Write or draw to explain.

9. **H.O.T.** Mrs. Duncan measured the lengths of a crayon and a pencil.
The pencil is twice as long as the crayon.
The sum of their lengths is 24 centimeters.
What are their lengths?

crayon: _____

pencil: _____

10. ⭐ **Test Prep** Marita used unit cubes to measure the length of a straw.

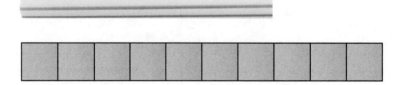

Which is the best choice for the length of the straw?

- ○ 1 centimeter
- ○ 3 centimeters
- ○ 7 centimeters
- ○ 10 centimeters

 TAKE HOME ACTIVITY • Have your child compare the lengths of other objects to those in this lesson.

FOR MORE PRACTICE:
Standards Practice Book, pp. P195–P196

Name _____

Measure with a Centimeter Ruler

Essential Question How do you use a centimeter ruler to measure lengths?

Listen and Draw REAL WORLD

Find three small objects in the classroom.
Use unit cubes to measure their lengths.
Draw the objects and write their lengths.

_____ centimeters

_____ centimeters

_____ centimeters

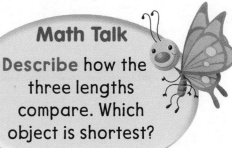

Math Talk

Describe how the three lengths compare. Which object is shortest?

HOME CONNECTION • Your child used unit cubes to measure the lengths of some classroom objects as an introduction to measuring lengths in centimeters.

Chapter 9

Model and Draw

What is the length of the crayon to the nearest centimeter?

Remember: Line up the left edge of the object with the first or zero mark on the ruler.

0 1 2 3 4 5 6 7 8 9 10 11
centimeters

_9_ centimeters

Share and Show

Measure the length to the nearest centimeter.

1.

_____ centimeters

☑ **2.**

_____ centimeters

☑ **3.**

_____ centimeters

Name _____

On Your Own

Measure the length to the nearest centimeter.

4.

_____ centimeters

5.

_____ centimeters

6.

_____ centimeters

7.

_____ centimeters

8.

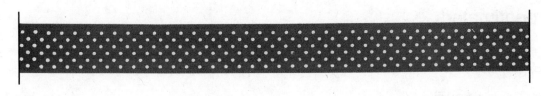

_____ centimeters

9. **H.O.T.** The crayon was on the table next to the centimeter ruler. The left edge of the crayon was not lined up with the zero mark on the ruler.

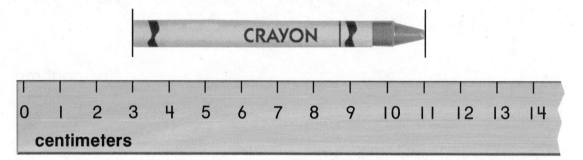

What is the length of the crayon? _____

Explain how you found your answer.

_____

_____

_____

10. ⭐ **Test Prep** Use a centimeter ruler to measure. Which is the best choice for the length of this string?

- ○ 1 centimeter
- ○ 4 centimeters
- ○ 7 centimeters
- ○ 10 centimeters

TAKE HOME ACTIVITY • Have your child measure the lengths of some objects at home using a centimeter ruler.

FOR MORE PRACTICE:
Standards Practice Book, pp. P197–P198

Name _____

Make Reasonable Estimates

Essential Question How can you use known lengths to estimate unknown lengths?

Listen and Draw

Find three classroom objects that are shorter than your 10-centimeter strip. Draw the objects. Write estimates for their lengths.

about _____ centimeters

about _____ centimeters

about _____ centimeters

Math Talk
Which object has the length closest to 10 centimeters? **Explain** how you know.

HOME CONNECTION · Your child used a 10-centimeter strip of paper to practice estimating the lengths of some classroom objects.

Chapter 9

four hundred twenty-one **421**

Model and Draw

This pencil is about 10 centimeters long.
Which is the most reasonable estimate
for the length of the ribbon?

7 centimeters

13 centimeters

20 centimeters

> The ribbon is longer than the pencil. 7 centimeters is not reasonable.

> The ribbon is not twice as long as the pencil. 20 centimeters is not reasonable.

The ribbon is a little longer than the pencil.
So, 13 centimeters is the most reasonable estimate.

Share and Show

✓ 1. The yarn is about 5 centimeters long. Circle the best estimate for the length of the crayon.

10 centimeters

15 centimeters

20 centimeters

✓ 2. The string is about 12 centimeters long.
Circle the best estimate for the length of the straw.

3 centimeters

7 centimeters

11 centimeters

On Your Own

3. The rope is about 8 centimeters long. Circle the best estimate for the length of the paper clip.

2 centimeters

4 centimeters

8 centimeters

4. The pencil is about 11 centimeters long.
Circle the best estimate for the length of the chain.

6 centimeters

10 centimeters

13 centimeters

5. The hair clip is about 7 centimeters long.
Circle the best estimate for the length of the yarn.

10 centimeters

17 centimeters

22 centimeters

6. The ribbon is about 13 centimeters long.
Circle the best estimate for the length of the string.

5 centimeters

11 centimeters

17 centimeters

PROBLEM SOLVING REAL WORLD

Circle the best estimate.

7. About how long is a new crayon?

  about 5 centimeters

  about 10 centimeters

  about 20 centimeters

8. About how long is a new pencil?

  about 20 centimeters

  about 40 centimeters

  about 50 centimeters

9. **H.O.T.** Mr. Lott bought a roll of tape. He used 280 centimeters of the tape. Now there are 220 centimeters of tape on the roll. How many centimeters of tape were on the roll when he bought it?

_____ centimeters

10. ⭐ **Test Prep** The length of the feather is about 7 centimeters.

Which is the best estimate for the length of the yarn?

- ○ 5 centimeters
- ○ 7 centimeters
- ○ 14 centimeters
- ○ 70 centimeters

TAKE HOME ACTIVITY · Give your child an object that is about 5 centimeters long. Have him or her use it to estimate the lengths of some other objects.

FOR MORE PRACTICE:
Standards Practice Book, pp. P199–P200

Name _____

Centimeters and Meters

Essential Question Why is measuring in meters different from measuring in centimeters?

Listen and Draw REAL WORLD

Draw or write to describe how you measured each distance.

Distance 1

Distance 2

FOR THE TEACHER • Each small group uses a 1-meter piece of yarn to measure a distance marked on the floor with masking tape. Repeat for a different distance.

Math Talk
Describe how the length of your piece of yarn is different from the length of a centimeter.

Chapter 9

Model and Draw

I **meter** is the same as
100 centimeters.

The real door is about 200 centimeters tall.
The real door is also about 2 meters tall.

Share and Show

Measure to the nearest centimeter.
Then measure to the nearest meter.

Find the real object.	Measure.
chair 1.	_____ centimeters _____ meters
teacher's desk ✓ 2.	_____ centimeters _____ meters
wall ✓ 3.	_____ centimeters _____ meters

On Your Own

Measure to the nearest centimeter.
Then measure to the nearest meter.

Find the real object.	Measure.
4. **chalkboard**	_____ centimeters _____ meters
5. **bookshelf**	_____ centimeters _____ meters
6. **table**	_____ centimeters _____ meters
7. **bulletin board**	_____ centimeters _____ meters

PROBLEM SOLVING

8. **H.O.T.** Jason and his dad are walking next to a barn. They want to measure the length of the barn. Would the length be a greater number of centimeters or a greater number of meters?

_____

Explain your answer.

_____

_____

_____

_____

9. ⭐ **Test Prep** Use a centimeter ruler to measure.

Which is the best choice for the length of the pencil?

- ○ 30 centimeters
- ○ 25 centimeters
- ○ 20 centimeters
- ○ 15 centimeters

TAKE HOME ACTIVITY • Toss a small object and have your child measure the distance it travels in centimeters and in meters.

428 four hundred twenty-eight

FOR MORE PRACTICE:
Standards Practice Book, pp. P201–P202

© Houghton Mifflin Harcourt Publishing Company

Name _____

Act It Out • Length

Essential Question How can acting it out help
you solve a problem?

Eli wants to measure the distance around
a can of soup. He has a ruler, a yardstick,
a piece of string, and a marker. How should
he measure this distance?

🔑 Unlock the Problem REAL WORLD

What do I need to find?

_____

_____

What information do I need to use?

Eli has _____

_____

_____

Show how to solve the problem.

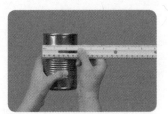

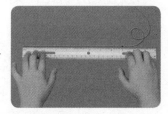

It is difficult to
measure a curved surface
with a flat tool.

You can find
the distance around the can
with the string. Then measure
the string with the ruler.

HOME CONNECTION • The *act it out* strategy is one that can help your
child to choose the best measurement tool for the situation.

© Houghton Mifflin Harcourt Publishing Company

Try Another Problem

- What do I need to find?
- What information do I need to use?

inch ruler   **yardstick**   **meterstick**   **string**

1. Selena wants to measure the length of the classroom in meters. What should she use from the box above to find the length? Describe how to find the length.

   Selena should use _____.

   _____

   _____

   _____

Choose the better measurement tool. Explain your choice.

2. Joseph wants to measure the length of a sidewalk. Which tool should he use: an inch ruler or a yardstick?

   Joseph should use _____ because

   _____

   _____

Math Talk

Explain how you chose the measurement tool for Exercise 1.

Share and Show

Choose what to use to measure the length. Then measure. Describe how you measured.

| inch ruler | yardstick | string | centimeter ruler |

3. Measure the length of a wall in your classroom.

What to measure with: _____

Length: _____ _____

How I measured: _____

_____

_____

4. Measure the distance around a pencil holder in inches.

What to measure with: _____

Length: _____ _____

How I measured: _____

_____

_____

On Your Own

Solve. Write or draw to explain.

5. Samir has a poster that is 41 inches long. His brother's poster is 27 inches long. His sister's poster is 31 inches long. How much longer is Samir's poster than his brother's poster?

_____ inches longer

6.  **H.O.T.** The chart shows the beads that Lisa had. Then she gave 6 beads to Ali and 3 beads to Kim. How many beads does Lisa have now?

Color	Number
pink	45
purple	28

_____ beads

7. ⭐ **Test Prep** Michael wants to measure some books to find a book that is 20 centimeters long. Which is the best tool for him to use?

○ yardstick

○ inch ruler

○ color tiles

○ centimeter ruler

 TAKE HOME ACTIVITY • Have your child list some objects that he or she would use a yardstick to measure.

FOR MORE PRACTICE:
Standards Practice Book, pp. P203–P204

Vocabulary

Use a word in the box to complete each sentence.

| foot |
| yard |
| inch |

1. A _____ is longer than a foot. (pp. 409–411)

2. An _____ is shorter than a foot. (pp. 405–408)

Concepts and Skills

Use a unit cube. Measure the length in centimeters. (pp. 413–416)

3.

_____ centimeters

Measure the length to the nearest centimeter. (pp. 417–420)

4.

_____ centimeters

Measure the length to the nearest inch. (pp. 397–400)

5.

_____ inches

Fill in the bubble for the correct answer choice.

6. Measure the length of the pen to the nearest inch.

Which is the best choice for the length of the pen? (pp. 397–400)

○   1 inch

○   3 inches

○   6 inches

○   10 inches

7. Sandra has a blue pencil and a red pencil.

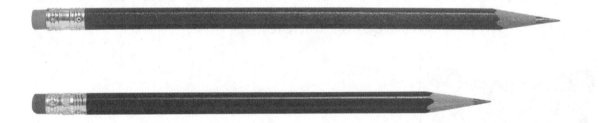

Jessie gives Sandra a green pencil that is shorter than the red pencil. Which sentence is true? (pp. 381–384)

○   The green pencil is the same length as the blue pencil.

○   The green pencil is shorter than the blue pencil.

○   The green pencil is longer than the blue pencil.

○   The green pencil is the same length as the red pencil.

Fill in the bubble for the correct answer choice.

8. Use a centimeter ruler to measure the length of the paintbrush to the nearest centimeter.

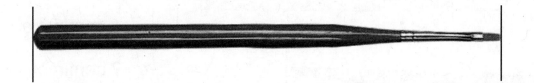

Which is the best choice for the length of the paintbrush? (pp. 417–420)

○ 13 centimeters

○ 18 centimeters

○ 21 centimeters

○ 23 centimeters

---

9. The paper clip is about 4 centimeters long. Which is the best estimate for the length of the string? (pp. 421–424)

○ 20 centimeters

○ 9 centimeters

○ 4 centimeters

○ 3 centimeters

Short Answer

10. The craft stick is about 12 centimeters long. Circle the best estimate for the length of the clothes pin.

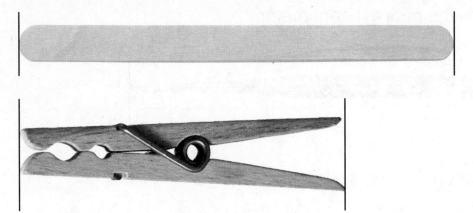

6 centimeters

9 centimeters

11 centimeters

Explain how you chose your estimate.

_____

_____

_____

Performance Task

11. Measure the length of the straw to the nearest centimeter.

_____ centimeters

Describe another way to measure the length of the straw and the tool you would use.

_____

_____

_____

Chapter 10

Weight, Mass, and Capacity

Curious About Math with Curious George

Most oranges grown in the United States are grown in California and Florida. Oranges are eaten as fruit and are used for juice. If 2 oranges weigh about 1 pound, about how many pounds do 8 oranges weigh?

Name _____

Show What You Know

Compare Weights

Circle the object that is heavier.
Put an X on the object that is lighter.

1.   2.

Use a Balance

Use and real objects. Measure with ▪.

Object	Measurement
3. markers	about _____ ▪
4. eraser	about _____ ▪

Use Nonstandard Units to Measure Capacity

Use and real objects. Measure with 🥤.

Container	Measurement
5. travel cup	about _____ 🥤
6. mug	about _____ 🥤

 Family note: This page checks your child's understanding of important skills needed for success in Chapter 10.

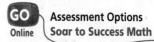

Review Words
weight
heavier
lighter

Vocabulary Builder

Visualize It

Fill in the graphic organizer to describe how the **weights** of two different objects compare. Use the review words.

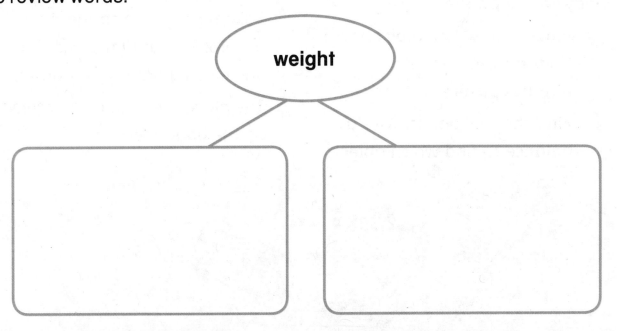

weight

Understand Vocabulary

Use review words to complete the sentences.

1. The stapler is _____ than the eraser.

2. The eraser is _____ than the stapler.

GO Online • eStudent Edition • Multimedia eGlossary

Game Heavier or Lighter?

Materials

- 12 ● • 12 ○ • ⚖

Play with a partner.

① Place your ● on a picture. Your partner places a ○ on another picture.

② Find the real objects. Use a balance to find which object is heavier. The player with the heavier object leaves the counter on that picture.

③ Take turns choosing the first picture. Play until there is only one picture without a counter.

④ The player with more counters on the board wins.

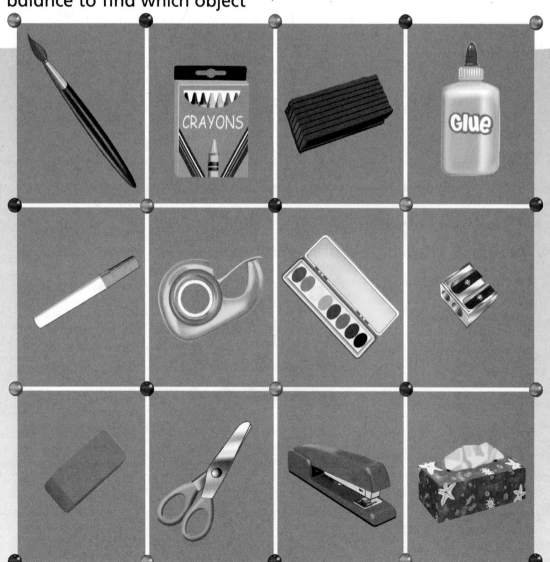

Name _____

Ounces and Pounds

Essential Question How can you choose and use units to measure weights of objects?

Listen and Draw · REAL WORLD

Draw and label the things the children bought.

Devin's Bag	Casey's Bag

FOR THE TEACHER • Read the following problem. Devin and Casey each bought two school supplies. Devin bought heavy items and Casey bought light items. They bought a pencil, a bottle of glue, a pair of scissors, and a box of 24 crayons. Have children weigh each item on a balance with cubes, and then draw the two items in the correct bag for each.

Math Talk
How did you decide which items to draw in each bag?

Model and Draw

Weight is the measure of how heavy an object is.

Use **ounces** to measure the weight of a light object.

Use **pounds** to measure the weight of a heavier object.

I pound is the same as 16 ounces.

A strawberry weighs about 1 ounce.

A grapefruit weighs about 1 pound.

Share and Show

Math Board

	Find the object.	Choose the unit.	Measure.
1.	scissors 	(ounce) / pound	about __5__ ounces
2.	stapler	ounce / pound	about _____ _____
✓ 3.	book	ounce / pound	about _____ _____
✓ 4.	eraser	ounce / pound	about _____ _____

On Your Own

Find the object.	Choose the unit.	Measure.
pack of pencils 5.	ounce pound	about _____ _____
notebook 6.	ounce pound	about _____ _____
full lunch box 7.	ounce pound	about _____ _____
marker 8.	ounce pound	about _____ _____
tape dispenser 9.	ounce pound	about _____ _____

Solve. Write or draw to explain.

10. **H.O.T.** Each book weighs 10 ounces. Each notepad weighs 5 ounces. How much does the box of crayons weigh?

_____ ounces

11. Fred has 3 baseballs. Each baseball weighs 6 ounces. What is the total weight of the baseballs?

_____ ounces

12. ⭐ **Test Prep** Each book weighs about 2 pounds. There are 4 books in the stack. About how much does the stack of books weigh?

- ○ 2 pounds
- ○ 4 pounds
- ○ 8 pounds
- ○ 12 pounds

TAKE HOME ACTIVITY • Choose three objects. Ask your child if ounces or pounds is the better unit for measuring each.

FOR MORE PRACTICE:
Standards Practice Book, pp. P209–P210

Name _____

Grams and Kilograms

Essential Question How can you choose and use units to measure mass?

Listen and Draw  REAL WORLD

Use a balance and cubes to compare two objects.
Draw those objects.

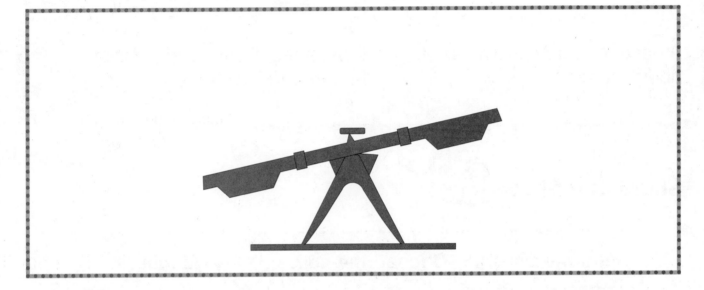

 FOR THE TEACHER • Have children find two classroom objects and balance each object with cubes. Then have children draw the objects on the balance pans to represent how their objects compared. Have them repeat the activity with two different objects.

Math Talk
How could you find items lighter than a dictionary?

Model and Draw

Use **grams** and **kilograms** to measure **mass**.
Mass is the amount of matter an object has.

Use grams to measure the mass of a light object.	Use kilograms to measure the mass of a heavier object.
A baseball card has a mass of about 1 gram.	A baseball bat has a mass of about 1 kilogram.

1 kilogram is the same as 1,000 grams.

Share and Show

	Find the object.	Choose the unit.	Measure.
1.	**crayon**	gram kilogram	about _____ _____
✓2.	**dictionary**	gram kilogram	about _____ _____
✓3.	**scissors**	gram kilogram	about _____ _____

Name _____

On Your Own

Find the object.	Choose the unit.	Measure.
stapler 4.	gram kilogram	about _____ _____
pack of paper Wide Ruled Notebook Paper 100 Sheets 5.	gram kilogram	about _____ _____
folder 6.	gram kilogram	about _____ _____
tape dispenser 7.	gram kilogram	about _____ _____
shoe 8.	gram kilogram	about _____ _____

PROBLEM SOLVING

REAL WORLD

Solve. Write or draw to explain.

9. **H.O.T.** The total mass of an eraser and a glue stick is 71 grams. The mass of the glue stick is 48 grams. What is the mass of the eraser?

_____ grams

10. The mass of each pen is 15 grams. What is the mass of 3 pens?

_____ grams

11. ⭐ **Test Prep** Ms. Walsh has a new bowling ball. Which is most likely the mass of the bowling ball?

- ○ 5 kilograms
- ○ 15 grams
- ○ 60 grams
- ○ 800 kilograms

TAKE HOME ACTIVITY · With your child, look for packaged foods that are measured in grams. Have him or her compare items by holding them, and then by comparing the measurements on the labels.

448 four hundred forty-eight

FOR MORE PRACTICE:
Standards Practice Book, pp. P211–P212

Name _____

Cups and Quarts

Essential Question How can you choose and use units to measure the capacities of containers?

Listen and Draw  REAL WORLD

Draw containers that can hold more than a small paper cup.

FOR THE TEACHER • Fill the small cup with water or rice and pour it into a larger container. Discuss with children how the fact that the larger container is not full means that it is larger, or holds more, than the small cup. Then have children find and draw containers that hold more than a small paper cup.

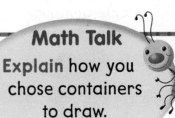

Math Talk
Explain how you chose containers to draw.

Capacity is the amount a container can hold.

Use **cups** to measure the capacity of a small container.

Use **quarts** to measure the capacity of a larger container.

I quart is the same as 4 cups.

This milk carton holds about 1 cup. | This milk carton holds about 1 quart.

Share and Show

Math Board

Find the container.	Choose the unit.	Measure.
1. juice carton 	cup quart	about _____ _____
2. pail	cup quart	about _____ _____
✓ 3. cereal bowl	cup quart	about _____ _____
✓ 4. detergent jug	cup quart	about _____ _____

Name _____

On Your Own

Find the container.	Choose the unit.	Measure.
vase 5.	cup quart	about ____ _____
mug 6.	cup quart	about ____ _____
yogurt container 7.	cup quart	about ____ _____
bucket 8.	cup quart	about ____ _____
water bottle 9.	cup quart	about ____ _____

Solve. Write or draw to explain.

10. Beth has four soup mugs. Each soup mug has a capacity of 2 cups. What is the total capacity of the soup mugs?

_____ cups

11. **H.O.T.** The table shows the juice that Ms. Tyson put in the punch bowl. The punch bowl is half full. What is the capacity of the punch bowl?

Juice in Punch Bowl	
Juice	**Amount**
apple	4 cups
grape	3 cups
cherry	3 cups

_____ cups

12. ⭐ **Test Prep**   Each jug holds about 2 quarts of water. Jake wants to take 6 quarts of water on a camping trip. How many jugs of water should he take?

- ○ 2 jugs
- ○ 3 jugs
- ○ 6 jugs
- ○ 12 jugs

 TAKE HOME ACTIVITY • Choose three containers. Ask your child if a cup or a quart is a better unit for measuring the capacity of each one.

FOR MORE PRACTICE:
Standards Practice Book, pp. P213–P214

Name _____

Milliliters and Liters

Essential Question How are milliliters and liters alike? How are they different?

Listen and Draw  REAL WORLD

Use a scoop and water to compare the capacities of two containers. Draw each container in the correct space.

less capacity	more capacity

FOR THE TEACHER • Give children a variety of containers (e.g., a half-gallon milk jug, a cereal bowl, a saucepan). Have children select 2 containers, measure how many scoops of rice or water each container can hold, and draw the containers to show how the capacities compare.

Math Talk
Name some containers that have a very small capacity.

Milliliters and **liters** are also units of capacity.

I milliliter is a small amount. I milliliter is about 20 drops of water.

I liter is the same as 1,000 milliliters.

This bottle can hold about 1 liter.

Share and Show

	Find the container.	Choose the unit.	Measure.
1.	**storage bin**	milliliter liter	about _____ _____
2.	**spoon**	milliliter liter	about _____ _____
✓ 3.	**paper cup**	milliliter liter	about _____ _____
✓ 4.	**bucket**	milliliter liter	about _____ _____

On Your Own

Find the container.	Choose the unit.	Measure.
soda bottle 5.	milliliter liter	about _____ _____
vase 6.	milliliter liter	about _____ _____
milk jug 7.	milliliter liter	about _____ _____
mug 8.	milliliter liter	about _____ _____
aquarium 9.	milliliter liter	about _____ _____

TAKE HOME ACTIVITY • With your child, look at labels on containers at the grocery store. Find containers with capacities less than 1 liter.

© Houghton Mifflin Harcourt Publishing Company

FOR MORE PRACTICE:
Standards Practice Book, pp. P215–P216

Name _____

✓ Mid-Chapter Checkpoint

Concepts (pp. 441–455)

Find the object.	Choose the unit.	Measure.
box of crayons 1.	ounce pound	about _____ _____
pencil 2.	gram kilogram	about _____ _____

Find the object.	Choose the unit.	Measure.
glass 3.	cup quart	about _____ _____
waste basket 4.	milliliter liter	about _____ _____

⭐ **Test Prep**

5. Which is most likely the weight of the baseball? (pp. 441–444)

- ○ 5 ounces
- ○ 5 pounds
- ○ 50 ounces
- ○ 50 pounds

Name _____

Choose the Unit

Essential Question How do you decide which unit to use to measure?

Listen and Draw REAL WORLD

Compare weights of objects to the weight of a stapler.
Compare capacities of containers to the capacity of a jar.

less than	more than

less than	more than

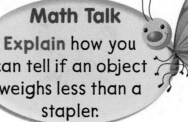

Math Talk

Explain how you can tell if an object weighs less than a stapler.

FOR THE TEACHER • Show children a stapler. Have them name and draw a classroom object that weighs less than the stapler and a classroom object that weighs more than the stapler. Repeat for containers that hold less than and more than a jar.

Model and Draw

Think about the weight of an object or the size of a container to help you decide which unit to use to measure.

> Use small units for light objects and for small containers.

> Use larger units for heavy objects and for large containers.

Share and Show

Circle the better unit of measure for the weight or the mass of the object.

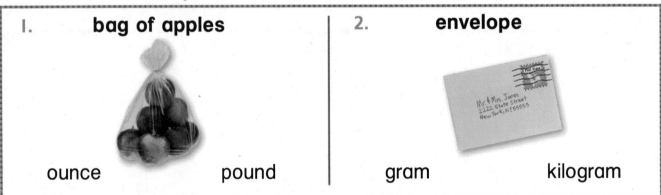

1. **bag of apples**

ounce   pound

2. **envelope**

gram   kilogram

Circle the better unit of measure for the capacity of the container.

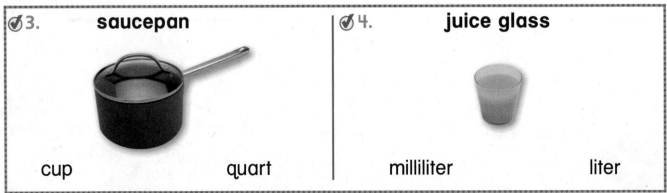

☑ 3. **saucepan**

cup   quart

☑ 4. **juice glass**

milliliter   liter

On Your Own

Circle the better unit of measure for the weight or
the mass of the object.

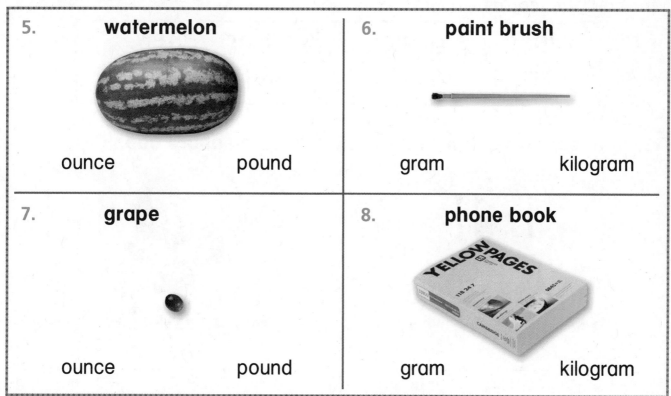

5. watermelon

ounce   pound

6. paint brush

gram   kilogram

7. grape

ounce   pound

8. phone book

gram   kilogram

Circle the better unit of measure for the capacity of
the container.

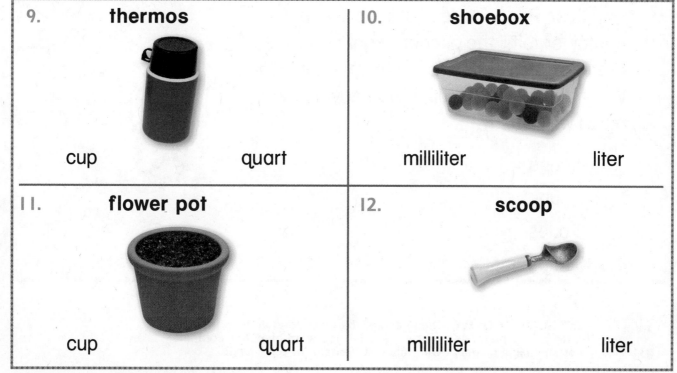

9. thermos

cup   quart

10. shoebox

milliliter   liter

11. flower pot

cup   quart

12. scoop

milliliter   liter

H.O.T. Use the words in the box. Write all of the units that could be used.

cup	gram	kilogram	liter
milliliter	ounce	pound	quart

13. **measure weight or mass**

_____

_____

14. **measure capacity**

_____

_____

15. ⭐ **Test Prep** Kyle is using a 1-cup container to fill the pitcher. Right now, there are 2 cups of juice in the pitcher. When the pitcher is full, about how much will it hold?

○ 2 cups

○ 8 cups

○ 20 cups

○ 80 cups

TAKE HOME ACTIVITY · Name one of the measuring units in the box at the top of this page. Ask your child to tell you what object or container he or she might measure with this unit. Repeat for other units.

FOR MORE PRACTICE:
Standards Practice Book, pp. P217–P218

Name _____

Act It Out • Measurement

Essential Question How can acting it out help you choose a measuring tool?

Ann wants to find the capacity of this pitcher. She has a ruler, a scale, and a liter container. Which measuring tool should she use?

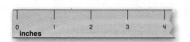

Use a ruler to measure length.

Use a scale to measure weight.

Use a liter container to measure capacity.

🔑 Unlock the Problem

What do I need to find?

which ___measuring tool___

Ann should use to find the amount of water the pitcher will hold

What information do I need to use?

Ann has ___a ruler, a scale,___

___and a liter container.___

Show how to solve the problem.

Use a _____
to measure capacity.

HOME CONNECTION • Your child used the act it out strategy to help him or her determine the best measuring tool to use to measure length, weight, and capacity.

Try Another Problem

Choose the best tool to use to measure.

- What do I need to find?
- What information do I need to use?

1. Kristin wants to find how tall the pitcher is. Which measuring tool should she choose? Explain.

Kristin should use _____ because

_____

_____

_____

2. Brad wants to find how heavy the pitcher is. Which measuring tool should he choose? Explain.

Brad should use _____ because

_____

_____

_____

Math Talk
Explain how you decided which measuring tool to use for Exercise 2.

Share and Show

Choose the best tool to measure.

ruler

scale

liter container

---

3. Maya wants to know how heavy her lunchbox is. Which tool should she use?

_____

4. Gabe wants to know how much water this fish bowl will hold. Which tool should he use?

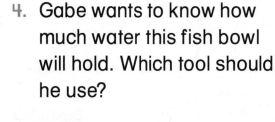

_____

---

5. Jim wants to know how much water this pot will hold. Which tool should he use?

_____

6. Jenna wants to know how wide her book is. Which tool should she use?

_____

☑ 7. Lee wants to know how long her pencil is. Which tool should she use?

_____

☑ 8. Neil wants to know how heavy the bag of oranges is. Which tool should he use?

_____

On Your Own

Choose a way to solve.
Write or draw to explain.

9. One box of books weighs 26 pounds. Another box of books weighs 35 pounds. How much do the two boxes of books weigh in all?

_____ pounds

---

10. **H.O.T.** Rebecca needs 900 milliliters of water. She has a pitcher with 650 milliliters of water and a cup with 120 milliliters of water. How many more milliliters does she need?

_____ more milliliters

---

11. ⭐ **Test Prep** Emma collected 12 oak leaves. She collected twice as many maple leaves as oak leaves. How many leaves did she collect in all?

- ○ 12
- ○ 24
- ○ 36
- ○ 48

TAKE HOME ACTIVITY • Ask your child to name objects or containers that he or she could use a scale, an inch ruler, or a liter container to measure.

FOR MORE PRACTICE: Standards Practice Book, pp. P219–P220

Chapter 10 Review/Test

Vocabulary

Use a word in the box to complete each sentence.

| milliliter |
| pound |
| capacity |

1. One _____ is about 20 drops of water. (pp. 453–455)

2. _____ is the amount a container can hold. (pp. 449–452)

Concepts (pp. 441–455)

Find the object.	Choose the unit.	Measure.
dictionary	ounce pound	about _____ _____
scissors	gram kilogram	about _____ _____
mug	cup quart	about _____ _____
pitcher	milliliter liter	about _____ _____

3.
4.
5.
6.

Fill in the bubble for the correct answer choice.

7. Sarah wants to measure the weight of her backpack. Which unit should she use to measure its weight? (pp.457–460)

○ pound
○ liter
○ cup
○ quart

8. The total mass of a pencil and an eraser is 45 grams. The eraser has a mass of 25 grams.

What is the mass of the pencil? (pp.445–448)

○ 20 grams
○ 30 grams
○ 60 grams
○ 70 grams

9. James made a pitcher of lemonade for himself and three friends. Which is most likely to be the capacity of the pitcher? (pp.449–452)

○ I cup
○ 2 cups
○ I quart
○ 10 quarts

Name _____

Fill in the bubble for the correct answer choice.

10. Kristi wants to balance a toy boat with some blocks. The boat weighs 16 ounces. Each block weighs 2 ounces.

How many blocks are needed? (pp.441–444)

- ○ 2 blocks
- ○ 8 blocks
- ○ 14 blocks
- ○ 16 blocks

11. Ava is drinking a glass of apple juice. Which is most likely the capacity of her glass? (pp.453–456)

- ○ 15 milliliters
- ○ 25 liters
- ○ 200 milliliters
- ○ 500 liters

12. Oscar is drinking milk in the cafeteria. Which is most likely the capacity of his milk carton? (pp.449–451)

- ○ 50 quarts
- ○ 10 liters
- ○ 3 milliliters
- ○ 1 cup

Short Answer

13. Each box of crayons weighs 4 ounces. How much does the glue bottle weigh? Explain.

_____

_____

_____

Performance Assessment

14. Jenna wants to buy a fish bowl and some fish. First, she measures the fish bowl.

   What measurement should she find?

_____

_____

   Name the tool she can use to measure.

   Describe how she can use the tool.

_____

_____

_____

_____

Curious About Math with
Curious George

A sundial shows the time using the position of the sun. It has numbers around it, like a clockface. What numbers are on a clockface?

Show What You Know ✓

Order Numbers to 100 on a Number Line

Write the number that is just before, between, or just after.

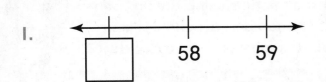

1. [ ]   58   59

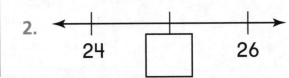

2. 24   [ ]   26

Nickels

Count by fives. Write the total value.

3.

_____   _____   _____   _____   _____ total

Time to the Hour

Write the time shown on the clock.

4.    5.    6.

      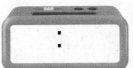

Family note: This page checks your child's understanding of important skills needed for success in Chapter 11.

GO Online   Assessment Options   Soar to Success Math

Vocabulary Builder

Review Words
skip count
pattern
count on

Visualize It

Fill in the graphic organizer.
Show ways to **skip count**.

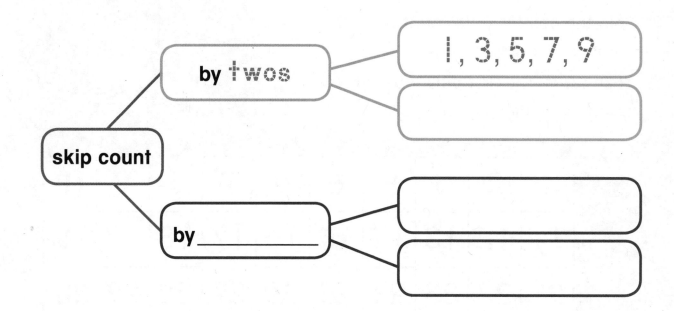

skip count

by twos — 1, 3, 5, 7, 9

by _____

Understand Vocabulary

Write the missing numbers in each counting **pattern.**

1. **Skip count** by tens. 25, ____, ____, 55, ____, ____, 85, ____

2. **Skip count** by fives. 10, 15, ____, ____, ____, 35, ____, ____

3. **Count on** by ones. 40, ____, ____, ____, 44, ____, 46, ____

Game

5 and 10 Count

Materials • 1 ▢ • 1 ▢ • ◉

Play with a partner.

① Spin the pointer on ◉ for your starting number. Put your cube on the number.

② Spin the pointer. Skip count by that number two times.

③ Take turns. The first player to get to 100 wins. Play again.

1	2	3	4	**5**	6	7	8	9	**10**
11	12	13	14	**15**	16	17	18	19	**20**
21	22	23	24	**25**	26	27	28	29	**30**
31	32	33	34	**35**	36	37	38	39	**40**
41	42	43	44	**45**	46	47	48	49	**50**
51	52	53	54	**55**	56	57	58	59	**60**
61	62	63	64	**65**	66	67	68	69	**70**
71	72	73	74	**75**	76	77	78	79	**80**
81	82	83	84	**85**	86	87	88	89	**90**
91	92	93	94	**95**	96	97	98	99	**100**

Name _____

Dimes, Nickels, and Pennies

Essential Question How can you find the total value of a group of dimes, nickels, and pennies?

Listen and Draw REAL WORLD

Sort the coins. Then draw the coins.

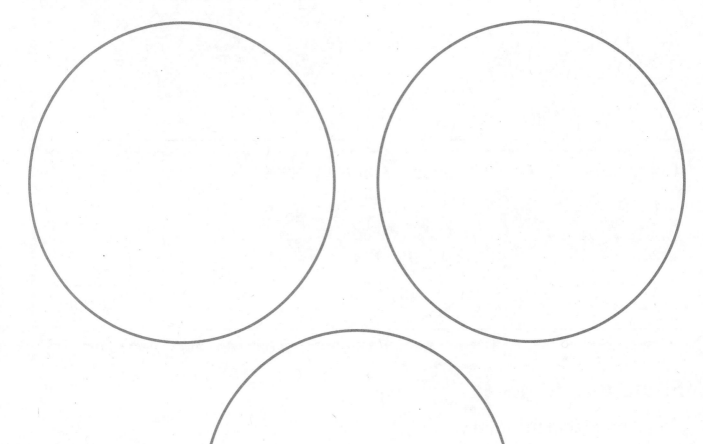

FOR THE TEACHER • Distribute play coins of dimes, nickels, and pennies and discuss their values. Have children sort the coins and draw them inside the three circles. Have children label the drawings with the numbers *1*, *5*, or *10* to indicate the cent value of each coin drawn.

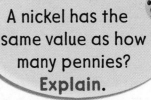
Math Talk
A nickel has the same value as how many pennies?
Explain.

Chapter 11

Model and Draw

dime	¢ is a **cent sign**.	**nickel**	**penny**
10 cents = 10¢		5 cents = 5¢	1 cent = 1¢

Count dimes by tens.

10¢, 20¢, _____

Count nickels by fives.

5¢, 10¢, _____

Count by tens.   Count by fives.   Count by ones.

10¢, 20¢, 25¢, _____

☐

total value

Share and Show   Math Board

Count on to find the total value.

✓ 1.

_____

☐

total value

✓ 2.

_____

☐

total value

474 four hundred seventy-four

© Houghton Mifflin Harcourt Publishing Company

On Your Own

Count on to find the total value.

3.

_____

total value ☐

4.

_____

total value ☐

5.

total value ☐

6.

total value ☐

7.

total value ☐

8.

total value ☐

PROBLEM SOLVING

Choose a way to solve.
Write or draw to explain.

9. Maggie had 5 nickels in her pocket. She gave 2 nickels to her sister. What is the total value of the coins in Maggie's pocket now?

_____

10. Jake has 2 dimes in his desk and 6 dimes in his hand. What is the total value of the coins Jake has?

_____

11. **H.O.T.** Draw two ways to show 25¢.
You can use dimes, nickels, and pennies.

12. ⭐ **Test Prep**   Sue has these coins. How much money is this?

- ○ 4¢
- ○ 30¢
- ○ 40¢
- ○ 80¢

TAKE HOME ACTIVITY • Show your child a collection of five coins, with dimes, nickels, and pennies. Ask your child to find the total value.

FOR MORE PRACTICE:
Standards Practice Book, pp. P225–P226

Name _____

Half Dollars and Quarters

Essential Question How can you find the total value of a group of coins?

Listen and Draw REAL WORLD

Sort the coins. Then draw the coins.

FOR THE TEACHER • Distribute play coins of half dollars and quarters and discuss their values. Have children sort the coins and draw them inside the two boxes. Have them correctly label the drawings with *25¢* or *50¢*.

Math Talk

Describe how the value of a half dollar is greater than the value of a quarter.

half dollar

50 cents

50¢

quarter

25 cents

25¢

50¢, 75¢, 85¢, _____

[ ] total value

Share and Show

Count on to find the total value.

1.

_____

[ ] total value

2.

_____

[ ] total value

3.

_____

[ ] total value

On Your Own

Count on to find the total value.

4.

_____

total value

5.

_____

total value

6.

total value

7.

total value

8.

total value

PROBLEM SOLVING REAL WORLD

Read the clue. Choose the name of a coin from the box to answer the question.

| nickel half dollar |
| quarter |

9. I have the same value as 5 pennies.

   What coin am I?

   _____

10. I have the same value as 25 pennies.

    What coin am I?

    _____

11. I have the same value as 5 dimes.

    What coin am I?

    _____

12. **H.O.T.** I have the same value as a group of 4 nickels and 5 pennies.

    What coin am I?

    _____

13. ⭐ **Test Prep** Tom gives these coins to his brother.

    How much money does Tom give to his brother?

    ○ 15¢

    ○ 30¢

    ○ 55¢

    ○ 75¢

TAKE HOME ACTIVITY · Have your child find the total value of a combination of coins up to 99¢.

480 four hundred eighty

Name _____

Count Collections

Essential Question How do you order coins to help find the total value?

Listen and Draw REAL WORLD

Line up the coins from greatest value to least value. Then draw the coins in that order.

greatest   least

greatest   least

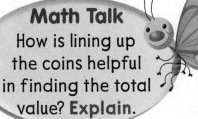

Math Talk
How is lining up the coins helpful in finding the total value? **Explain.**

FOR THE TEACHER • Give each child four or five play coins of different values. Have children order their coins and then draw them. Have children trade sets of coins and repeat.

Chapter 11

Order coins from greatest value to least value.
Then find the total value.

Count the cents.
25, 50, 60, 61, 62

_____
total value

Share and Show

Draw and label the coins from greatest
to least value. Find the total value.

Remember: Write the
cent sign (¢).

I.

_____

✓2.

_____

✓3.

_____

482 four hundred eighty-two

On Your Own

Draw and label the coins from greatest
to least value. Find the total value.

4.

_____

5.

_____

6.

_____

7.

_____

8.

_____

Solve. Write or draw to explain.

9. Paulo has these coins.

He spends 1 quarter. How much money does he have left? _____

---

10. These coins are in Rachel's bank.

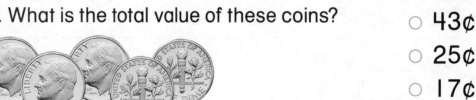

Rachel adds 1 nickel to her bank.
How much money is in Rachel's bank now?   _____

---

11. **H.O.T.** Bobby has only nickels and dimes.
He has twice as many nickels as dimes.
The total value of his coins is 60¢.
What coins does Bobby have?

_____ nickels _____ dimes

---

12. ⭐ **Test Prep** Tyler has these coins in his
pocket. What is the total value of these coins?

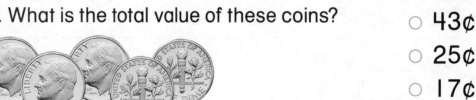

- ○ 50¢
- ○ 43¢
- ○ 25¢
- ○ 17¢

TAKE HOME ACTIVITY · Have your child draw and label
coins with a total value of 72¢.

FOR MORE PRACTICE:
Standards Practice Book, pp. P229–P230

Name _____

Find a Pattern • Money

Essential Question How can finding a pattern help you solve a problem?

Doug has 6 dimes.
He wants to trade them for pennies.
How many pennies should he get?

Unlock the Problem REAL WORLD

What do I need to find?

how many pennies

Doug should get

What information do I need to use?

Doug has __6__ dimes.

I dime equals __10__ pennies.

Show how to solve the problem.

You can find a pattern. Complete the table.

dimes	1	2	3	4	5	6
pennies						

Doug should get _____ pennies.

HOME CONNECTION • Your child found a pattern to solve a problem.
The pattern for this problem is shown in a table.

Try Another Problem

Find a pattern. Complete the table.

- What do I need to find?
- What information do I need to use?

1. Emily has 5 dimes. She wants to trade them for nickels. How many nickels should she get?

dimes	1	2	3	4	5
nickels	2				

Emily should get _____ nickels.

2. Joe has 6 nickels. He wants to trade them for pennies. How many pennies should he get?

nickels	1	2	3	4	5	6
pennies	5					

Joe should get _____ pennies.

Math Talk

How did finding a pattern help you solve the second problem? **Explain.**

Name _____

Share and Show

Find a pattern. Complete the table.

☑ **3.** Val has 4 quarters. She wants to trade them for nickels. How many nickels should she get?

quarters	1	2	3	4
nickels				

Val should get _____ nickels.

☑ **4.** Travis has 8 dimes. He wants to trade them for pennies. How many pennies should he get?

dimes	1	2	3	4	5	6	7	8
pennies								

Travis should get _____ pennies.

---

5. Colleen has 3 half dollars. She wants to trade them for nickels. How many nickels should she get?

half dollars	1	2	3
nickels			

Colleen should get _____ nickels.

On Your Own

Solve. Write or draw to explain.

6. There are some books about animals and 275 books about sports at the library. There are 687 books about animals and sports at the library altogether. How many books about animals are at the library?

_____ books

7. 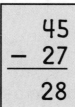 Use addition to check Frank's work. If there is an error, rewrite the problem to show the correct difference.

$$\begin{array}{r} 45 \\ -\ 27 \\ \hline 28 \end{array}$$

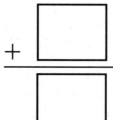

8. ⭐ **Test Prep** Rose has 7 nickels. She wants to trade those nickels for pennies. How many pennies should she get?

- ○ 35
- ○ 30
- ○ 14
- ○ 5

TAKE HOME ACTIVITY • Have your child explain how he or she solved Exercise 8.

488 four hundred eighty-eight

© Houghton Mifflin Harcourt Publishing Company

FOR MORE PRACTICE:
Standards Practice Book, pp. P231–P232

Name _____

One Dollar

Essential Question How can you show the value of one dollar with coins?

Listen and Draw  REAL WORLD

Draw the coins. Write the total value.

_____

_____

Math Talk
How many pennies have the same value as 80¢? **Explain.**

FOR THE TEACHER • In the first box, have children draw eight nickels and then count to find the total value. In the second box, have children draw eight dimes and then count to find the total value.

One **dollar** has the same value as 100 cents.

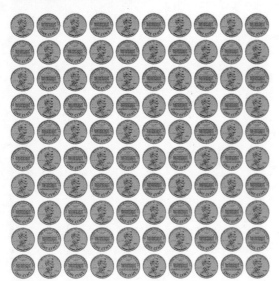

$1.00 = 100¢

dollar sign $\longrightarrow$ $\llcorner$ decimal point

The decimal point separates the dollars from the cents.

Share and Show

Draw the coins to show $1.00. Write the total value.

Count 100 cents to make one dollar.

1. half dollars

_____

✓ 2. quarters

_____

✓ 3. dimes

_____

On Your Own

Circle coins to make $1.00.
Cross out the coins you do not use.

4.

5.

6.

7.

TAKE HOME ACTIVITY • Have your child draw a group of
coins to show $1.00.

Chapter 11 • Lesson 5

FOR MORE PRACTICE:
Standards Practice Book, pp. P233–P234

four hundred ninety-one **491**

Mid-Chapter Checkpoint

Concepts and Skills

Count on to find the total value. (pp. 473–476)

1.

□

total value

Find a pattern. Complete the table. (pp. 485–488)

2. Joel has 7 dimes. He wants to trade them for nickels. How many nickels should he get?

dimes	1	2	3	4	5	6	7
nickels							

Joel should get _____ nickels.

Count on to find the total value. (pp. 477–480)

3.

□

total value

4. ⭐ **Test Prep** Mary used these coins to buy a folder. What is the total value of these coins? (pp. 481–484)

○ 30¢
○ 52¢
○ 60¢
○ 70¢

Name _____

Telling Time

Essential Question How do you tell time to the hour and half hour on a clock that has only an hour hand?

Listen and Draw REAL WORLD

Write the rest of the numbers on the clockface.

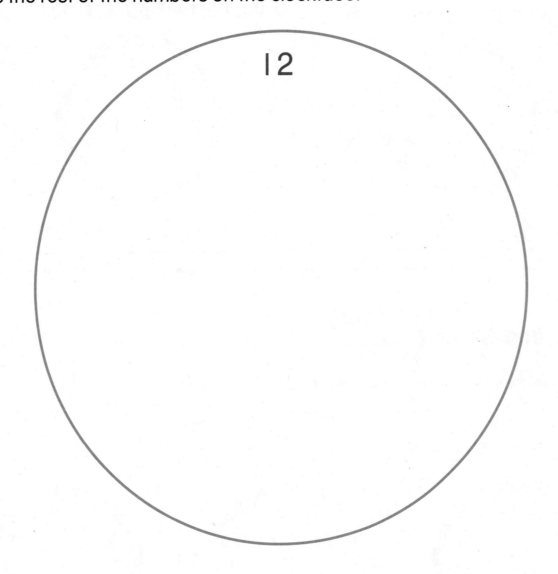

Math Talk
Explain how a clockface is similar to a number line.

HOME CONNECTION • This activity is a review of the face of an analog clock. Your child will use both analog and digital clocks to tell time in the next few lessons.

Model and Draw

The **hour hand** moves from one number to the next number as 1 **hour** passes.

The hour hand on this clock is pointing to the 3. This means that the time is about 3 o'clock.

3:00

The hour hand moves halfway from one number to the next number as a **half hour** passes.

The hour hand on this clock is halfway between 10:00 and 11:00. It is **half past** 10:00.

half past 10:00

Share and Show

Look at where the hour hand points. Write the time.

1.

_____

☑ 2.

_____

☑ 3.

_____

On Your Own

Look at where the hour hand points. Write the time.

4.

_____

5.

_____

6.

_____

7.

_____

8.

_____

9.

_____

10.

_____

11.

_____

12.

_____

PROBLEM SOLVING

REAL WORLD

13. It is half past 9:00. Draw the hour hand to show the time.

14. It is 7:00. Draw the hour hand to show the time.

15. H.O.T. Write your own problem about a time like the ones above. Explain how to solve.

_____

_____

_____

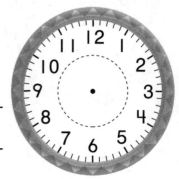

16. ⭐ **Test Prep** What time is shown on this clock?

○ 10:00   ○ half past 10:00

○ 11:00   ○ half past 11:00

TAKE HOME ACTIVITY • Say a time, such as 3:00. Ask your child to describe where the hour hand points at this time.

FOR MORE PRACTICE:
Standards Practice Book, pp. P235–P236

Name _____

Time to the Hour and Half Hour

Essential Question How do you tell time to the hour and half hour on an analog clock?

Listen and Draw REAL WORLD

Draw the hour hand to show each time.

FOR THE TEACHER • Call out times to the hour and to the half hour. Begin with 3:00. Have children draw the hour hand to show the time. Repeat the activity for half past 5:00, 11:00, and half past 8:00.

Math Talk
Describe where the hour hand points to show half past 4:00.

It takes 5 **minutes** for the **minute hand** to move from one number to the next number on a clockface.

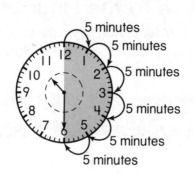

5 minutes
5 minutes
5 minutes
5 minutes
5 minutes
5 minutes

Trace the clock hands to show 4:00 and 4:30. Write the times.

4:00

4:30

The 30 tells you that the time is 30 minutes after the hour.

Share and Show Math Board

Look at the clock hands. Write the time.

1.

:

✓ 2.

:

✓ 3.

:

Name _____

On Your Own

Look at the clock hands. Write the time.

4.

:

5.

:

6.

:

7.

:

8.

:

9.

:

H.O.T. Look at the time. Draw the hour hand and the minute hand to show the same time.

10.

7:30

11.

2:00

12.

11:00

PROBLEM SOLVING

REAL WORLD

Write Math

13. **H.O.T.** Allie eats lunch when the hour hand points halfway between the 11 and the 12, and the minute hand points to the 6. When does Allie eat lunch? Show the time on both clocks.

How do you know what time to write in the digital clock? Explain.

_____

_____

_____

14. ⭐ **Test Prep** Reggie's guitar lesson starts at 10:30. Which clock shows this time?

○    ○

○    ○

TAKE HOME ACTIVITY · Have your child explain how he or she completed the exercises on this page.

FOR MORE PRACTICE:
Standards Practice Book, pp. P237–P238

Name _____

Time to 5 Minutes

Essential Question How do you tell and show time to five minutes?

Listen and Draw  REAL WORLD

Draw the hour hand and the minute hand to show the time.

 FOR THE TEACHER • Read the following story and have children draw the hour and minute hands to show each time. Sofia goes to music at 10:30. She goes to the playground at 11:00. She eats lunch at 11:30. Show the times Sofia does these things.

Math Talk
Describe where the minute hand points to show half past the hour.

Chapter 11

five hundred one **501**

Model and Draw

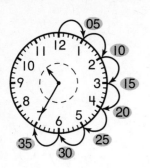

You can skip count by fives to help you tell time.

What does it mean when the minute hand points to the 7?

Skip count by fives until you reach the 7.

The hour hand points between the 10 and the 11. The minute hand points to the 7.

The time is ___10:35___.

Share and Show

Math Board

Look at the clock hands. Write the time.

1.

2.

3.

4.

✓5.

✓6.

On Your Own

Look at the clock hands. Write the time.

7.

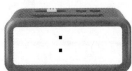

8.

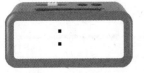

9.

10.

11.

12.

H.O.T. Look at the time.
Draw the minute hand to show the same time.

13.

14.

15.

Draw the minute hand to show the time.
Then write the time on the clock.

16. My hour hand points between
the 8 and the 9. My minute hand
points to the 5. What time do
I show?

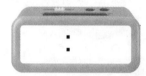

17. **H.O.T.** How many minutes does it take for the minute
hand to travel around the clock from 12 to 12?

_____

18. ⭐ **Test Prep** What time is shown on this clock?

○ 1:45

○ 12:45

○ 12:09

○ 9:05

TAKE HOME ACTIVITY · Have your child draw a large blank clockface
and use two pencils as clock hands to show some different times.

FOR MORE PRACTICE:
Standards Practice Book, pp. P239–P240

Time to the Minute

Essential Question How do you tell and show time to the minute?

Listen and Draw REAL WORLD

Write the times in the digital clocks.
Then label the clocks.

_____

_____

_____

_____

FOR THE TEACHER • Write *Luke*, *Beth*, *Kelly*, and *Mike* on the board. Have children write the time for each analog clock in the digital clock below it. Read the story and have children write the name to show which child does an activity at that time. Luke plays football at 3:25. Beth eats lunch at 11:45. Kelly sets the table at 6:30. Mike eats breakfast at 8:15.

Math Talk
Where does the minute hand point to show 15 minutes past the hour? Explain.

Model and Draw

Each mark along the circle of the clockface stands for
1 minute. Find the minutes past 9:00 to tell the time.

First, count by fives.

Then, count on by ones.

Share and Show

Look at the clock hands. Write the time.

1.

2.

3.

4.

✓ 5.

✓ 6.

© Houghton Mifflin Harcourt Publishing Company

On Your Own

Look at the clock hands. Write the time.

7.

☐ : ☐

8.

☐ : ☐

9.

☐ : ☐

10.

☐ : ☐

11.

☐ : ☐

12.

☐ : ☐

H.O.T. Look at the time.
Draw the minute hand to show the same time.

13.

14.

15.

PROBLEM SOLVING

REAL WORLD

Write Math

16. **H.O.T.** Look at the clocks to see when Rachel started each activity.

ate a snack

played ball

read a book

Write the times of the activities in order.
Start with the thing Rachel did first.

first

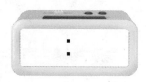

second

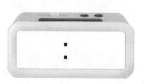

third

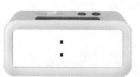

17. ⭐ **Test Prep** What time is shown on this clock?

- ○ 12:30
- ○ 3:06
- ○ 6:03
- ○ 6:30

TAKE HOME ACTIVITY • Name a time to the minute. Ask your child to describe where the clock hands point for this time.

508 five hundred eight

© Houghton Mifflin Harcourt Publishing Company

FOR MORE PRACTICE:
Standards Practice Book, pp. P241–P242

Name _____

Units of Time

Essential Question How can you compare days, weeks, months, and years?

Listen and Draw REAL WORLD

Look at the times shown on both kinds of clocks.
Draw lines to match the times on the clocks.

 5:21 •

 7:30 •

1:45 •

11:05 •

 •

 •

•

 •

HOME CONNECTION • This activity is a review of telling time on analog and digital clocks. Your child has learned about telling time to the hour, half hour, 5 minutes, and minute.

Math Talk
Describe how a digital clock and an analog clock are different.

Model and Draw

Days, **weeks**, **months**, and **years** are used to measure time.

Maria had a library book for 12 days.

Is this **more than, less than,** or **the same as** 1 week?

Time Relationships
There are 60 minutes in 1 hour.
There are 24 hours in 1 day.
There are 7 days in 1 week.
There are about 4 weeks in 1 month.
There are 12 months in 1 year.

12 days is _____ 1 week.

Share and Show

Write **more than, less than,** or **the same as** to complete the sentence.

1. Ellie and a friend drew pictures for 25 minutes.

   This is _____ 1 hour.

✓2. Mitch and his family were on vacation for 2 weeks.

   This is _____ 7 days.

✓3. The map was on the classroom wall for 1 month.

   This is _____ 3 weeks.

On Your Own

Write **more than, less than,** or **the same as** to complete the sentence.

Time Relationships
There are 60 minutes in 1 hour.
There are 24 hours in 1 day.
There are 7 days in 1 week.
There are about 4 weeks in 1 month.
There are 12 months in 1 year.

4. Christopher had a rock collection for 1 year.

 This is _____ 12 months.

5. Snow was on the ground for 2 weeks.

 This is _____ 1 month.

6. Pete and his family were at the park for 4 hours.

 This is _____ 1 day.

7. Judy stayed with her grandparents for 10 days.

 This is _____ 1 week.

8. Jen worked on a puzzle for 60 minutes.

 This is _____ 1 hour.

PROBLEM SOLVING  REAL WORLD

Write Math

Circle to show your answer.

9. Claudia and her uncle plan to bake a cake. Which is the better way to measure the time it will take to bake the cake?

weeks   minutes

10. Anthony and his family went camping. Which is the better way to measure the time they were camping?

minutes   days

11. **H.O.T.** Wesley was at camp for 3 weeks. Mark was at camp for 19 days. Who was at camp for a greater amount of time? _____

Explain how you found your answer.

_____

_____

_____

12. ⭐ **Test Prep** Kelly visited her grandmother for 7 days. Which amount of time is the same as 7 days?

○ 1 hour
○ 1 month
○ 1 day
○ 1 week

TAKE HOME ACTIVITY · Use strips of paper to make a matching game that will help your child review the time relationships in this lesson.

FOR MORE PRACTICE:
Standards Practice Book, pp. P243–P244

✓ Chapter 11 Review/Test

Vocabulary

Use a term in the box to complete each sentence.

dime
dollar
minute hand
hour hand

1. One _____ has the same value as 100 cents. (pp. 489–491)

2. The value of one _____ is 10¢. (pp. 473–476)

3. At half past 2:00, the _____ points halfway between the 2 and the 3. (pp. 493–496)

Concepts and Skills

Count on to find the total value. (pp. 477–480)

4.

☐

total value

Draw and label the coins from greatest to least value. Find the total value. (pp. 481–484)

5.

_____

Fill in the bubble for the correct answer choice.

6. The clock shows the time that the museum opens. What time is shown? (pp. 497–500)

○ 8:00

○ 9:00

○ 10:00

○ 12:00

---

7. The play begins at 8:30. Which clock shows 8:30? (pp. 497–500)

○

○

○

○

---

8. The clock shows the time that soccer practice starts. What time is shown on the clock? (pp. 501–504)

○ 7:23

○ 6:20

○ 5:30

○ 4:35

Fill in the bubble for the correct answer choice.

9. Lindsey wants to buy lemonade that costs one dollar. Which coins could she use to buy the lemonade? (pp. 489–491)

- ○ 4 nickels
- ○ 4 pennies
- ○ 4 quarters
- ○ 4 dimes

10. Pete went to softball camp for 10 days. Which of these is more than 10 days? (pp. 509–512)

- ○ 1 week
- ○ 1 day
- ○ 1 month
- ○ 1 hour

11. The train left the station at the time shown on the clock. What time is shown on the clock? (pp. 505–508)

- ○ 2:57
- ○ 3:11
- ○ 3:55
- ○ 11:15

Short Answer

12. Find a pattern. Complete the table.
Adam has 7 dimes. He wants to trade them
for nickels. How many nickels should he get?

dimes	1	2	3	4	5	6	7
nickels							

Adam should get _____ nickels.

What skip counting pattern did you use in this table?

_____

Performance Task

13. Draw and label the coins from greatest
to least value. Find the total value.

_____

How would the total value be different if a quarter
was added to the amount above? Explain.

_____

_____

_____

Geometry and Patterns

Curious About Math with
Curious George

A wind farm is a group of wind turbines used to make electricity. Each of these wind turbines has 3 blades. How many blades are on 2 turbines? 3 turbines? 4 turbines?

Name _____

Show What You Know ✓

Sort by Color, Size, or Shape

Draw an X on the one that does not belong.

1.
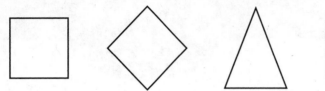

2.
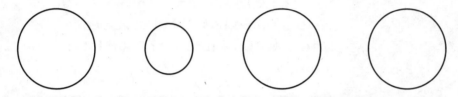

3.
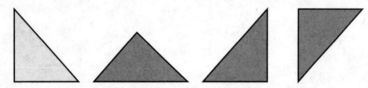

Identify Shapes

Circle all the shapes that match the shape name.

4. triangle

5. rectangle

Growing Patterns

Look for the pattern. Circle to show what comes next.

6.
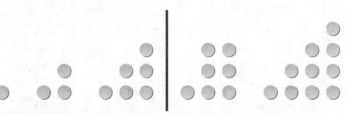

Family note: This page checks your child's understanding of important skills needed for success in Chapter 12.

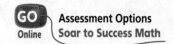

GO Online   Assessment Options
Soar to Success Math

© Houghton Mifflin Harcourt Publishing Company

Name _____

Review Words
pattern
shape
rectangle
triangle
square

Vocabulary Builder

Visualize It

Fill in the graphic organizer.

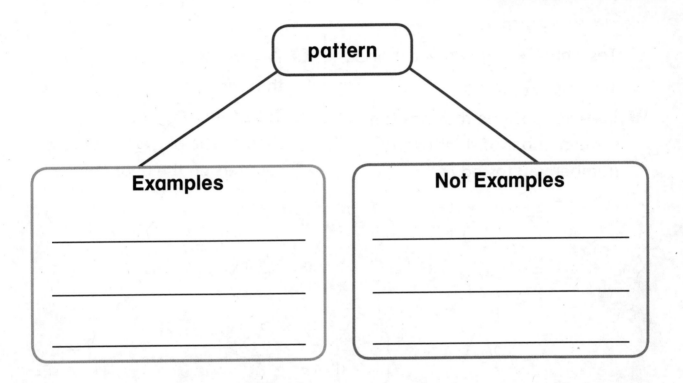

pattern

Examples
_____
_____
_____

Not Examples
_____
_____
_____

Understand Vocabulary

Draw a **shape** to match each label.

rectangle   **triangle**   **square**

Count the Sides

Materials • 1 • 10 ⚫ • 10 🔵

Play with a partner.

1. Toss the . If you toss a 1 or a 2, toss the again.

2. Look for a shape that has the same number of sides as the number you tossed.

3. Put one of your counters on that shape.

4. Take turns. Cover all the shapes. The player with more counters on the board wins.

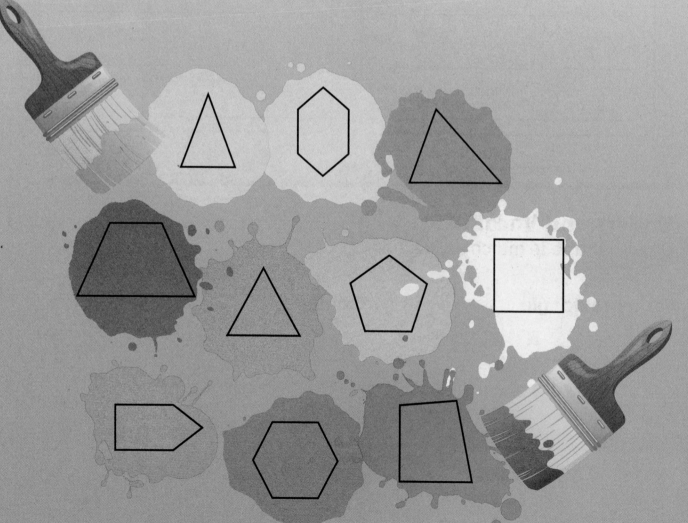

Name _____

Three-Dimensional Shapes

Essential Question What are the names of some three-dimensional shapes?

Listen and Draw REAL WORLD

Draw a picture of an object that has the shape shown.

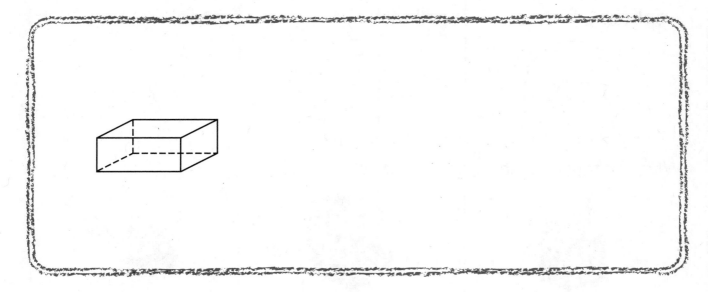

FOR THE TEACHER • Have children look at the first shape on the page. Ask children to name items that have this shape, for example, a cereal box or an eraser. Have each child draw a picture of a real-life object that has the shape. Repeat for the second shape on the page.

Math Talk
Describe how the two shapes are alike. Describe how they are different.

These are solid or three-dimensional shapes.

cube	rectangular prism	square pyramid
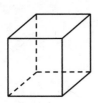	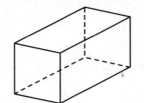	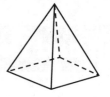

sphere	cylinder	cone
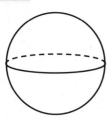	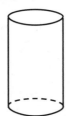	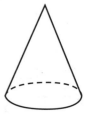

Which of these objects has the shape of a cube?

Share and Show

Circle the objects that match the shape name.

☑ 1. sphere

☑ 2. square pyramid

© Houghton Mifflin Harcourt Publishing Company

On Your Own

Circle the objects that match the shape name.

3. cylinder

4. rectangular prism

5. cone

6. cube

7. **H.O.T.** Circle the shapes that roll.
Draw an X over the shapes that do not roll.

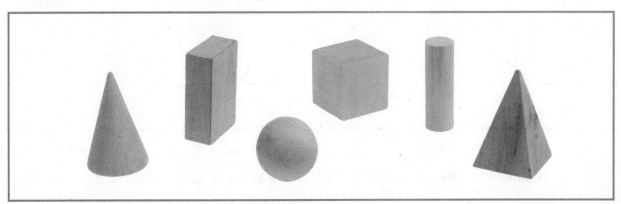

8. Ryan traced around the bottom of each block. Match each block with the shape Ryan drew.

9. **H.O.T.** Julio used cardboard squares as the flat surfaces of a cube. How many squares did he need to use?

_____ squares

10. ⭐ **Test Prep** Which of these shapes is a cone?

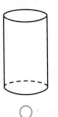
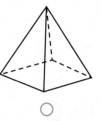

○   ○   ○   ○

TAKE HOME ACTIVITY • Ask your child to show you something that has the shape of a cylinder.

FOR MORE PRACTICE:
Standards Practice Book, pp. P249–P250

Name _____

Two-Dimensional Shapes

Essential Question What shapes can you name just by knowing the number of sides and vertices?

Listen and Draw REAL WORLD

Use a ruler. Draw a shape with 3 straight sides.
Then draw a shape with 4 straight sides.

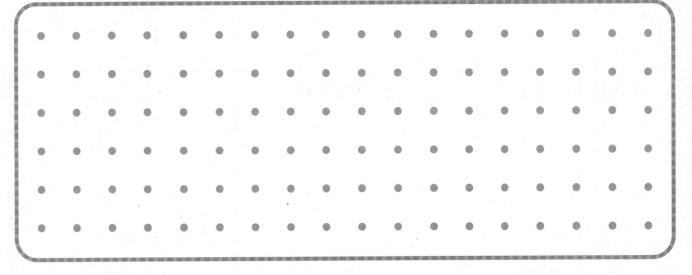

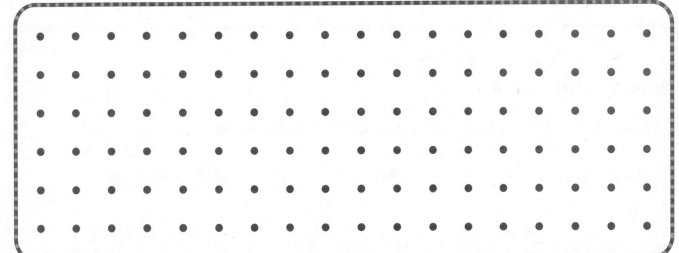

Math Talk
Describe how your shapes are different from the shapes a classmate drew.

FOR THE TEACHER • Have children use rulers as straight edges for drawing the sides of plane shapes. Have children first draw a plane shape that has 3 sides. Then have children draw a plane shape that has 4 sides.

Chapter 12

Model and Draw

These are plane or two-dimensional shapes.
You can count **sides** and **vertices** to name
these shapes.

triangle

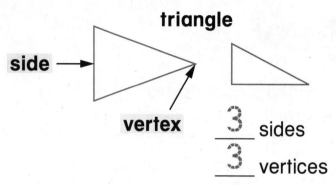

side →

vertex

$\underline{3}$ sides

$\underline{3}$ vertices

quadrilateral	pentagon	hexagon
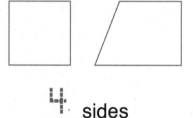	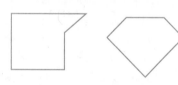	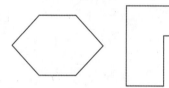
$\underline{4}$ sides	____ sides	____ sides
____ vertices	____ vertices	____ vertices

Share and Show

Write the number of sides and the number of vertices.

1. triangle

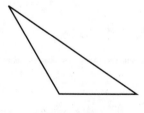

____ sides

____ vertices

✓ 2. hexagon

____ sides

____ vertices

✓ 3. pentagon

____ sides

____ vertices

Name _____

On Your Own

Write the number of sides and the number of vertices.

4. hexagon	5. square	6. quadrilateral
	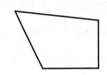	
____ sides ____ vertices	____ sides ____ vertices	____ sides ____ vertices
7. trapezoid	8. pentagon	9. rhombus
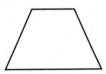		
____ sides ____ vertices	____ sides ____ vertices	____ sides ____ vertices
10. triangle	11. rectangle	12. hexagon
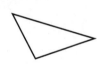		
____ sides ____ vertices	____ sides ____ vertices	____ sides ____ vertices

 Draw more sides to make the shape.

13. pentagon	14. quadrilateral	15. hexagon
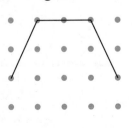	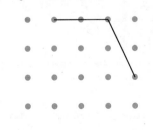	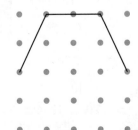

PROBLEM SOLVING REAL WORLD

Write Math

Solve. Draw or write to explain.

16. Jamie is making a hexagon and a pentagon with straws. He uses one straw for each side of a shape. How many straws does he need?

_____ straws

17. Mrs. Johnson buys 2 boxes of crayons. There are 8 crayons in each box. How many crayons are there in all?

_____ crayons

18. **H.O.T.** Ed draws a shape that has 4 sides. It is not a square. It is not a rectangle. Draw a shape that could be Ed's shape.

19. ⭐ **Test Prep** What is the shape of this sign?

○ quadrilateral

○ hexagon

○ pentagon

○ triangle

TAKE HOME ACTIVITY • Have your child show you an item that has the shape of a quadrilateral.

FOR MORE PRACTICE:
Standards Practice Book, pp. P251–P252

Name _____

Sort Two-Dimensional Shapes

Essential Question What is one way you can sort two-dimensional shapes?

Listen and Draw

Make the shape with pattern blocks.
Draw and color the blocks you used.

Use 1 block.

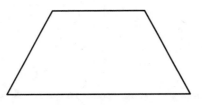

Use 2 blocks.

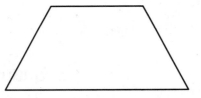

Use 3 blocks.

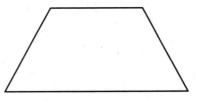

Math Talk
Describe how you could sort the blocks you used.

FOR THE TEACHER • Tell children that the shape shown three times on the page is a trapezoid. Have children use pattern blocks to make the trapezoid three times: first with one block, then with two blocks, and finally with three blocks.

Chapter 12

Model and Draw

Which shapes match the rule?

Shapes with more than
3 sides

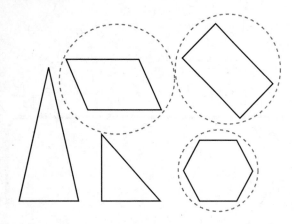

Shapes with fewer than
5 vertices

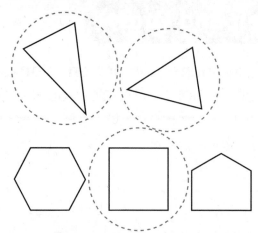

Share and Show

Circle the shapes that match the rule.

1. Shapes with 5 sides

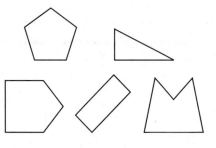

2. Shapes with more than
   3 vertices

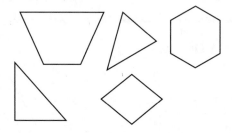

✓ 3. Shapes with fewer than
     4 vertices

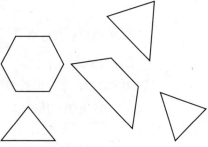

✓ 4. Shapes with fewer than 5 sides

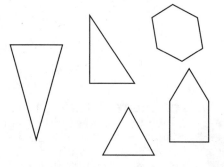

On Your Own

Circle the shapes that match the rule.

5. Shapes with 4 sides

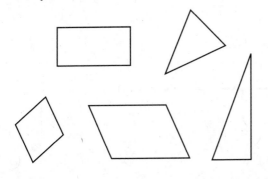

6. Shapes with more than 4 vertices

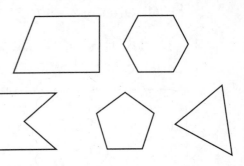

7. Shapes with fewer than 4 vertices

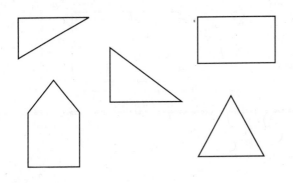

8. Shapes with fewer than 5 sides

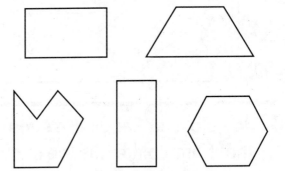

 Write a rule. Then circle the shapes that match the rule.

9. _____

_____

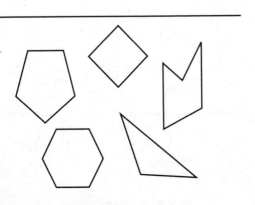

10. _____

_____

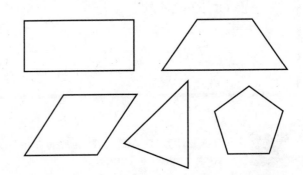

PROBLEM SOLVING

11. **H.O.T.** Sort the shapes.

  • Color the shapes red that match this rule.
    Red: Shapes with more than 4 sides

  • Color the shapes blue that match this rule.
    Blue: Shapes with fewer than 5 vertices

12. Jay plays baseball. He sees
    that home plate has the shape of
    a pentagon. How many vertices
    does home plate have?

    _____ vertices

13. ⭐ **Test Prep** Which of
    these shapes has fewer than
    4 vertices?

TAKE HOME ACTIVITY · Ask your child to draw three shapes that
each have 4 vertices.

© Houghton Mifflin Harcourt Publishing Company

FOR MORE PRACTICE:
Standards Practice Book, pp. P253–P254

Name _____

Symmetry

Essential Question How do you know if a shape
has a line of symmetry?

Listen and Draw

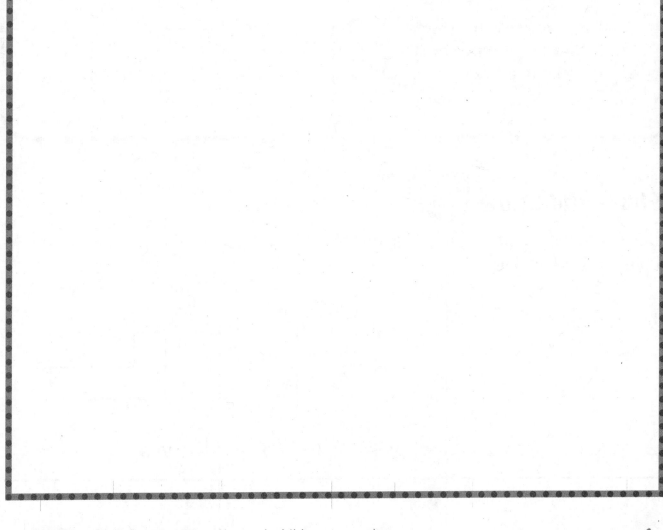

FOR THE TEACHER • Give each child a rectangular
piece of construction paper. Have each child fold the
paper in half and then cut out a shape along the
fold. Have children unfold their shape and look at
the two parts on either side of the fold. Then have
them glue their shape on the page and use a crayon
to show the fold line.

Math Talk
Describe how the
two parts of your
shape are alike.

Chapter 12

These shapes have a **line of symmetry**.

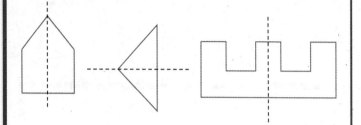

> When you fold the shape on the line, the two parts match exactly.

These shapes do not have a line of symmetry.

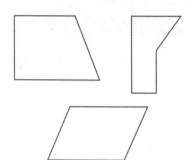

Share and Show

Does the shape have a line of symmetry?
If yes, draw the line.

1.

yes   no

2.

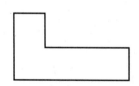

yes   no

3.

yes   no

4.

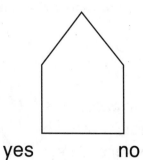

yes   no

☑ 5.

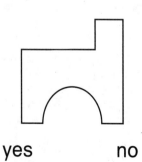

yes   no

☑ 6.

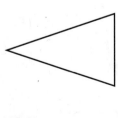

yes   no

Name _____

On Your Own

Does the shape have a line of symmetry?
If yes, draw the line.

7.

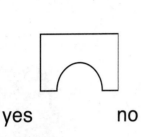

yes   no

8.

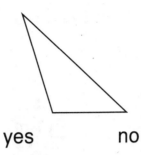

yes   no

9.

yes   no

10.

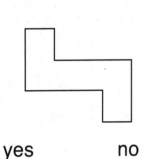

yes   no

11.

yes   no

12.

yes   no

Draw the matching part.

13.

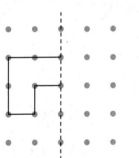

14.

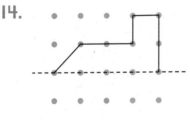

15.

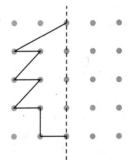

16. **H.O.T.** Draw a shape that has
a line of symmetry.

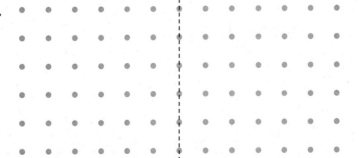

TAKE HOME ACTIVITY • Ask your child to show you how to make a shape with
line symmetry by folding and cutting a sheet of paper.

Chapter 12 • Lesson 4

FOR MORE PRACTICE:
Standards Practice Book, pp. P255–P256

Name _____

Mid-Chapter Checkpoint

Concept and Skills

Circle the objects that match the shape name. (pp. 521–524)

1. cylinder				
2. square pyramid				

Write the number of sides and the number of vertices. (pp. 525–528)

3. quadrilateral	4. pentagon	5. hexagon
____ sides	____ sides	____ sides
____ vertices	____ vertices	____ vertices

Test Prep

6. Which of these shapes has a
   line of symmetry? (pp. 533–535)

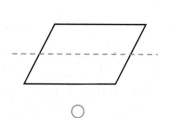   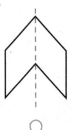   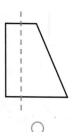   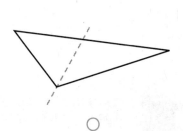

○   ○   ○   ○

Name _____

Algebra: Extend Growing Patterns

Essential Question How do you predict what is next in a pattern that is growing?

Listen and Draw

Use  to show the number pattern 2, 4, 6, 8, 10.
Draw the cube towers.

Math Talk
Describe the cube towers you built.

HOME CONNECTION • In this activity, your child used cubes to represent a growing pattern.

Model and Draw

You can predict what might come next in a pattern.

Describe how you think the pattern is growing. Then continue the pattern.

THINK:
Each step has 2 more squares than the last step. The squares are added to the side.

first   second   third   fourth   fifth

Share and Show   Math Board

Draw what might come next in the pattern.

1.

✓ 2.

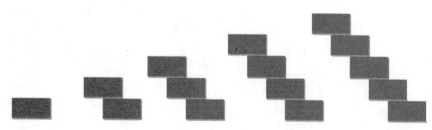

✓ 3.

Name _____

On Your Own

Draw what might come next in the pattern.

4.

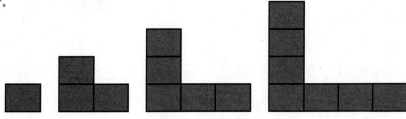

_____

5.

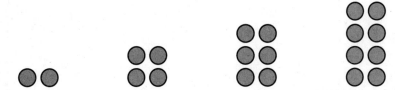

_____

6.

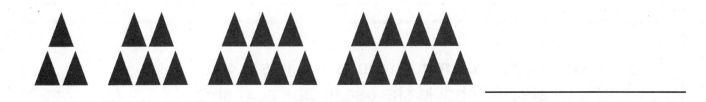

_____

7.

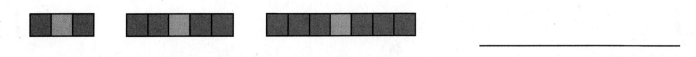

_____

8.

_____

9. 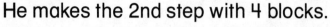 Bill makes a pattern with blocks.
He makes the 1st step with 2 blocks.
He makes the 2nd step with 4 blocks.
He makes the 3rd step with 6 blocks.
How many blocks should be in the 5th step?

_____ blocks

Draw a picture of what Bill's pattern might look like.

Describe how the pattern is growing.

_____

_____

10. ⭐ **Test Prep** Tina made a pattern with stickers.
How many stickers should she use for the next step
in the pattern?

○ 4

○ 5

○ 7

○ 10

TAKE HOME ACTIVITY · Use small objects, such as buttons, to make a growing
pattern. Ask your child to describe how the pattern grows.

FOR MORE PRACTICE:
Standards Practice Book, pp. P257–P258

Name _____

Find a Pattern • Number Patterns

Essential Question How can finding a pattern help you solve a problem?

Maya is making a pattern with blocks. The first row has 20 blocks, the second row has 18 blocks, and the third row has 16 blocks. How many blocks should be in the sixth row?

🔑 Unlock the Problem

What do I need to find?

_____

_____

What information do I need to use?

_____

_____

Show how to solve the problem.

first row	second row	third row	fourth row	fifth row	sixth row
20	18	16			

THINK: How do the numbers change?

A pattern in the numbers is _____

_____

There should be _____ blocks in the sixth row.

HOME CONNECTION • Your child used a diagram to show the problem. This helps your child find the pattern and then solve the problem.

Try Another Problem

Solve. Draw to show what you did.

• What do I need to find?
• What information do I need to use?

1. In a pattern, there are 3 cards in the first row, 6 cards in the second row, and 9 cards in the third row. How many cards are in the sixth row?

_____ cards

2. Darnell drew a cat pattern. He drew 4 cats in the first row. The number of cats goes up by 3 from row to row. How many cats are in the fourth row?

_____ cats

Math Talk

Explain how you solved the second problem.

Share and Show

Solve. Draw to show what you did.

✓ 3. Emily made a pattern with 2 pennies in the first row, 5 pennies in the second row, and 8 pennies in the third row. How many pennies should she put in the sixth row?

_____ pennies

✓ 4. Henry made a pattern. He used 3 cubes for the first tower, 5 cubes for the second tower, and 7 cubes for the third tower. How many cubes should he use for the seventh tower?

_____ cubes

---

5. Olivia used toy cars to make a pattern. She put 21 cars in the first row. She put 18 cars in the second row. She put 15 cars in the third row. In which row should there be just 9 cars?

_____ row

On Your Own

Solve. Write or draw to explain.

6. Patty has 75 beads for a necklace.
28 beads are red and the rest are blue.
How many blue beads does Patty have?

_____ blue beads

7.  H.O.T. Steve had 20 baseball cards. Then
he bought 4 baseball cards each week for three
weeks. How many cards did he have then?

_____ baseball cards

Explain how you solved the problem.

_____

_____

8. ⭐ **Test Prep** Madison made a pattern with
10 butterfly stickers in the first row, 13 stickers in
the second row, and 16 stickers in the third row.
How many stickers should be in the sixth row?

○ 39
○ 25
○ 22
○ 19

TAKE HOME ACTIVITY • Ask your child to draw a picture
to show the pattern in one of the problems in this lesson.

FOR MORE PRACTICE:
Standards Practice Book, pp. P259–P260

Name _____

Algebra: Find a Rule • Growing Patterns

Essential Question How do you find a rule
for a growing pattern?

Listen and Draw

Make towers with ▣ to show the number
pattern 2, 5, 8, 11. Draw the cube towers.

Math Talk
Describe how each
tower compares to
the one before it.

HOME CONNECTION • In this activity, your child
used cubes to represent a growing pattern.

In a growing pattern, the symbols or numbers change in a predictable way. The way they change is called a **rule**.

Look at how the pattern is growing. Write a rule for the pattern.

Rule:  Add 2 Xs.

Share and Show

Write a rule for the growing pattern.

1.

Rule: _____

2.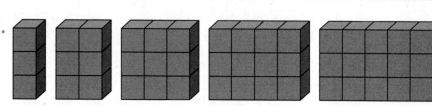

Rule: _____

3.

Rule: _____

Name _____

On Your Own

Write a rule for the growing pattern.

4. ⬤ ⬤⬤⬤ ⬤⬤⬤⬤⬤ ⬤⬤⬤⬤⬤⬤⬤
    ⬤ ⬤⬤⬤ ⬤⬤⬤⬤⬤ ⬤⬤⬤⬤⬤⬤⬤
    ⬤ ⬤⬤⬤ ⬤⬤⬤⬤⬤ ⬤⬤⬤⬤⬤⬤⬤
    ⬤ ⬤⬤⬤ ⬤⬤⬤⬤⬤ ⬤⬤⬤⬤⬤⬤⬤

Rule: _____

---

5. ▲   ▲ ▲   ▲ ▲ ▲   ▲ ▲ ▲ ▲
    ▲ ▲ ▲ ▲ ▲ ▲ ▲ ▲ ▲ ▲ ▲ ▲ ▲ ▲

Rule: _____

---

6. ◎ ◎◎ ◎◎◎ ◎◎◎◎ ◎◎◎◎◎
    ◎ ◎◎ ◎◎◎ ◎◎◎◎ ◎◎◎◎◎
    ◎ ◎◎ ◎◎◎ ◎◎◎◎ ◎◎◎◎◎
    ◎ ◎◎ ◎◎◎ ◎◎◎◎ ◎◎◎◎◎
    ◎ ◎◎ ◎◎◎ ◎◎◎◎ ◎◎◎◎◎

Rule: _____

---

7. **H.O.T.** Write a rule for the growing pattern.
    Explain how you found this rule.

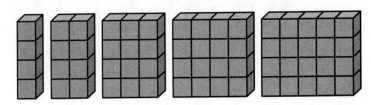

Rule: _____

_____

_____

_____

PROBLEM SOLVING

8. **H.O.T.** Draw your own growing pattern using small squares. Write a rule to describe your pattern.

Rule: _____

9. ⭐ **Test Prep** Which is a rule for this growing pattern?

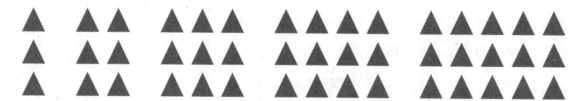

- ○ Add 1 triangle.
- ○ Add 2 triangles.
- ○ Add 3 triangles.
- ○ Add 6 triangles.

 TAKE HOME ACTIVITY • Ask your child to describe one of the patterns in this lesson.

FOR MORE PRACTICE: Standards Practice Book, pp. P261–P262

Name _____

Algebra: Explain Rules for Patterns

Essential Question How do you find and explain a rule for a growing pattern?

Listen and Draw

Make paper clip chains for the pattern.
Draw pictures to show what you did.

FOR THE TEACHER • Have children first make a chain with 3 paper clips. Then have them make more paper clip chains using the rule of adding 2 more paper clips for each new chain.

Math Talk
Describe the pattern using numbers. What would the next chain look like?

Find how the groups are growing.
Use numbers to find a rule for the pattern.

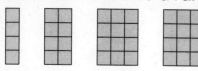

4   8   <u>1 2</u>   ___   ___   Rule: ____Add 4.____

Explain how you found the rule.

<u>4 squares are added each time and the numbers</u>

<u>also change by 4.</u>

Share and Show

Write a rule for the growing pattern.
Explain how you found the rule.

☑ 1. X   XXX   XXXXX   XXXXXXX

____   ____   ____   ____   Rule: _____

_____

_____

☑ 2.

____   ____   ____   ____   Rule: _____

_____

_____

On Your Own

Write a rule for the growing pattern.
Explain how you found the rule.

3.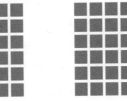

____ ____ ____ ____   Rule: _____

_____

_____

4.

____ ____ ____ ____   Rule: _____

_____

_____

5.  This pattern is both growing and repeating.

10 20 30 40 50

What is growing? _____

What is repeating? _____

What should be next in the pattern? _____ _____

What is a rule for the pattern? _____

_____

PROBLEM SOLVING

Write Math

6. Draw a growing pattern using small circles.
   Below each step, write a number to show the pattern.

_____   _____   _____   _____   _____

What is a rule for your pattern? _____

7. **H.O.T.** Describe why this is not a pattern.
   Then change one number to make a pattern.

20   22   24   26   29   30

_____

_____

8. ⭐ **Test Prep**   Which of these is the
   best rule for describing this pattern?

   ○ Add 4.

   ○ Add 3.

   ○ Add 2.

   ○ Add 1.

TAKE HOME ACTIVITY · Have your child draw a growing pattern
with squares using the rule Add 3.

552 five hundred fifty-two

FOR MORE PRACTICE:
Standards Practice Book, pp. P263–P264

© Houghton Mifflin Harcourt Publishing Company

Algebra: Find Missing Terms for Patterns

Essential Question How do you find missing terms in growing patterns?

Listen and Draw

Use numbers to describe the pattern.
Then write a rule for the pattern.

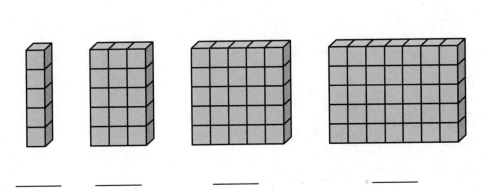

_____   _____   _____   _____

Rule: _____

FOR THE TEACHER • Ask children to count the number of blocks in each group and to write the number of blocks below the group. Ask them to write a rule to show how the numbers grow.

Math Talk
Describe how you found a rule for this pattern.

Each number or symbol in a pattern is called a **term**. Use a pattern rule to extend a pattern or to find a missing term.

THINK: How do the numbers change in the pattern?

32   37   42   47   _____   57   62   _____

A rule for the pattern is ___add 5___ .

So, the term after 47 is 5 more than 47, and the term after 62 is 5 more than 62.

32   37   42   47   _____   57   62   _____

Share and Show

Write the missing term. Then write a rule.

1. 22   26   30   34   38   _____

Rule: _____

2. 50   45   40   35   _____   25

Rule: _____

3. 36   38   40   _____   44   _____

Rule: _____

On Your Own

Write the missing term. Then write a rule.

4. 426 427 428 429 _____ 431

    Rule: _____

5. 51 61 71 81 91 _____

    Rule: _____

6. 112 110 108 _____ 104 _____

    Rule: _____

7. 88 89 90 _____ 92 _____

    Rule: _____

8. 70 65 60 55 _____ 45

    Rule: _____

9. **H.O.T.** Write the missing terms. Explain how
   you found the missing terms for the pattern.

    _____ 43 46 49 _____ _____ 58

    _____

    _____

    _____

    _____

PROBLEM SOLVING

REAL WORLD

Solve. Write or draw to explain.

10. Mr. Lee had a collection of horseshoes. He gave 44 horseshoes to a neighbor. Now Mr. Lee has 36 horseshoes. How many horseshoes did Mr. Lee have to start with?

_____ horseshoes

11. **H.O.T.** Jack wrote a growing number pattern. The second term is 4 and the sixth term is 16. Write a pattern that could be Jack's pattern.

_____ _____ _____ _____ _____ _____

12. ⭐ **Test Prep** What is the missing term for this pattern?

9   14   19   24   _____   34

- ○ 25
- ○ 29
- ○ 33
- ○ 35

TAKE HOME ACTIVITY · Ask your child to choose one pattern in this lesson and tell you what the next term should be for that pattern.

556 five hundred fifty-six

Chapter 12 Review/Test

Vocabulary

Use a word in the box to complete each sentence.

| cube |
| quadrilateral |
| sphere |
| pentagon |

1. A basketball has the shape

   of a _____. (pp. 521–524)

2. A _____ has 5 sides and 5 vertices. (pp. 525–528)

3. A _____ has 4 sides and 4 vertices. (pp. 525–528)

Concepts and Skills

Does the shape have a line of symmetry?
If yes, draw the line. (pp. 533–535)

4.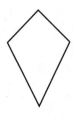

yes   no

5.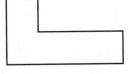

yes   no

6.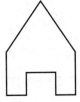

yes   no

7. Draw what might come next in the pattern. (pp. 537–540)

Fill in the bubble for the correct answer choice.

8. **Which of these shapes is a cube?** (pp. 521–524)

 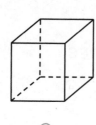  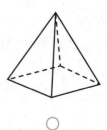

○   ○   ○   ○

9. **Which of these shapes has fewer than 5 vertices?** (pp. 529–532)

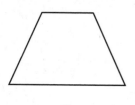   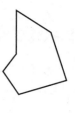

○   ○   ○   ○

10. **Which of these shapes has a line of symmetry?** (pp. 533–535)

○ 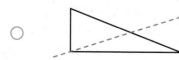   ○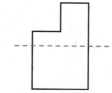

○ 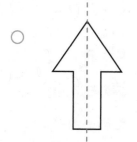   ○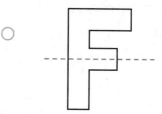

© Houghton Mifflin Harcourt Publishing Company

Name _____

Fill in the bubble for the correct answer choice.

11. Hunter is making a pattern with crayons. How many crayons should he use for the next step in the pattern? (pp. 537–540)

○ 7
○ 9
○ 11
○ 13

12. What is a rule for this pattern? (pp. 549–552)

23   33   43   53   63

○ Add 20.
○ Add 13.
○ Add 10.
○ Add 3.

13. What is the missing term in this pattern? (pp. 553–556)

18   21   24   27   ___   33

○ 25
○ 26
○ 28
○ 30

© Houghton Mifflin Harcourt Publishing Company

Short Answer

14. Reggie uses toothpicks to make a pentagon and a quadrilateral. How many toothpicks does he use?

Draw or write to explain your answer.

_____ toothpicks

Performance Task

15. Keira uses squares to make a growing pattern.
A rule for her pattern is Add 3.

Use squares to draw the first four terms of her growing pattern.

How many squares would you need to draw for the
sixth term in Keira's pattern? Explain how you know.

_____

_____

_____

_____

Picture Glossary

addend sumando

$$5 + 8 = 13$$

addends

array matriz

bar graph gráfica de barras

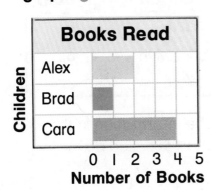

capacity capacidad

Capacity is the amount a container can hold.

cent sign signo de centavo

53¢

↑

cent sign

centimeter centímetro

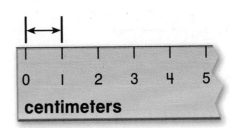

centimeters

compare comparar

Use these symbols when you **compare**: >, <, =.

241 > 234

123 < 128

247 = 247

cup taza

cone cono

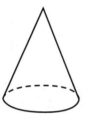

cylinder cilindro

cube cubo

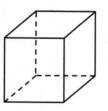

data datos

Favorite Lunch	
Lunch	Number
pizza	4
sandwich	6
salad	3

The information in the chart is called **data**.

day día

There are 24 hours in 1 **day**.

digit dígito

0, 1, 2, 3, 4, 5, 6, 7, 8, and 9 are **digits**.

decimal point punto decimal

$1.00
↑
decimal point

dime moneda de 10¢

A **dime** is worth 10 cents.

difference diferencia

9 − 2 = 7
↑
difference

dollar dólar

One **dollar** is worth 100 cents.

dollar sign signo de dólar

$1.00

↑
dollar sign

even par

2, 4, 6, 8, 10, . . .

even numbers

equal groups grupos iguales

These are 3 **equal groups**.

fact family familia de operaciones

5 + 6 = 11   11 − 6 = 5

6 + 5 = 11   11 − 5 = 6

A **fact family** is a set of related facts.

estimate estimar

When you **estimate**, you tell about how many.

foot pie

1 **foot** is the same length as 12 inches.

© Houghton Mifflin Harcourt Publishing Company

gram gramo

A baseball card has a
mass of about 1 **gram**.

half past y media

The time shown on this clock is
half past 10:00. It is halfway
between 10:00 and 11:00.

half dollar moneda de 50¢

A **half dollar** is worth 50 cents.

hexagon hexágono

A two-dimensional shape with
6 sides is a **hexagon**.

half hour media hora

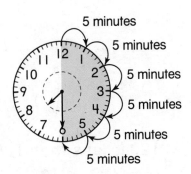

5 minutes
5 minutes
5 minutes
5 minutes
5 minutes
5 minutes

A **half hour** has 30 minutes.

hour hora

An **hour** has 60 minutes.

hour hand horario

hour hand

---

hundred centena

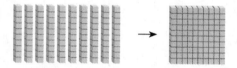

10 tens = 1 **hundred**

---

inch pulgada

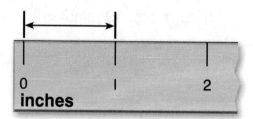

0　　　1　　　2
inches

is equal to (=) es igual a

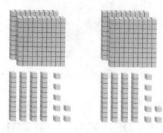

247 **is equal to** 247.
247 = 247

---

is greater than (>) es mayor que

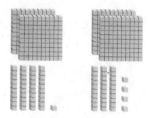

241 **is greater than** 234.
241 > 234

---

is less than (<) es menor que

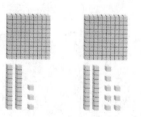

123 **is less than** 128.
123 < 128

is not equal to (≠) no es igual a

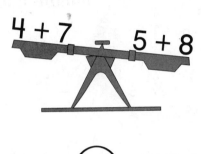

11 (≠) 13

line of symmetry línea de simetría

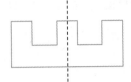

This shape has a **line of symmetry**. When you fold the shape on the line, the two parts match.

key clave

Number of Flowers Picked				
Jessie	☼	☼		
Inez	☼	☼	☼	☼
Paulo	☼	☼	☼	

Key: Each ☼ stands for 2 flowers.

The **key** shows how many each picture stands for.

liter litro

This bottle has a capacity of about 1 **liter**.

kilogram kilogramo

A baseball bat has a mass of about 1 **kilogram**.

mass masa

Mass is the amount of matter an object has. Use grams and kilograms to measure **mass**.

meter metro

I **meter** is the same length as 100 centimeters.

minute hand minutero

minute hand

milliliter mililitro

I **milliliter** is about the same amount as 20 drops of water.

month mes

There are about 4 weeks in I **month**.

minute minuto

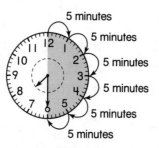

5 minutes
5 minutes
5 minutes
5 minutes
5 minutes
5 minutes

There are 30 **minutes** in a half hour.

multiplication sentence
enunciado de multiplicación

$2 \times 4 = 8$

multiply multiplicar

$$2 \times 4 = 8$$

Multiply to find how many in all.

ounce onza

A strawberry weighs about 1 **ounce**.

nickel moneda de 5¢

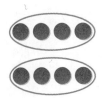

A **nickel** is worth 5 cents.

penny moneda de 1¢

A **penny** is worth 1 cent.

odd impar

1, 3, 5, 7, 9, 11, . . .

odd numbers

pentagon pentágono

A two-dimensional shape with 5 sides is a **pentagon**.

pictograph pictografía

Favorite Sandwich					
cheese	😊	😊			
ham	😊				
tuna	😊	😊	😊		

Key: Each 😊 stands for 5 children.

quart cuarto

4 cups = I **quart**

pound libra

A grapefruit weighs about
I **pound**.

quarter moneda de 25¢

A **quarter** is worth 25 cents.

quadrilateral cuadrilátero

A two-dimensional shape
with 4 sides is a
quadrilateral.

rectangular prism prisma
rectangular

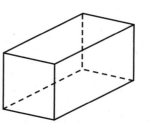

regroup reagrupar

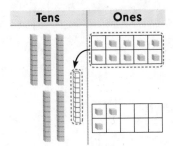

You can trade 10 ones for 1 ten to **regroup**.

rhombus rombo

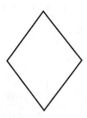

A two-dimensional shape with 4 equal sides is a **rhombus**.

rule regla

Rule: Add 2 triangles.

scale escala

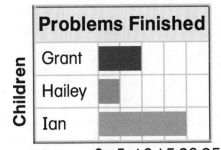

The **scale** shows you what numbers the lengths of the bars stand for.

side lado

This shape has 4 **sides**.

skip count contar salteado

A pattern of counting forward or backward

5, 10, 15, 20, 25, 30, . . .

sphere esfera

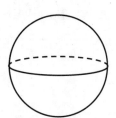

square pyramid pirámide cuadrada

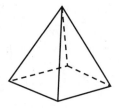

sum suma o total

$$9 + 6 = 15$$

sum

survey encuesta

Favorite Lunch	
Lunch	**Tally**
pizza	IIII
sandwich	⊞ I
salad	III

A **survey** is a collection of data from answers to a question.

term término

Each step in a pattern is a **term**.

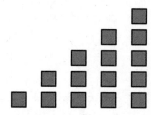

This growing pattern has 5 **terms**.

thousand millar

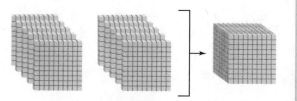

There are 10 hundreds in 1 **thousand**.

trapezoid trapecio

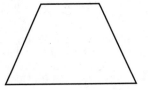

vertex/vertices
vértice/vértices

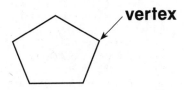

week semana

There are 7 days in 1 **week**.

yard yarda

1 **yard** is the same length as 3 feet.

year año

There are 12 months in 1 **year**.

Photo Credits